NEW ZEALAND
Rugby Greats
Vol: 3

NEW ZEALAND Rugby Greats

Vol: 3

Bob Howitt

Hodder Moa Beckett

Acknowledgements

There are a number of writers, publications and photographers the author wishes to thank, as follows:

Photographers: Peter Bush, John Selkirk, Andrew Cornaga (Photosport), Joanna Caird (Photosport), Neil McKenzie (Photosport), Ross Wiggins, Trevor Coppock, Mark Leech (UK), Mike Brett (UK), Wessel Oosthuizen (South Africa), Fotopacific, Vogel Photography, New Zealand Picture Library.

Publications: *New Zealand Herald*, *Sud Ouest* (France).

Authors: Lindsay Knight *(The Geriatrics)*, Alex Veysey *(Zinny – the Zinzan Brooke Story*; *The Game The Goal – the Grant Fox Story*; *Mexted – Pieces of Eight)*, Steven O'Meagher *(Fronting Up – the Sean Fitzpatrick Story)*, Chris Brown *(John Gallagher – the Million Dollar Man)*, Robin McConnell *(Iceman – the Michael Jones Story)*, Paul Thomas *(Kirwan – Running on Instinct)*, Trevor McKewen *(Real Men Wear Black)*, Wynne Gray *(Buck – the Wayne Shelford Story)*, Phil Gifford *(Smokin' Joe)*, Paul Lewis *(Brothers in Arms – the Alan and Gary Whetton Story)*, Nev McMillan and Clive Akers *(the New Zealand Rugby Almanack)*, Nev McMillan and the late Rod Chester *(the Encyclopedia of New Zealand Rugby)*, Pat Booth *(Jeff Wilson – The Natural)*.

ISBN 1-86958-478-3

© 1997 Bob Howitt

Published in 1997 by Hodder Moa Beckett Publishers Limited
[a member of the Hodder Headline Group]
4 Whetu Place, Mairangi Bay, Auckland, New Zealand

Printed through Colorcraft, Hong Kong

Contents

DEDICATION

To my wife Jenny

Introduction

It's 15 years since the second volume of *New Zealand Rugby Greats* was published. What incredible changes have occurred in the great game in that period.

South Africa has come in from the rugby wilderness, the World Cup has become a permanent fixture, the value of a try has increased from four points to five, the rules have undergone vast revision and, most dramatically of all, rugby has become professional.

Those 15 years have featured some of the All Blacks' greatest moments – triumph at the first World Cup tournament, an incredible sequence of 50 matches without defeat and, in 1996, an historic first series victory over the Springboks on South African soil.

So it is with great delight that I present the stories of 25 of the greatest All Blacks of the period, from Murray Mexted, Mark Shaw and John Ashworth, whose careers stretch back into the 1970s, through to the superstars of today, Jonah Lomu, Andrew Mehrtens, Sean Fitzpatrick, Olo Brown and Jeff Wilson.

The 25 subjects for this book were selected by the All Black coaches since 1982 – Peter Burke, Bryce Rope, Brian Lochore, Alex Wyllie, Laurie Mains and John Hart. To them, I say a big thank you, for their willing co-operation and for presenting me with such a superb blend of skilled and interesting footballers.

I was fortunate enough to be able to personally interview every one of the subjects in the early months of 1997, with the exception of London-based John Gallagher who answered my questions by phone. I was lucky that all the Japan-based subjects, John Kirwan, Joe Stanley, Graeme Bachop and Alan Whetton, happened to be in New Zealand early in the new year.

Of those Greats who have had books published on their careers I have sought to present a fresh side to their stories. The classic example is Gary Whetton who provided a remarkable postscript to his celebrated All Black career by sharing in a French club championship victory.

To the 25 Greats who so willingly made themselves available for interviews, I say thanks, guys. If a common thread emerged from the interviews, it was humility. I wrote in the introduction to volume one (written in 1975) that if one message came out of the book, it was that natural talent was a minor quality – that application, determination and self sacrifice were the qualities that took players to the top. Nothing has changed.

Bob Howitt
Auckland
April 1997

John Ashworth

It's hard to believe that a rugged prop who played 24 tests for the All Blacks and who caused uproar in Wales when he trampled one of their favourite sons, J.P.R. Williams, started his working career as a graphic artist.

A farmer now, he says that if he could manage his finances well enough to achieve early retirement, he would return to the world of art, to take up painting or sculpture.

That's John Ashworth, the loosehead prop who in the early 1980s formed part of the mighty All Black front row with Andy Dalton and Gary Knight – collectively known as the Geriatrics – that stood solid against every nation.

While Dalton and Knight were always men of the land, and readied themselves for their rugby careers as so many great New Zealand forwards before them had, through hard, manual farm work, Ashworth broke into the Canterbury team while working in the art department of a newspaper.

But he came to appreciate that graphic artists don't make All Black forwards. "I had to get rid of the soft hands and look the part," he says.

So he turned to truck driving and found that stacking pellets of wheat and barley added a physical hardness to him. But what really toughened him up was the seasonal job he took at the freezing works at Kaiapoi where he was required to stack frozen carcasses.

Determined to make up for lost ground, Ashworth supplemented his work at the freezing works by pounding the roads, to the point of becoming a running addict. He would regularly run up to 12 miles, determined to substitute extreme fitness for what he always considered to be a lack of natural ability.

"Many of the guys I played alongside at top level had far more natural talent than me," he says. "I was just a plodder who advanced step by step."

A plodder Ashworth may have considered himself but in 1978, and for five years from 1980, the New Zealand selectors rated him the best loosehead prop in the land; indeed, when the Geriatrics were at their best, Ashworth had few peers in the world.

The artist in Ashworth meant he performed best at grounds that evoked atmosphere, grounds that gave him a good feeling. As a consequence, he gave some of his finest performances at stadiums like Ballymore in Brisbane, but seldom at Athletic Park. "I played on adrenalin and emotion," says Ashworth. "How could you mentally prepare yourself in those cold, concrete dungeons in Wellington?"

Ashworth was never content to be just a scrummager. He wanted to contribute his share around the field. "I remember Eric Watson saying to me in 1979 that props were not expected to run with the ball. I never accepted that philosophy, which was the British approach. Their props were selected purely for the power of their scrummaging. All I wanted to do was get the scrum over and done with, and get out and run with the ball."

That attitude would see Ashworth play 126 games for Canterbury, which included the great Ranfurly Shield era when Grizz Wyllie reigned as coach, survive eight years as an All Black and round out his career on the Cavaliers tour of South Africa in 1986 at the age of 35. And he hasn't finished yet, having four times in the 1990s made the trek to Bermuda with the Classic All Blacks.

John's ancestors were early settlers in North Canterbury, establishing their homestead on the Main North Road between Leithfield and Amberley at what has become known as Ashworth's Corner. John, the eldest of five children, began his rugby, like most of the subjects in this book, at the age of five, remembering that he was "stuck in the scrum at hooker because they didn't know where else to put me!".

Ashworth began his secondary schooling at Rangiora High and finished it at Riccarton High, boarding at a private home from

John Ashworth

John Ashworth being used as a front of the lineout jumper during his first tour with the All Blacks – to France in 1977.   *Alain Bourron (Sud Ouest)*

Monday to Friday and taking the bus back to the family farm at weekends. He thrived at Riccarton, where the first XV coach was Sam Leary, the former New Zealand Universities and Canterbury fullback. Sport held a high priority and Ashworth enjoyed himself as a prop in the first XV.

As a student, the one subject at which he excelled was art, so it was no surprise when, upon leaving college, he enrolled at the Wellington Polytechnic to study commercial art. "With hindsight," he says, "I would have been better taking an agricultural course at Lincoln College but Wellington seemed a good opportunity at the time."

Although his rugby developed reasonably promisingly – at 19 he made the Wellington College Old Boys senior team, as a lock – his lifestyle left a lot to be desired. There was, he recalls, too much beer and not enough nourishing food going into the Ashworth body. "I ended up seriously run down and eventually had to go home to recuperate on mum's home cooking!"

In 1970, back in his home environment, fortified, he made solid progress in rugby. From the tiny Kowai club, he won selection for Country Colts and then Canterbury Colts. At the time he was working for *The Press* newspaper, first in the advertising department, then in the art department.

It made sense to move into the city where he joined the Linwood club, which he describes as "perhaps the most significant step of my entire rugby career." Linwood was prospering in those days, fielding a senior team overflowing with Canterbury representatives, most notable among them All Black hooker Tane Norton, flanker John Phillips and halfback Brent Elder. "Playing for Linwood, with the calibre of players there," says Ashworth, "had a profound effect on me and on the commitment I realised was essential to get me to the top."

Because he was close to being Linwood's tallest forward at 6ft 2in (1.88m), Ashworth was occasionally used as a lock, often jumping at No 5 in the lineout. By 1972, however, he had established himself at loosehead prop, the position in which he would gain world-class status. Such recognition lay well ahead. In 1972, he can recall Ken Jane, the Linwood coach, describing him as "too soft".

'Soft' he may have been, but he wasn't beyond a good scrap. Those were the days, he recalls, when the macho attitude flourished in the front row. "Props were always trying to put one over on their opposites," he says. "I can recall Wayne Louden and I finishing up with two black eyes each – and we were clubmates! It was a Linwood trial and we were vying for the right to prop with Tane (Norton)."

He progressed from Canterbury B in 1972 to the Canterbury A squad in 1973, getting outings against Mid-Canterbury, Otago and Southland. However, his opportunities over the next few seasons were few because, from 1974, Canterbury boasted a pair of All Black props, Billy Bush and Kerry Tanner.

Although some astute observers rated Ashworth ahead of Tanner as a loosehead prop, he remained in his shadow until 1976 when Tanner toured South Africa with J.J. Stewart's All Blacks. In his absence, Ashworth enjoyed a full season of representative play. Well, enjoyed is perhaps not the most appropriate word. Ashworth felt he played some of his worst rugby in 1976. That was about the time he decided to exchange office life for manual work and toughen himself up.

Although Ashworth wasn't that satisfied with his form in those years, the New Zealand selectors obviously identified him as a player with potential, placing him in the All Black trials (at Athletic Park) in 1975 and 1976.

A country lad again by 1977, Ashworth resisted the urge to link with Wyllie's club, Glenmark, instead joining Kaiapoi, a club with a rocky recent background. From the time Ashworth became a member, Kaiapoi enjoyed a boom period through until 1983 when it appropriately celebrated its centenary by winning the North Canterbury championship.

Being an All Black trialist and a Canterbury player didn't guarantee Ashworth instant status in the country where the selector-coach Alistair Hopkinson, the former All Black prop, omitted him from his team for the big annual clash with Town. Jimmy Stubbs, a long-serving Country front rower, was preferred.

But it was Ashworth, not Stubbs, who found himself assembling in Auckland in October for the All Black tour of Italy and France. Other rookies in that team, coached by Jack Gleeson and captained by Graham Mourie, were Gary Knight and Andy Dalton.

Ashworth was grateful that Mourie was on hand for his debut against the Italian President's XV at Padua. "We were struggling dreadfully," he says. "I think it was six-all when Mourie came on as a replacement and promptly scored two tries. He saved me the embarrassment of starting my All Black career with a loss."

While Dalton and Knight would participate in the test series, which was squared, Ashworth went through that first tour as one of the midweek brigade, understudy at loosehead prop to Brad Johnstone. "That suited me fine," he says. "I've always been a plodder and have always had to work hard at anything to make progress. While I was proud to be an All Black, I wondered if I had a tiger by the tail. Would I justify my selection or be a oncer?"

Johnstone would provide one of the more memorable episodes of the visit to France. "Most of the guys found meal times a source of huge frustration," says Ashworth. The service was painstakingly slow, and those who didn't like rare steaks had to settle for bland pasta. One evening, Brad Johnstone reached breaking point. After waiting for ninety minutes, he took one look at what was on his plate, and tipped it upside down on the table, to the horror of the waiters. "The food wasn't what hungry All Blacks wanted," says Ashworth, who identifies France as one of the first countries he would visit now. Upon his return to New Zealand in '77, Ashworth found he was tipping the scales at 18st (115kg) because of all the bread he had eaten.

His fear of being an All Black 'oncer' vanished when he was selected for the 1978 Bledisloe Cup series against the Wallabies in New Zealand, marking a charismatic character with whom he would form a solid friendship, Stan Pilecki. "We had a mutual understanding," says Ashworth, "On the field, if he hit me, I hit him, and that was the end of that. Off the field, we both enjoyed socialising. We were still playing against each other at test level in 1985."

Although the All Blacks won that '78 series and Ashworth scored a try in the third test, the heavy (30-16) loss at Eden Park inevitably meant heads would roll. Two who were dropped for the tour of the United Kingdom later that year were Ashworth and Brian McKechnie. Ironically, they would provide the most lasting headlines of the tour, after being called up as replacements for injured players. McKechnie came in for Bevan Wilson, Ashworth for Rod Ketels.

Ashworth didn't have long to brood over his rejection, Ketels dropping out soon after the touring team's assembly in Auckland. Russ Thomas, the manager, phoned and told him, "You're in!" "How long before I have to commit myself?" inquired Ashworth, who had made work arrangements. "About twenty minutes," replied Thomas.

What a tour it would be, one which would incite extreme passions, particularly in Wales. There would be high drama in almost every international until finally coach Jack Gleeson (who within 12 months would die of cancer) became the first New Zealand coach to achieve a Grand Slam in the UK.

Ashworth, who had the unique experience of being a reserve for the entire Grand Slam, experienced a most bizarre tour, starting it and finishing it amid controversy.

In the tour opener against Cambridge University, Ashworth had the misfortune to pack down against a player who had contracted a dreadful facial rash of the herpes strain. The infection was transmitted to Ashworth who in turn, during training, passed it on to Knight. Andy Haden was also infected.

Knight was the worst sufferer of the scrumpox, being admitted to hospital in Dublin when on the brink of collapse. He had to wear bandages on his face for the remainder of the tour.

John Ashworth

The All Blacks, specialising in last-minute escape acts, defeated Ireland 10-6 (through a late try by Dalton), Wales 13-12 (through a late penalty goal by McKechnie after Haden had sensationally thrown himself out of a lineout), England 16-6 and Scotland 18-6 (securing victory through another late try, by Bruce Robertson).

While Haden's 'dive' had stirred up passions in Wales, the All Blacks had come through their near two-month tour remarkably intact. The tabloids of Fleet Street had been starved of sensationalism. The diplomacy of manager Thomas and the discipline of the All Blacks under Gleeson had denied them the sort of headings on which they thrive.

All that would change at Bridgend, after Ashworth's boot inflicted serious damage to the face of J.P.R. Williams, Bridgend's most celebrated international. Emotions were running high that day. This was Welsh rugby's last opportunity to bring down the '78 All Blacks who had defeated Cardiff, West Wales, Wales (outrageously, the Welsh claimed) and Monmouthshire. Bridgend, which was celebrating its centenary, believed it had the team to salvage Wales' rugby pride.

The game was an ugly, brawling affair from the start. Gleeson, the most mild mannered of men, was incensed. "They started kneeing our players and collapsing scrums," he said. "Our policy throughout was no punching, fighting or backchatting, but against Bridgend our boys could tolerate it no longer."

It was in this atmosphere, then, on a typically dark, murky Welsh mid-winter afternoon, that Ashworth stood on Williams' face at a ruck. Ashworth recalls the incident: "JPR was lying on the ball, hugging it, refusing to roll away. He was a fullback who'd always wanted to be a loose forward. As I went over the top of him I tried to flick the ball back. Obviously, my boot came in contact with his face. There was no malice intended. I have never kicked anyone deliberately on a rugby field."

Williams' cheek was punctured by a sprig and it required seven stitches to repair the wound. He was off the field for 12 minutes.

The raking, played and replayed on television, was big news in the papers the next day, with Ashworth branded a villain. The incident had an unfortunate sequel when Williams' father, Dr Peter Williams, addressing the centenary dinner that evening, said he regretted having encouraged his sons to play rugby. His comments sparked a walkout by not only the All Blacks but several Bridgend players as well.

Three days later, Ashworth had his role as a permanent Saturday reserve interrupted when Brad Johnstone was injured playing against the Barbarians at Cardiff Arms Park. After the Bridgend incident, the Welsh were aggrieved that Ashworth should be considered for the tour finale at all, and booed him loudly as he ran on to the field. Two years later, in 1980, Ashworth would return to Wales with the All Blacks, the tour that had been arranged to commemorate the centenary of rugby in that country. This time, Bridgend had not been allocated a game, but Ashworth suggested to the team management that it might be an appropriate gesture to make a social call on the club.

"We felt it would show goodwill and heal any ill feeling that might still exist," says Ashworth. On the night, Ray Harper, the manager, Graham Mourie, the captain, Andy Haden, Gary Knight, Andy Dalton, Frank Oliver and Bernie Fraser joined Ashworth at the Bridgend club.

"We weren't entirely sure how we would be received," says Ashworth. "When we arrived, Andy Haden suggested to the driver that he should turn the bus around and leave the engine running, just in case!

"In the event, we were received graciously. Dr Williams was there along with JPR who was still talking like Prince Charles. I felt a lot happier after that tour than I had in 1978."

Tours by New Zealand to Europe were two-a-penny in the late 1970s, placing pressure on players who, as amateurs, received no more than the modest daily allowance determined by the IRB. Ashworth was one who on a number of occasions gave a higher priority to his farmwork than his rugby. He declared himself unavailable for the tour of England and Scotland in 1979. He would also pull out of the 1981 tour of France, the 1983 tour of England and Scotland and the 1984 tour of Fiji for the same reason. Had he remained available for everything, his final tally of test appearances might have been closer to 40 than 24.

He did, however, undertake two tours of Australia, in 1980 and 1984, appearing in all six tests. The '80 tour was significant because it was the first time he had overtaken Brad Johnstone as New Zealand's No 1 loosehead prop. Although the outcome of the series was a huge disappointment, he found Australia an excellent country

John Ashworth

They would become known as the The Geriatrics. From left, Gary Knight, Andy Dalton and John Ashworth providing the foundation of the All Black scrum in the early 1980s.   Peter Bush

to tour. "You're only three hours from home," he says. "The food's good, they speak English and you're never going to suffer from hypothermia."

Far from suffering hypothermia, Ashworth struggled to handle the heat in Townsville. "It was so hot I had to change my jersey after the warm-up!"

Another game he remembers with some amusement was that against ACT at Canberra. "We actually fielded five front rowers and three locks in our pack that afternoon. One of them was Andy Haden, who came on as a replacement for Hika Reid. He'd been standing in the dressing room eating a pie when our coach Eric Watson told him he was required. A few minutes after he came on the field, he threw up!"

Watson insisted his players practise at the time the next match was kicking off. As a consequence, Ashworth and company had to sacrifice many of the benefits of touring they might otherwise have enjoyed. "I toured Australia twice and I only once visited a farm and I haven't been on Sydney Harbour yet!"

After the disappointments of 1980, when the Bledisloe Cup was claimed by the Aussies, Ashworth enjoyed continuing success as an All Black through until his international career wound up after the 1985 season. Although there were a couple of hiccups, the All Blacks won every series he participated in – against the Springboks in 1981, the Australians in 1982, the Lions in 1983, the French and the Australians again in 1984 and England in 1985.

Almost throughout that term his front row colleagues were Andy Dalton and Gary Knight. They might have been dubbed something romantic like The Three Musketeers but John Brooks of the *Press* newspaper of Christchurch is held responsible for giving them the Geriatric tag. At a press conference during the '83 Lions tour, he implied that some of the All Blacks were getting on a bit. "What *about* their age?" came back Dalton, the skipper. "Well," said Brooks, "some are saying that some of you are getting a bit geriatric."

When Dalton joined his players in the team bus, he told them that "those press so-and-sos are calling us geriatrics." The title stuck. Senior citizens by international rugby standards they might have been but by 1985, when Ashworth was 35 and Knight and Dalton both 33, the All Black team of which they were such integral members was still winning, still standing solid against all comers.

Their togetherness as a threesome was never better exemplified than in the dramatic third test against the Springboks at Eden Park in 1981. It became known as the Flour Bomb test, and no one understood that better than Knight who had one of the flour bombs, dropped from the Cessna that buzzed the ground incessantly, land on him.

"It really only dazed me," Knight said later, "but it did shake me up." Momentarily confused, Knight decided he had had enough. "Let's pull the pin," he said. "I've had my eyes gouged in France, had scrum pox in Britain, been food poisoned in Australia and struck by a fence post in Fiji. Now I'm not even safe in my own country. I'm off."

Ashworth listened compassionately and decided the brotherhood of the 'geriatric' front row should take over. He put his arm around Knight's broad shoulders and said, "You're hanging in here with us, mate." When Allan Hewson struck the winning goal half an hour later, Knight was there to celebrate a famous test and series victory.

A marvellous part of Ashworth's career was the winning and defending of the Ranfurly Shield with a champion Canterbury side. He'd moved to Hawke's Bay by 1985 and so missed the epic

John Ashworth

John Ashworth was a tight forward who liked to run with the ball as he demonstrates here against the Lions in the fourth test at Eden Park in 1983. Others, from left, are Gary Knight, Graham Price and Andy Dalton. John Selkirk

provincial match of the century when Auckland finally ended the great era but he'd extracted huge satisfaction and enjoyment out of the "log" by then. "The shield was a bonus for me, really," he says. "I'd been involved in first-class rugby for ten years when we won it."

Ashworth gives credit to Alex Wyllie for making it all possible. "He was an absolute perfectionist in his approach as a coach," says Ashworth. "He demonstrated uncanny timing in peaking his side for its most important engagements."

When Manawatu challenged in 1983, it pitted Ashworth against Knight. There were problems. Knight's teammates were helping him build some 'hate' against his cobber for the next day. "What happens?" he says. "The phone goes and it's Ash. He wanted to know if I was coming out to the farm to help him crutch his sheep. And he looked offended when I wouldn't talk to him during the match!"

At the beginning of 1985, Ashworth and his family moved north after undertaking to purchase a 240 hectare farm at Takapau in central Hawke's Bay, land Ashworth was attracted to while staying with his brother-in-law at Dannevirke. In one sense, Ashworth wasn't too distraught when the All Black tour of South Africa, for which he had been selected, was abandoned in such sensational circumstances because it allowed him to focus on his new farm. While Hawke's Bay rugby folk were delighted to welcome an All Black to their area, he was available for only two games that season (including the crunch encounter against Taranaki which determined the winner of Division Two – Hawke's Bay lost!).

Few people, including most of the players, knew exactly what was going on as the Cavaliers tour of 1986 unfolded. When Ashworth farewelled his wife at Takapau to head to Wellington for the assembly, he said to her, "Don't be surprised if I telephone later to say another tour's off." In Wellington, he was handed his air tickets. "Only then," he says, "did I appreciate that I was on my way to South Africa." And his motivation for going? "My rugby career wouldn't have been complete if I hadn't been to South Africa."

It was appropriate that wives were able to join the players on the Cavaliers tour. "In my case," says Ashworth, "I wouldn't have been able to participate in all the rugby I did if I hadn't had such a capable partner. Running a farm can be a 24-hour job. So it was great that Joanne could join me."

It was expected that the Geriatrics would comprise the front row for the series against the Springboks but Northern Transvaal flanker Burger Geldenhuys ruined that planning when he shattered Andy Dalton's jaw with a rogue punch in the tour's second game, ending Dalton's active participation. Ashworth and Knight's front row partner thus became Hika Reid, although for the final test the now veteran Ashworth was replaced by Steve McDowell.

It didn't matter to Ashworth that a two match ban was imposed on the Cavaliers upon their return, because he slid quietly out of top-level rugby. He managed a couple of club matches for Takapau but within a year had turned his attentions to coaching, helping out with the club under-19s. He has since coached the Hawke's Bay Colts, the Southern club in Dannevirke and various age group sides in southern Hawke's Bay.

But his greater passion is in following the careers of his sons Leith, who is in the first XV at Palmerston North Boys High School, Tyler, a prop with the Hereworth College first XV, and five-year-old Shay.

Graeme Bachop

There is an elite band of individuals who have been selected to wear the All Black jersey before representing their province. Robert Wilson achieved it in 1884, George Dickinson (who was also to play cricket for New Zealand) in 1922 and Grahame Thorne in 1967.

The only other player in 113 years who has managed to win over the national panel before convincing the local selectors of his worth is Graeme Bachop. His fairytale rise from club player to international happened at the age of 20 in 1987, a few months after New Zealand had dazzled the rugby world with their immaculate play at the first World Cup.

David Kirk, who captained that famous team and whose charismatic nature did so much to advance the popularity of the game, took off for Oxford University late in the season as a Rhodes Scholar, leaving a significant vacancy in the All Blacks for the tour of Japan. Co-coaches John Hart and Alex Wyllie decided it was an excellent opportunity to 'blood' a newcomer, and the footballer they elevated to instant stardom was Bachop who'd performed so effectively for their New Zealand Colts team that same season.

Bachop didn't let them down, slotting easily into the All Black machine, although if he thought his new status would assure him of recognition back home, he was mistaken. The Canterbury coach, Doug Bruce, stayed faithful to Bruce Deans at halfback, lengthening the bizarre nature of Bachop's career.

By the end of the 1988 season, by which time he had undertaken

Graeme Bachop . . . one of only four players to wear the All Black jersey before turning out for their province.   Andrew Cornaga (Photosport)

Graeme Bachop

two overseas tours as an All Black, Bachop had played one game for Canterbury! It was, he admits, a perplexing stage of his career.

He came under pressure to move to other unions. John Hart suggested that if the frustration of warming the reserves bench for Canterbury was becoming unbearable, he should move to Auckland where his talents would certainly be appreciated.

He considered the offers, discussed the issue with 'Grizz' Wyllie, whose Canterbury teams had achieved greatness in the 1980s, and opted to stay put.

In the finish, it all worked out for the best. By the time he relocated himself in Japan in 1995 he had chalked up 71 appearances for Canterbury and had participated in 31 tests for his country, winning recognition at the third World Cup in South Africa as arguably the finest scrumhalf in the game.

There were to be extreme highs and lows in the career of the man who came to be known as Grim.

Lyttelton isn't one of the more fashionable towns in New Zealand but the seaside suburb of Christchurch has made a significant contribution to New Zealand rugby. When the All Blacks toured Britain and France in 1972-73 the coach was Bob Duff who resided in, and was later to become deputy mayor of, Lyttelton.

Duff's team fired the enthusiasm of five-year-old Graeme Bachop who also lived in Lyttelton. Along with the rest of the family, Graeme got up in the middle of the night during that tour to cheer on the All Blacks. Graeme, the second youngest of seven children, amused his family when he stood up during one of the internationals and declared, "I'm going to be an All Black!"

The Bachops' father Norman was a New Zealander but their mother Timi, who was born in Tahiti and raised in Rarotonga, claimed a grandfather who was Western Samoan. That gave the Bachop children one-sixteenth Samoan blood, enough to qualify Stephen for that nation's World Cup team in 1991.

A watersider, Norman Bachop was a committeeman of the Lyttelton Rugby Football Club and, naturally, a great supporter of his four sons, who all played for the club. Brian and Tony, the two eldest boys, made it to the seniors but Graeme and Stephen, the two who would aspire to international status, switched to the Linwood club as teenagers to further their careers.

Rugby Greats

When Graeme arrived at Linwood, to join the under-16s, he could pass only one way, a serious shortcoming for an aspiring halfback, but the problem was soon remedied when he came under the influence of Brent Elder, the former Canterbury and Wairarapa representative.

Bachop is hugely appreciative of the encouragement and guidance he received at Linwood from Elder. "He could see I had the ability," says Bachop. "It was a case of putting it together. He taught me so much, when to use my flair, when to try and dominate. I was pretty timid at fifteen, but he encouraged me to start barking at the forwards."

It wasn't long before the Bachop brothers began to get noticed. Graeme was used by the Canterbury under-16 coach, but as a first-five, the halfback slot going to a likely lad by name of Jon Preston. It would take Bachop several years before he would shrug off the challenge of Preston.

In 1983, Preston was at halfback and Bachop at first-five in the South Island under-16 team which defeated North in the curtainraiser to the Canterbury-Auckland Ranfurly Shield contest at Lancaster Park. Although he contributed a dropped goal, it's fair to say he hadn't yet made a name for himself – he was listed in the programme as Graham Bauchop. Two years later when he was a reserve for South Island under-18 he would appear in the programme as Graeme Gachop!

Bachop's natural talent was obvious from a young age and as a 16-year-old he was taken to the national provincial sevens tournament at Feilding. He learnt several years later that that was where Alex Wyllie first underlined him as a player of the future. By the time he was 18 he had won his way into the New Zealand touch team alongside Joe Stanley.

The provincial match of the century took place at Lancaster Park in 1985 when Auckland held on desperately to win the Ranfurly Shield from Canterbury. Bachop was on the field that day, at halfback for Canterbury against Auckland in the colts curtainraiser. Among his opponents were Michael Jones and Zinzan Brooke.

Promising as he was, Bachop didn't force Canterbury coach Doug Bruce into acts of recklessness in 1986 or 1987. Bruce was more than content to have Bruce Deans firing out passes behind the Canterbury scrum. Backing him up was Alan Lindsay, who surely holds the

Graeme Bachop

Canterbury record for time spent on the reserves bench. That left Bachop to serve his apprenticeship with the Colts.

The circumstances were to alter dramatically late in the 1987 season, however, when Bachop was fast-tracked into the All Blacks. His opportunity came after he attended the national colts trials and coaching school at Porirua. "Someone whispered to me that I was a player the selectors were interested in," says Bachop. "Encouraged, I put my body on the line in the trial, which I had to do because our team spent most of the game defending."

Bachop was duly selected for the Colts along with his brother Stephen. It was an excellent team with which to be associated, being jointly coached by John Hart and Alex Wyllie, who had come on to the national panel to assist Brian Lochore. "They instilled so much confidence in me," says Bachop. "Believing in yourself is a major part of playing rugby at that level, and I responded to their encouragement."

Recovering from a surprise first-up loss to Wairarapa-Bush, the Colts team of '87 developed into a formidable combination, winning their 'test' against the Australians at Takapuna by 37 points to 12.

Bachop marked Ricky Stuart who was being billed as the next Australian halfback (but who would make his mark in league). "He was a quality player," says Bachop, "behind a strong pack. But our loose forwards (Robin Brooke at No. 8, Duane Monkley and Kevin Schuler) were brilliant and set up the victory."

After that, it was life as normal for Bachop – club action with the Linwood senior team and representative outings for the Canterbury Colts. There was no reason to expect that in a few months his life would be changed forever as he was projected into the national limelight.

Bachop the carpenter was earning some overtime money one Sunday in September when the All Black team to tour Japan was announced on radio, and he was in it! "It didn't take the media long to track me down," he says. "Suddenly, I was in the spotlight. They took me down to Latimer Square for the interviews. I've never been particularly comfortable in front of television cameras, so you can imagine how I felt on that occasion. I was Graeme Who?"

His selection delighted the Bachops – "a great sporting family," says Graeme – and the whole of the Lyttelton community. "The people of Lyttelton are very close, and they respond when one of their people is recognised. I kept receiving all these cheques in the mail, many of them from watersiders who obviously didn't have a lot of money. Their generosity was greatly appreciated."

Because he'd sidestepped the system to reach the All Blacks – leap-frogging Andrew Donald and Dean Kenny who'd played in the trials – he didn't know anyone when the All Blacks assembled, apart from a couple of the Canterbury players, among them fellow halfback Bruce Deans. "Buck Shelford, the captain, had never heard of me," says Bachop, "and most of the players didn't know who I was which was rather daunting."

Eager to justify his selection, Bachop was depressed after the first training session in Auckland. "I stuffed everything up," he says. "I put the ball into the scrums too quickly and rolled passes along the ground to Grant Fox. I was too nervous." With encouragement from Hart and Wyllie, Bachop soon settled down and by the time he arrived in Japan he'd overcome his nervousness and was operating like a true All Black.

Bachop was to have a luxurious entry into international rugby. In his first two outings, against a Japanese Selection and the Asian Barbarians, the All Blacks scored a total of 35 tries without conceding one. While it would have been hard for any player not to excel in the circumstances, Bachop, who basically concerned himself with the rapid despatch of the surfeit of possession the All Black forwards claimed, won admiring reviews for his performances.

Being an All Black didn't alter Bachop's status around Canterbury significantly in 1988, although he was introduced to the representative squad at Lindsay's expense. The No 9 jersey remained the exclusive property of Bruce Deans, however.

The All Black selectors were prepared to back their investment and Bachop was reserve to Deans for the tests against Wales. Three days before the Auckland international (June 11) Bachop celebrated his 21st birthday. It was also selector Lane Penn's birthday, which merited a party. "We were made to drink rum and eat half of the birthday cake each," said Bachop. "As it was as hard as rock, that was quite a challenge!"

By the time he headed for Australia with Buck Shelford's men in June, Bachop still had not represented his province. But he was an All Black and that was the ultimate for an eager young Kiwi. His six

Graeme Bachop

Graeme Bachop, doing what a halfback should do best – clearing the ball as swiftly as possible to his backline. Andrew Cornaga (Photosport)

outings yielded him seven tries at such unfashionable rugby settings as Perth, Singleton, Canberra, Townsville, Gosford and Melbourne. "It was," he says, "not easy to perform immediately at that level when I wasn't getting any representative rugby back home."

The Rugby Annual lavished praise on him: "Bachop . . . something of a gamble but came through mightily. Got only the six lesser games but revealed a snappy pass and an elusiveness that brought him seven tries." In a quagmire against ACT, Bachop demonstrated the skills that would, in time, carry him into the top echelon of rugby halfbacks. Not only was his passing assured in the most trying of conditions, he dribbled the ball almost 50 metres for an exceptional try.

In August of '88 he finally made his Canterbury debut, against Bay of Plenty at Lancaster Park when Deans was carrying an injury. Thrilled to finally wear the red and black jersey, Bachop says he was ready when the occasion came. "Before every game, when I was a reserve, I would prepare as if I was going on. For so long I never did because Bruce was so resilient."

When Frank Jack took over as Canterbury coach in 1989, Bachop was his preferred halfback, but it didn't help when the side lost all five matches in the South Pacific championship series. Bachop was returned to the reserves bench, as back-up to Deans, for the NPC.

Rugby Greats

If that was a setback, his career was to take off spectacularly when the All Blacks toured Wales and Ireland, for he would displace Deans from the test line-up. Which was quite something in a Wyllie-coached team, considering that Deans had played in every one of Canterbury's Ranfurly Shield defences from 1982 to 1985 and in every test since Wyllie had become All Black coach at the beginning of 1988.

Apart from finding the fanaticism of the Welsh hard to bear, Bachop loved every minute of the tour, and of course his elevation to test status was the icing on the cake. It was a sensationally good team with which to be associated. "Of all the teams I have played in," says Bachop, "the All Blacks of 1988 and 1989 were the greatest. You just knew they were never going to lose. The players weren't cocky, they placed pressure on themselves to keep winning." And win they did, the All Blacks sweeping through both countries, winning all 14 matches.

Bachop was overcome with nerves when he ran on to Cardiff Arms Park for his test debut. "I could hardly breathe," he says. "It was the most nervous I have ever been. I remember Steve McDowell asking me if I was all right. It was all I could do to answer him."

Once the adrenalin kicked in with the referee's first blow on the whistle, Bachop relaxed. He went on to give an accomplished performance, capping it with a try. "I couldn't believe how quickly the game went. When the final whistle sounded, I thought it was for the next play."

He was lucky to survive the Dublin international after his head came violently into contact with an Irish player's hip. "It was dark and I was dazed and I seemed to be lost for a while. Fortunately, our physio produced some smelling salts which brought me around. I remember giving Foxy a pass from which he scored, only to have it ruled out when the touch judge intervened."

The highlight of the Barbarians game at Twickenham was a triple scissors move, involving Zinzan Brooke, Craig Innes and Bachop, which produced an important try for Brooke. It was an old Canterbury move which Bachop called. "I think the code name was Varsity," he says. "It's an oldie but a goodie and it worked to perfection that day, allowing us to come home unbeaten."

Bachop has only the highest of praise for skipper Shelford. "He was an incredible leader, an individual with great mana. If a game wasn't going right, he would call the guys together and say, 'Right, this is what we're going to do.' He never lost as an All Black captain, and I personally believe it was a mistake to drop him in 1990. We missed him at the World Cup the next year."

After the frustrations of the previous three seasons, 1990 was a delight for Bachop. With Deans having retired, he finally established himself as Canterbury's first-choice halfback. And as an All Black he was at halfback in all seven tests (against Scotland and Australia at home and against France at Nantes and Paris).

If that was the good news, the bad news was that the wheels on the mighty All Black machine were beginning to loosen and pretty soon would fall off. The team that had been invincible since '87 dropped the third test of the Bledisloe Cup series to Australia at Athletic Park and then lost two of the warm-up games in France. The next season they would lose to the Wallabies twice more, most disastrously in the World Cup semi-final in Dublin.

"Everyone's had a go at trying to account for the All Blacks' downfall," says Bachop. "I just feel that because they had been together for so long, they were beginning to get stale. Probably the mistake was in not making changes, but when you string together fifty successive victories, it's hard to toss players out."

Bachop identifies the referees as a major cause of the New Zealanders' problems at Toulon and Bayonne in France. "They wouldn't allow us to develop second or third phase ball," he says. "It's hard to score from set play against determined opponents. It was entirely different in the tests, with neutral referees. We got our second phases going and won both internationals easily."

Of the World Cup campaign of 1991, Bachop remembers only the loss to Australia and the sense of despair and disappointment that engulfed the team afterwards. "The Aussies were better prepared than us, and blew us away. We didn't have any answers."

Bachop found it incredibly difficult to come up for another international midweek, but with a number of changes (notably Jon Preston and Walter Little coming in as the five-eighths) the All Blacks managed to put away Scotland to secure the bronze medal.

In the wake of the World Cup disasters, vast changes swept through the All Black scene. Laurie Mains replaced Alex Wyllie as coach, Gary Whetton was unwanted as a player or captain and Ant Strachan was suddenly in vogue as a halfback.

Rugby Greats

Bachop was still in the picture but was to lose valuable ground at a halfbacks' meeting, convened by Lin Colling, in Napier at the time of the trials. Bachop had rushed back from representing his country at the Hong Kong sevens tournament and, jetlagged, had difficulty focusing on Colling's words.

"I gather I received a poor report for attitude," says Bachop. "It was probably justified but I was dreadfully tired. That session was the last thing I needed. All I wanted to do was sleep."

Bachop was given the first test of the Mains era, against the World team at Christchurch, but an inglorious loss saw Strachan introduced for the remainder of the series. Bachop was then dropped altogether, being replaced by his old Canterbury rival Jon Preston, for the tests against Ireland and for the tour of Australia and South Africa.

He did get to Australia, for the match aganst ACT at Canberra when the touring party was beset with injuries. It was a significant occasion, being the first time he and his brother Stephen (who had gone to the '91 World Cup with Western Samoa) had operated together as All Blacks. But that was to be it for Graeme internationally until 1994.

"I was an All Black reject at twenty-four," he says. "It was hard facing people, although life went on. A lot said I deserved to be there. But the selectors didn't think so."

Bachop admits that it took some time before he wanted to be back in the All Blacks. "It probably sounds odd, but for a long time I couldn't get rid of the rejected feeling."

Come 1994 and he decided to do something about his career, to try and kick-start it back into life. After 11 years with Linwood he moved to the High School Old Boys club, not for the social facilities but to link, as a player, with Andrew Mehrtens. "I had a few sleepless nights before I made the decision to move," he says. "Mehrts had come into the Canterbury side in 1993 and I could see he was the first-five of the future. I felt it was in my interests to work with him."

The other individual at HSOB who would help shape his destiny was Steve Hansen, who would become assistant coach of Canterbury. "He really helped get me back on track," says Bachop. "The 'want' to be an All Black returned.' Bachop doesn't believe his rugby changed, only the determination to re-establish himself at the top.

He became aware that Laurie Mains was showing interest again. Although he missed selection for the main trial in Napier, where Stu

30

Graeme Bachop

Forster and Junior Tonu'u were the halfbacks, he was delighted to be named a reserve (behind Forster) for the tests against France, and even more delighted when, after the team had suffered a couple of embarrassing losses, he was returned to the test No 9 jersey.

Mains explains that there were aspects of Bachop's play the selectors considered weaknesses. "He rarely ran down the left side of the field from a ruck or maul. He had a favourite side for kicking and a favourite side for running, which made him rather predictable. Once we drew his attention to these traits, he worked on them and became a far more rounded footballer."

A nice aspect of his return to international duty was teaming up with brother Stephen for the series against the Springboks and the spectacular Bledisloe Cup test in Sydney. "It was good to be back," he says. "Not many make it back after being dropped."

The second 40 minutes in Sydney would reveal the high-powered, attacking rugby the All Blacks would produce with such devastating effect at the World Cup. "Even though it was a loss, it pointed the way to go," says Bachop. "We played that spell at incredible pace, which is how I enjoy my rugby."

While on the rugby 'scrapheap' in 1993 and into 1994, Bachop had

Try coming up for Graeme Bachop against Canada at Eden Park in 1995.

Andrew Cornaga (Photosport)

given serious consideration to his future as he was struggling to survive as a carpenter. He'd asked his former Canterbury colleague Andrew McCormick to inquire if there was a Japanese club interested in his services, which resulted in an approach during the Hong Kong sevens tournament early in 1994.

By the time he returned to All Black duty, he was committed to moving to Japan at the conclusion of the 1994 season to work and play rugby for the Sanix club of Fukuoka. Although he dearly wanted to participate in the third World Cup, future security was his first priority. He and his wife Angela flew away to a new culture, leaving Laurie Mains to convince the NZRFU he was worthy of selection in 1995 even though resident outside New Zealand.

Mains won his argument, and Bachop returned not only for the World Cup campaign but stayed for the Bledisloe Cup games in '95 as well. It was a most satisfactory outcome all round. Thanks in no small part to the input of Bachop – who rivalled Springbok Joost van der Westhuizen as the most commanding halfback at the World Cup – the All Blacks produced rugby of divine quality, sweeping aside opponent after opponent until the tragic stumble against the South Africans in the tournament final.

Bachop was rooming with Mehrtens in Johannesburg when the poisoning hit 48 hours before the grand final. "Andrew was the first one to be affected," he says. "After that, they dropped like flies. It was a nightmare after everything had been going along so sweetly. Although I suffered comparatively mildly, I was drained of energy during the game.

"After the disappointments of 1991, all I wanted to achieve in rugby was a World Cup win. We had the team and the tactics to succeed, but sadly, it wasn't to be."

Finally, in August 1995, after two cracking victories over Australia, Bachop returned to Japan where he has had the satisfaction of assisting his Sanix team to complete a spectacular rise from fifth division to the first division in four years. Also involved with the club are former All Blacks Mark Finlay and Jamie Joseph.

Graeme and Angela's son Taylor was born (in Christchurch) in June, 1996.

Robin Brooke

Hauling a television set up to Auckland Hospital was a challenging task, but the least Robin Brooke felt he could do after learning that his brother Zinzan was to be confined to his bed for several days. It was early June, 1992.

Zinzan, a proven international rugby player who'd been on the scrapheap since New Zealand's demise at the second World Cup the previous October, had undergone surgery for a gash on his leg which had become deeply infected.

Being restricted to a hospital bed can be a lonely existence. Hence the request for the TV set which Robin dutifully hooked up and tuned in.

The brothers chatted for a while, the previous Saturday's test match at Carisbrook in which the All Blacks had narrowly escaped defeat against Ireland the major topic.

With the time approaching 6 o'clock, Robin suggested it was time to be getting home.

"Why don't you hang around for the sports news," said Zinzan, obviously eager for company, "and see how many test players get dumped."

Their interested heightened when the news headlines informed them that the All Black selectors had made sweeping changes for the second test at Athletic Park.

They tried to guess who the new players would be, while waiting with fascination for the team announcement. Two names that didn't figure among their list of possibilities were their own.

Getting ready for the World Cup tournament in 1995. Campaign manager Brian Lochore chats with, from left, Graeme Bachop, Ian Jones (obscured) and Robin Brooke. *Andrew Cornaga (Photosport)*

Robin Brooke didn't absorb the names of all the newcomers – there were six – because he was totally flabbergasted when he heard his name read out (as a replacement for Blair Larsen).

"I was absolutely stunned," he admits. "I had no inkling whatsoever that the selectors were even considering me."

However, his mind did go back to a telephone call he had received while staying at Zinzan's flat in Rome at the beginning of the year. The caller hadn't identified himself to Zinzan. He wanted to speak to Robin. Zinzan didn't mind the snub until he learned that the caller was the new All Black coach Laurie Mains.

"Laurie Mains? What the hell does he want?" asked Zinzan.

"He suggests I break my contract with the Brescia club and get back to New Zealand in time for the trials."

"Did he say he wanted me to come back, too?"

"No."

"Well, if you're going, I'm going."

And they returned together, not, as it turned out, in time for the trials from which the All Black squad for the centenary matches against the World XV (and subsequently the Irish series) was chosen

Robin Brooke

but certainly in time to qualify for the major happening of the 1992 season, the tour of Australia and South Africa.

That was the event Robin thought Mains was luring him back home for, the big tour for which 30 players would be selected. Instead, he was suddenly a test player. He could scarcely believe it.

A few others were having trouble comprehending it, as well. Former test winger Stu Wilson wrote in his column in Truth, "Robin Who?"

"I had my first knocker before I'd even played," he said.

As he reflected on his sensational elevation to international status, Robin Brooke felt that he owed a vast debt of gratitude to the Japanese motor firm of Mazda. No, he didn't drive one of their models. But what they had done, which had given him his big break, was whisk his eldest brother Marty off to Japan with an offer that, as they put it so sweetly in the Mafia movies, was "too good to refuse".

Until Marty exited the scene midway through the 1990 season, Robin was in danger of becoming a professional reserve for Auckland. It seems incredible, in hindsight for someone who was to make such a huge impression at international level, that Robin Brooke would be used only five times by Auckland in three full years after debuting as a 20-year-old in 1987.

He admits to becoming thoroughly frustrated warming the reserves bench while his brother Marty and Gary Whetton forged an impressive locking combination. "In the finish," he says, "I started going out nightclubbing on Friday nights – I knew I was never going to be needed."

And he wasn't. Not at all in 1988. Only four times in 1989, of which two were as a reserve. And once in 1990, until in August of that year Marty said "sayonara".

Robin Brooke would make dramatic progress as a lock once involved consistently at top representative level, and Mains would file his name under the Must Have category after observing him in action during 1991.

When Mains stepped aside, World Cup glory so agonisingly denied him, after the 1995 season he would state that Brooke's skills combined with his mental and physical hardness made him the best in the world in his position. "The All Blacks," said Mains, "were seldom as effective when Robin was not playing. Even if I had to pay the food bill, he would be my choice for any tour where the tests were demanding."

Food bill. Now there's a good nickname. It was acquired by Brooke after he'd completed a 13-match tour of the UK without playing a game. But we'll come to that later!

The middle of five sons (and one daughter) born to Sandy and Hine Brooke, who all grew up on a farm at Ahuroa, about 20 kilometres inland from Puhoi north of Auckland, Robin would distinguish himself early in life with his prowess as an athlete.

Marty and Zinzan had been pretty accomplished performers on the athletic track, but Robin would not only eclipse their achievements but those of every other Northlander in his age bracket.

Records in the discus, the shot put, the javelin and the long jump at Mahurangi College and Northland-wide were held by Marty and Zinzan. Robin set fresh marks in the lot, several of which still stand.

Then when he went off to the nationals in his early teens he created records for the discus (extending the old mark by almost 20cm) and the shot put.

When international sprint star Alan Wells appeared at a widely promoted athletics meeting in Whangarei he almost had the limelight stolen away from him by Robin who won his 100 metre dash, in the prelude to the big sprint of the afternoon, in 11.65s.

Because of his involvement in athletics, and also basketball, Robin was a later developer at rugby than his brothers had been. Which doesn't mean he didn't still do the traditional Kiwi thing of being involved in the national game from the age of five.

The Brooke family rugby show used to swing into action on Saturday mornings, on behalf of the Puhoi club. "Mum was the manager and dad the coach," recalls Robin. "Dad was an excellent coach who shaped our rugby for many years. He had been a useful footballer himself." As a lock, Sandy Brooke had played a number of games for the Barbarians alongside such greats as Tiny White and Peter Jones.

"On Saturday mornings Marty and Zinny and myself would jump into dad's Holden Kingswood and head for the rugby, picking up numerous kids along the way. There was always a big drum of cocoa on board which I usually found more appealing than the rugby!"

It wasn't until his fifth form year that Robin began to focus his

Robin Brooke

attentions seriously on rugby. By then he was established in the Mahurangi College first XV and word was spreading that another quality product had been produced by the Brooke rugby-making family of Ahuroa.

As a 15-year-old he had the thrill of playing at Eden Park prior to the third Wallaby test in 1982, a member of the North Island under-16 team, a side from which surprisingly few players have gone on to achieve national recognition.

The next year he was pulling on the black jersey for the first time, as a New Zealand under-17 representative, sharing in the victory over Australia, again at Eden Park. That team, coached by former All Black winger Ralph Caulton, featured Stephen Bachop at first-five.

Brooke made rapid progress in 1984. In September, he locked the North Island under-18 scrum at Carisbrook with Steve Gordon, a team whose reserves featured Daryl Halligan and Errol Brain. This was after he'd been named player of the tournament at the Northern Region under-18 event in Opotiki.

From there he was selected in the New Zealand schools team that undertook a seven-week tour of the UK and Holland, under the coaching expertise of Graham Henry. Although the players had to contribute to the funding, it was too good an opportunity to miss, especially with internationals scheduled for Murrayfield, Lansdowne Road, Cardiff Arms Park and Twickenham.

Brooke celebrated his 18th birthday on the tour which he recalls as "an incredible experience". Their first stop was Disneyland. Throughout the UK the players were billeted for all the midweek games and accommodated in hotels for the internationals.

The winning touch that Henry would bring to the Auckland representative team rubbed off on to his schoolboys. They won 11 of their 12 matches, losing only to Wales, when, according to Brooke, "nothing went right." Scotland was beaten 37-6, Ireland 20-3 and England 12-6 but the scoreline against Wales was a disappointing 9-12.

His schooling completed, and with the his parents selling the farm at Ahuroa, Brooke moved down to Auckland, to study building at Carrington Tech. It was natural that he would follow Marty and Zinzan to the Marist club. The year he joined them, 1985, they were starting to advance promisingly up the rugby ladder. It was to be Marty's first year as an Auckland representative while Zinzan would make an impression as a New Zealand Colt.

Robin, still only 18, was nurtured that first season in the Marist thirds, the team from which John Kirwan had been so sensationally plucked two years earlier by Auckland coach John Hart. Brooke didn't make quite such an instant impact, but he was soon called on by the Auckland Colts selector.

In 1986, he joined his brothers in the Marist senior team. Within a year the trio would take the field on the same afternoon for Auckland.

For Brooke, 1987 was a season of spectacular progress and thrilling success, one which pointed to a long and distinguished career at representative level. But the early flattery would only deceive. In April, with his brother Marty, and Mata'afa Keenan, sidelined with injury, he was introduced by Auckland coaches Maurice Trapp and Bryan Williams for the South Pacific Championship series, making his debut against Queensland on Eden Park.

What a galaxy of talent surrounding the 20-year-old lock. "Fourteen All Blacks and me," he recalls. "Well, some of them, like Michael Jones and brother Zinny, wouldn't actually become internationals until the World Cup kicked off the next month, but I was definitely the odd man out." Thirteen of the players around him that afternoon were to contribute to New Zealand's World Cup triumph.

Brooke's was disadvantaged by having to pack on the loosehead (or left) side of the scrum, having played all his rugby to that point on the tighthead side. The privilege of packing there belonged to Gary Whetton.

"I honestly couldn't push with my left shoulder," says Brooke, "which upset our loosehead prop, Steve McDowell. In the finish he became really annoyed and, as one scrum was going down, he grabbed me by the hair and said, 'Push, you bastard, push!'"

Notwithstanding Brooke's personal difficulties, Auckland produced dazzling rugby to hammer Queensland 43-18, the highlight being John Kirwan's 70-metre try.

Brooke was retained for the next three matches, against Fiji, Canterbury and the NPC clash with Wairarapa-Bush, but with his brother Marty soon returned to full fitness, he would be given only one further outing that season, a notable one in the Ranfurly Shield defence against East Coast.

Robin Brooke

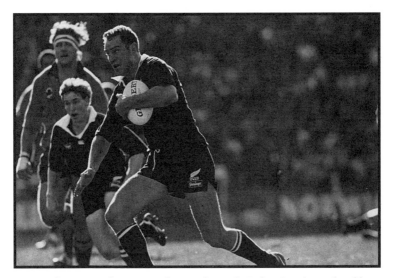

Proving he's more than just a lineout forward, Robin Brooke makes like a midfielder against Australia at Eden Park in 1995.   *Joanna Caird (Photosport)*

It was notable because Robin played at No. 8, Zinzan on the side of the scrum and Marty at lock. Perhaps not too surprisingly, because Robin and Marty were vying for the same spot, it would be the only occasion the three brothers would be selected for the same Auckland line-up, although they did have a couple of onfield reunions in 1989 when Robin got involved as a replacement.

Although largely neglected by the Auckland coaches, Brooke was snapped up by the New Zealand Colts bosses John Hart and Alex Wyllie and used as a No. 8 in the test against Australia at Takapuna, contributing handsomely to the side's decisive 37-12 victory.

It was a display which led to him being named one of New Zealand's five most promising players in the *Rugby Almanack*.

More than satisfied at the direction in which his career was headed, Brooke accepted an invitation to play the off-season in Italy, with the Livorno club. He reminds you, rather pointedly, that Livorno is where the high-powered liqueur Sambuca is made. Without quite re-creating all the events that led to the Decline and Fall of the Roman Empire, Brooke does imply that an excess of the good life did nothing to enhance his status as a rugby player in 1988.

"When I arrived back home, I was pushing the scales beyond

eighteen stone and was in anything but peak condition," he says. "Auckland was flush with locks at the time – Gary Whetton, brother Marty, Mata'afa Keenan and Rob Cheval – and I rather fell behind." Trapp and Williams, the Auckland coaches, didn't concern themselves at all with an overweight Brooke in '88. However, what might have been an entirely anonymous year for him was salvaged through participation in the New Zealand Maori tour of Italy, France, Spain and Argentina.

"What a great experience that was," he says. "The social element was fantastic while the rugby took on all the aspects of a boxing tour!"

Brooke says that after coach Mattie Blackburn had gone to considerable lengths to outline acceptable standards of behaviour, at the first port of call, L'Aquila in Italy, Mike Te Paa, the giant front-rower from North Harbour, stayed up all night drinking rum and strumming a guitar.

"Mattie blew him up at the first training session," says Brooke, "but Mike was unfazed. It was a wonderfully relaxed tour, a real hoot."

In the second match, at Toulon, three players were sent off and the whole game degenerated into a running battle. "There were," says Brooke, "loads of fights, especially in France and Argentina. It was good fun at the time. Maoris enjoy a Wild West shoot-out and we all stuck together which resulted in some spectacular all-ins. I'm sure it wouldn't be acceptable now but it made for a memorable tour in 1988!"

The three Brooke brothers regularly operated together, Marty and Robin at lock with Zinzan on the side of the scrum, the No. 8 jersey being the property of the skipper Buck Shelford.

Back home in 1989 – the year in which Marist won the Auckland senior club championship for the first time in 39 years – Brooke was condemned to the reserves bench for Auckland, being selected for only the Barbarians and Mid-Canterbury matches.

"There was a group of us who sat out most games on the bench – Mark and John Carter, Craig Dowd, Olo Brown and me," Brooke recalls. "I ate a lot of chocolate bars and started going out on Friday nights. It was a frustrating time in my career during which I seriously contemplated a move to North Harbour or Otago. Upon reflection, I probably should have gone, but I respected my spot on the reserves bench. I knew that if I made Auckland I was basically in the All Blacks."

The breakthrough didn't come until midway through 1990 when brother Marty forsook mashed potatoes for rice, heading to Japan when a major career opportunity was offered by Mazda. His departure saw Robin team up with Gary Whetton and play the last nine matches of the season.

Brooke established himself during 1991 as one of the foremost locks in New Zealand. The *Rugby Annual* noted that he was "consistently the stand-out performer in the pack" while the *Rugby Almanack* observed that "Brooke's consistent displays must surely earn him national selection before long." Fine sentiments, but not ones supported by national coach Alex Wyllie who, at a cost, stuck with his tried and true performers.

Brooke says he gave himself a reasonable chance of making the World Cup squad in '91 but when he missed out he elected to spend another summer in Italy, this time with the Brescia club in the north. He was enjoying his existence and was reasonably fit but was not concerning himself greatly about events in New Zealand, until the call came in from Laurie Mains.

"That put a whole new complexion on things," he says. "If the All Black coach was suggesting I return New Zealand, I felt it was a sensible thing to get down there as swiftly as possible."

Brooke's test debut was on a typically murky Wellington winter's day, with Athletic Park being lashed by a cold southerly. It didn't dampen the All Blacks' spirit, though. With six changes from Carisbrook – Olo Brown and Matthew Cooper were also making their test debuts, and John Timu, Michael Jones and Mike Brewer had been recalled – the team blitzed Ireland in the second half, recording a record 59-6 victory.

If the victory was sweet, even sweeter afterwards for Brooke was hearing coach Mains announce that everyone who'd played that day was "in" for the tour of Australia and South Africa.

Someone who hadn't played and who was plainly on the outer with the selectors was Zinzan. But thanks to some serious lobbying by All Black skipper Sean Fitzpatrick, both Brooke brothers were among the 30 named for the big trip. By the time of the second test in Australia they would both be in the test fifteen.

Rugby Greats

Robin Brooke soars high to secure possession against Italy at Bologna in 1995.

Mark Leech (Photosport)

Brooke came to admire coach Mains, as a forward finding him technically outstanding. "We trained our arses off in Australia," he says. "I learnt, for the first time in my life, how far I could push myself. Although I think I might have discovered a fresh limit at Taupo the next February! The training paid off with classic victories in the third test in Sydney (Brooke marking Rod McCall throughout the series) and against the Springboks at Ellis Park."

The All Blacks' first try against the Springboks in Johannesburg came when brother Zinzan audaciously took a quick tap and surged through to the goalline, catching the South Africans napping. Brooke remembers saying to him, "No, no, no, no!"

"But he did, and he scored," says Robin. "That's his trademark."

The *Rugby Annual* identified the brothers Brooke as "the superstars of the famous victory over South Africa. Robin Brooke was still going like a human dynamo when most of the others were, in Mains' words, 'absolutely knackered'."

It was on that tour that Brooke first encountered lifting in the lineouts. "They had it down to an art form," he says, "which is how come these two 6ft 3in locks cleaned us out in the Junior Springboks game. Thank goodness we're all now allowed to be lifted."

Things went pretty sweetly for Brooke in 1993. He appeared in all the domestic internationals, against the Lions, the Wallabies and the Western Samoans, and helped Auckland through to another NPC title, although there was the small hiccup of the loss of the Ranfurly Shield (after nine years and 61 defences) to Waikato.

In listing him as a player of the year, the *Rugby Annual* identified him as the outstanding player in all five domestic tests. "It was a measure of the esteem in which his teammates held him," the editor noted, "that whenever the All Blacks faced a pressure lineout, they invariably threw to Brooke."

Brooke's glorious season began to come seriously unstuck in the NPC final against Otago at Eden Park when he "blew" his calf muscle.

"I'd never torn a muscle in my life," he says, "so it was a mystifying and traumatic happening. And unfortunately I didn't receive the treatment most appropriate to such an injury."

The All Blacks assembled a week later to prepare for the tour of England and Scotland, and the medical panel, noting a straight-forward calf muscle tear, cleared Brooke to tour. He would be ready for action within a fortnight of arriving in the UK, they concluded.

Well, not only was Brooke not playing within a fortnight, he completed the entire seven-week rugby expedition without once taking the field. Blair Larsen was taken along as a temporary replacement and he also stayed for the full tour.

Brooke's unusual status earned him the nickname of 'Foodbill'. His continuing presence became something of an embarrassment to manager Neil Gray who ruled after the sixth match at Galashiels that he had to return home, after he'd failed yet another fitness test.

Gray organised for Brooke to head for the airport when the team departed by coach for Glasgow. That was the theory. But when the over-zealous duty boys threw Brooke's bags in with the team luggage, which went on ahead, he was obliged to travel to Glasgow too, missing his scheduled flight.

Somehow after that, he managed to escape the manager's attention and survived right through to the Barbarians match at Cardiff, the 13th game of the tour!

Without potting anyone, Brooke claims the medical advice he received for the calf injury was "all wrong".

"I was initially advised to walk on the leg when I should have been resting it. And soon after my arrival in the UK, I was being ordered to jog. I could feel the muscle pulling as I moved. I was assured it was scar tissue that would break and heal. It broke all right, worse than before. And in a different place. In the finish, my calf muscle was like mincemeat."

The agony continued back in New Zealand as Brooke sought to put the frustrations of the UK tour behind him and build up for the new season. However, the Auckland team had taken on a new trainer who seemed to think he was preparing a class of Carl Lewis sprinters.

"I blew the other calf then," recalls Brooke. "It had become overloaded when I started favouring the original injury. My calves were in a hell of a mess."

In despair, Brooke tried physiotherapists, naturopaths, masseurs and healers, but nothing fixed the trouble with any permanency, although his legs held together well enough for Mains to use him in the second and third tests against the Springboks. "I wasn't right, but I was hanging together," he says.

It was damage a long way from his calves that kept him out of the Bledisloe Cup international in Sydney, though – this time the All Black skipper's head causing Brooke's cheekbone to cave in during the third Bok test. He suffered a dropped eyeball.

At season's end, and determined to be in condition for the World Cup, Brooke resumed his search for the panacea that would allow him to reproduce his best form. Through his girlfriend Hailey (they were married at the beginning of 1996) he was introduced to a Tongan masseur, Koni Talea.

"He couldn't believe the mess my legs were in," says Brooke. "It took several months but he finally got them sorted out, in time for the World Cup."

A rehabilitated Robin Brooke survived the brutal summer training camps and was champing at the bit, ready for World Cup action, until the unbelievable happened. In running around the Takapuna Golf Course in Auckland, the day before departure for South Africa, he felt a tweak in his calf muscle again.

"I couldn't believe it. Not again, I thought. This is too bad to be true. Zinzan was in a fight against time to get his Achilles tendon sorted out and now I was crocked too."

Robin Brooke

For a couple of weeks, as the tournament swung into action, the Brooke brothers became known as the Broke brothers.

It's history now that they both returned to action – to the intense relief of coach Laurie Mains – in the record-shattering romp against the Japanese at Bloemfontein, going on to perform starring roles against Scotland, England and South Africa in the play-offs.

Robin Brooke's participation in the tournament was secured after a dramatic (and painful) session on a treadmill in Johannesburg. After a South African doctor had advised that he return to New Zealand, it was former All Black doctor Lawrie 'Spock' Knight who suggested that the trouble was almost certainly deep scar tissue around the nerve. "He convinced me I could run through it," says Brooke. "To cut a long story short, I did, to the immense relief of the All Black management, and myself."

Calf muscle injuries are a thing of the past now for Brooke who in 1996 participated in all 10 tests – locking the scrum with Ian Jones and bringing his number of test appearances to 32 – and enjoyed overwhelming success at every level.

The All Blacks won a historic first series in South Africa and took out the Bledisloe Cup and the Tri-Nations series, Auckland reclaimed the Ranfurly Shield and bagged a fourth straight NPC; and (although because of his national commitments he didn't get to play for them) Marist won the prestigious Gallaher Shield as Auckland's premier club.

A builder with Fletchers until 1991, Brooke is now a director of his own building company, one which early in 1997 had four houses under construction in west Auckland.

Having played a leading role in the WRC negotiations in 1995, Brooke enjoys life as a professional rugby player. He has his own personal trainer (Lee Parore at Les Mills) and finds it much easier to balance sporting and personal commitments, with his income assured.

Zinzan Brooke

The T-shirt Zinzan Brooke was wearing said it all: UNFINISHED BUSINESS FINISHED. SCORE SETTLED. It was a T-shirt Brooke could wear proudly, because the dropped goal and the desperate final tackle he produced in the dying moments of 1996's most important rugby international, at Pretoria's Loftus Versfeld, had made it possible for the All Blacks to indeed finish their unfinished business.

Brooke was one of the players who had stood dejectedly on Ellis Park 14 months earlier ruminating on what might have been as the Springboks and their ecstatic supporters celebrated the winning of the third World Cup. After 100 minutes of total commitment, the scoreboard read: South Africa 15, New Zealand 12.

"I don't think I have ever experienced such intense disappointment as I did at that moment," says Brooke. "After the frustrations of the 1991 campaign, the winning of the third World Cup was the fiercest ambition I have known. All things being equal, I am positive the All Blacks would have won the final. All things *weren't* equal. We lost. End of story."

Well, not quite end of story. End of that story, for sure. The Springboks were crowned world champions and will remain world champions until the title is fought for again, in Wales in 1999.

But once the dust settled in Johannesburg in '95, the All Blacks filled themselves with resolve: There was a tour of South Africa on the books for 1996. They couldn't take away the Springboks' world crown but they could eke a special revenge by becoming the first New

Zinzan Brooke

Helping finish the unfinished business. Zinzan Brooke knows the significance of the dropped goal he's just landed against the Springboks at Pretoria in 1996. It put his team seven points ahead and helped secure a famous first series win in South Africa.   John Selkirk

Zealand team to win a series on South Africa soil.

They would prove they were the superior rugby team.

Fourteen months on and the All Blacks are leading the Springboks 30-26 with about five minutes to play in the second test of the series at Pretoria, one test in the bag. Five minutes to guts it out, five minutes to finally achieve that which had eluded the All Black touring teams of 1928, 1949, 1960, 1970 and 1976.

The heat has sapped the New Zealanders' energy, the altitude is burning their lungs, the Springboks, determined not to become the first team to drop a series to the All Blacks at home, are readying themselves for a final assault.

The All Blacks drive into a ruck on the 22, secure the ball, Justin

Marshall has it and, there, behind him, screaming for it, is Zinny, readying himself to drop a goal.

"It was the obvious thing to do," says Brooke, "because a goal of any sort put us seven points ahead. It meant the Springboks then had to score a try and convert it. Even if my kick missed, they were committed to a 22 drop-out which would have given us back possession."

Not every footballer would be capable of such cool, calculated reasoning five minutes from the finish of a contest between the world's two most powerful teams, played throughout at a frenetic pace. Not every loose forward would would be capable of drop-kicking a goal in such circumstances. Few would ever contemplate it.

The Springboks' hearts would have sunk with Brooke's goal, but they weren't about to concede victory. Enough time remained for them to salvage a draw and keep the series alive through to the final international at Ellis Park.

Those final moments seemed like an eternity to the All Blacks as the Springboks battered away at their goalline, forcing a series of scrums and penalties. Each desperate thrust was met by equally desperate defence. One more penalty. Time is up, surely. Hold them out this one last time and victory is assured.

A John Kirwan saying flashed into Brooke's mind: A champion is a player who gets up when he knows he can't. "Before their last tap and charge, I was on my knees. I remember saying to Olo (Brown) I didn't think I could get up. But Olo, Craig (Dowd) and myself managed to lift ourselves for one last effort."

Ruben Kruger, the great flanker, had scored a try in identical circumstances earlier in the spell because Brooke had lunged at the Springbok forwards' wedge, as they drove from a tap penalty, too high, and been pushed back. "I knew I had to go around the legs this time," he said, "and bring down the first player. This time we were able to stop the move stone dead."

The Springboks fell short of the goalline at which point referee Didier Mene's whistle blew for fulltime, the All Blacks victors by seven points. Series secured. Unfinished business finished.

Time to celebrate. Celebrate? Some of the All Blacks could scarcely lift themselves off the turf. Many were close to exhaustion. Skipper Sean Fitzpatrick would describe it unhesitatingly as the most

Zinzan Brooke

physically sapping game he had ever been involved in.

Then from the sidelines came the sound of a haka. Eric Rush and Jonah Lomu were leading it, from the reserves' bench. "It was," says Brooke, "a very special moment, rather symbolic. At that moment, I think we all began to appreciate what we had achieved."

Brooke and his fellow All Blacks, their exhaustion temporarily placed on hold, moved across to acknowledge the thousands of Kiwis in the crowd. "Every New Zealander jumped up," says Brooke. "They were waving flags and they were incredibly happy. It was a great moment. It was how I had wanted it to be at the end of the World Cup."

If 1995 had been the year of the Great Disappointment for Brooke, 1996, by which time he had reached the mature age for an international footballer of 31 and was captaining Auckland and Auckland Blues, would be the one of Endless Celebrations. For everything in rugby Zinzan Valentine Brooke was associated with in that year turned to gold. The Auckland Blues won the first Super 12 series, his Auckland Marist club won the Gallaher Shield, Auckland reclaimed the Ranfurly Shield (after dropping it while Brooke and co were in South Africa) and won a fourth straight NPC ttitle and the All Blacks not only created history against the Springboks but took out the Tri-Nations championship undefeated and won both Bledisloe Cup encounters.

The dust jacket of Brooke's autobiography *Zinny*, written by Alex Veysey and published in 1995, said his was the story of a back country farmboy who brought his home paddock skills to the city and prospered. He certainly did that. Because of his prodigious range of skills and contribution to the All Blacks' greatness in 1996 he was arguably, at the time of writing this book, and with Jonah Lomu sidelined with a serious kidney disease, the most celebrated rugby personality in the world.

Zinzan, the shortest, definitely the most competitive, and probably the most naturally talented, of the five sons and one daughter born to Sandy and Hine Brooke of Ahuroa, near Puhoi, about 30 minutes' drive north of Auckland, demonstrated exceptional abilities from an early age.

That unusual name of his should be explained. He was christened Murray Zinzan Brooke, Zinzan being a family name. It survived until he found himself surrounded by Murrays at school at Ahuroa. His teacher asked if any of the kids wanted to change their names. "Just call me Zinzan," said Murray Brooke. It stuck. He eventually changed his name by deed-poll to Zinzan Valentine Brooke, that distinctive middle name relating to the fact that his birthday is February 14, Valentine's Day.

He loved shearing. By the time he was 14, he could get through 300 sheep in a day. "I think in those days I wanted to be a Golden Shears champion." he says. "The All Blacks weren't a serious consideration. I loved the oily smell and feel of the wool and the battle with the rams and the cranky ewes."

His earliest rugby, in the red and white jersey of the Puhoi club, was courtesy of his father, who was the coach, and his mother, who was the team manager. "Mum stressed that enjoyment was as important as achievement," he says. "That's something which has stayed with me in my sport and in my life. I still play my best rugby when I allow myself to cut loose naturally and play with freedom and instinct. Graciousness in defeat was another of mum's messages."

Brooke left Mahurangi College at 15, the same age at which he made his senior club rugby debut for Warkworth (and scored three tries against Kaipara Flats). A year later he packed down at prop for the North Island under-16 team against the South at Lancaster Park and in 1982 he pulled on the black jersey of New Zealand for the first time for the under-17 international against Australia, again in Christchurch, again at prop.

About this time the family sold the farm at Ahuroa and moved to Warkworth. Zinzan was posted to Carrington Polytech in Auckland, to study plumbing.

Fate determined that he would play for the Marist club, not Ponsonby. Because of the enterprise of Eddie Kohlhase (who'd been in the same North Island under-18 squad as Zinzan), Brooke joined the Marist club. "I was going to bus to the Ponsonby club for training, but Eddie said he'd pick me up and take me to Marist," says Brooke. "Suited me fine. When he arrived, there was another guy in the car with a surfboard. His name was John Kirwan, a butcher, and he was chasing a spot in the third grade team."

It was Eddie Kohlhase's father Eric who decided that Brooke wasn't a tight forward. In 1984 he made him a blindside flanker in the Marist

Zinzan Brooke

thirds (the team from which Kirwan had been plucked by Auckland coach John Hart the season before). He also allowed him to kick the goals. "From my earliest days, I loved kicking goals," says Brooke. "I once landed a goal from halfway for Mahurangi College. When I played in Italy I had a better success ratio than Naas Botha and when I later represented Auckland I would always join Grant Fox for kicking sessions after training."

Brooke's career began to take off in 1985, initially through sevens. He performed so effectively for Marist at the annual Taupiri event, finding the games "a magic experience", that he was named player of the tournament. Whereupon John Hart asked him if he would like to be in the Auckland sevens team. "Would I *what?*" Brooke said to himself. It was the beginning of a six-year love affair with sevens. "The game was made for me," he says. "It allowed me to express myself totally on a rugby field, to run, dummy, sidestep, work scissors, do everything."

Mid-year, he was named in the New Zealand Colts, as a flanker. The captain was a likely lad from Otago called Mike Brewer and the backline included Greg Cooper, Bernie McCahill, John Schuster and Marty Berry.

Elder brother Marty made his Auckland representative debut in 1985 and Brooke would join him the next season. But before that he experienced the exhilaration of playing for a winning New Zealand team at the Hong Kong sevens festival. A team that was led by Wayne Smith and also featured Buck Shelford, David Kirk, Frano Botica and Craig Green eliminated Fiji in the semi-finals and dealt to the French Barbarians in the final.

Brooke's first-class debut had come in 1985, when he was 20, for a Marist President's XV against a Condors selection that included the legendary Puma Hugo Porta and two of his countrymen Ernesto Ure and Juan Lanza. More significant, though, was his arrival on the representative scene with Auckland in 1986, courtesy of the Cavaliers who were away doing their thing (to the frustration of coach Hart) in South Africa. "I'm sure I would have spent a lot longer waiting in the wings if Alan Whetton hadn't taken off with the Cavaliers," says Brooke.

He kicked off his career on an appropriate international note, against Fiji in Suva. Torrential rain and fired up opponents made this a daunting occasion for the Aucklanders but thanks to the boot of Greg Cooper, they escaped with a 15-10 win. Brooke's involvement lasted until Whetton returned. Then it was a regular seat on the reserves' bench.

His leadership qualities were given an airing in July when he captained the New Zealand Colts. It was to be a humbling experience. Being an ignorant Aucklander, he blissfully invited Wellington to take first advantage of a roaring northerly gale at Athletic Park. Big mistake – by halftime Wellington led 40-nil! The wind abated in the second spell and the Colts finished up losing 52-6.

Further embarrassment followed when they were battered 35-11 by their Australian counterparts at the Sydney Cricket Ground. Starring for Aussie was Ricky Stuart and handling the goalkicking for New Zealand was Daryl Halligan, individuals who would become star performers in Sydney league.

Brooke would come desperately close to joining them. He wasn't too enthusiastic about an offer he received from Eastern Suburbs in 1986 but four years later, convinced that league offered him greater financial security than rugby, he did sign with Manly. He signed at the same time as Matthew Ridge, the package worth $A118,000 plus a few trimmings. It was agreed they would make a joint announcement after Auckland's game against New Zealand Maori at Eden Park. But when the moment arrived, and following Ridge's revelation, Brooke said nothing. He'd gone cold on the idea. "Graham Lowe insisted he didn't want me switching to league unless I wanted to play the game more than rugby," says Brooke. "I agonised over it. Although rugby didn't offer the same tangible rewards, there was the camaraderie of the game, the great personal relationships. And then I'd have had to learn a whole new game. So I changed my mind. Graham Lowe was great about it all. He said he would never jeopardise my rugby career, so the contract just disappeared."

The final trial in May of 1987 from which the All Black World Cup squad would be selected offered only passing interest to Brooke. While his career with Auckland was developing promisingly, to the extent that the day following the trial (when all the guns would be absent) he was going to captain Auckland in a South Pacific Championship match against Canterbury, he didn't consider he rated nationally.

Zinzan Brooke

Buck Shelford, Michael Jones, Alan Whetton, Andy Earl and Brett Harvey were the loose forwards in the final trial while Mike Brewer (then injured), Paul Renton, the veteran Mark Shaw, Harvey and Tony Thorpe were the loosies called to an earlier trial in Hamilton. Zinzan Brooke wasn't in the picture.

Brooke was working away as a plumber when an official of the Auckland Rugby Union telephoned to ask if he was available to act as a reserve for the Black team at the trial in Whangarei. "It occurred to me that I was something of an afterthought," says Brooke, "someone who lived reasonably handy to Whangarei. I accepted, reminding the official that I would need to be back in town to captain Auckland the next afternoon."

Brooke stripped and took his place in the grandstand from where he watched Andy Dalton's shadow test team deal to Andy Donald's hopefuls. He'd had an entertaining few days in Whangarei, now he just wanted to get back to Auckland and focus on the Canterbury game.

Well, Auckland took on Canterbury without Zinzan Brooke because at the ritzy function which followed the trial – when Moet and Chandon was as plentiful as Steinlager – he was named in the World Cup squad. Brett Harvey was out. Zinzan Brooke was in.

"It was a strange atmosphere," recalls Brooke, "with the selected players reluctant to begin celebrating because they felt sorry for those who'd missed out. I had to get outside and release some of the jubilation that was in me. I grabbed my Marist mate Bernie McCahill, who'd been selected too, and we hurried out into the main street and shouted to the stars."

Brooke's participation in rugby's greatest event wasn't vast. He was given the one outing, as an openside flanker in the pool match against Argentina on a sparkling afternoon at Athletic Park. He was luckier than Bruce Deans, Frano Botica and the injured skipper Andy Dalton who didn't get to take the field once in the tournament.

Because he was the only Maori in the starting fifteen he was also given the honour of leading the haka. That was a worry, because he didn't know it. So he practised in front of a mirror and it went all right on the day. "It wasn't a Buck haka," he says. "Buck was the greatest haka leader of them all."

Brooke felt he'd performed his duties adequately in the unfamiliar

Bloodied but not beaten – Zinzan Brooke in action against the Springboks during the 1994 series in New Zealand.   *Photosport*

No 7 jersey, so was disappointed to read a newspaper column in which former openside specialist Graham Mourie poured cold water on his performance. "He possesses special skills," wrote Mourie, "but he will never make it as an openside flanker." The comments hurt, Brooke says, because that day he was playing the position by instinct.

While he may not have set the world on fire as an openside flanker, he had arrived as an All Black. "The World Cup campaign taught me what was required to be an All Black – not just any All Black, but a good one."

Brooke would start being a good All Black later that year in Japan, when Buck Shelford launched his unbeaten reign as captain. In the meantime, there was the notable occasion when all three Brooke brothers, Marty, Robin and Zinzan, took the field in the same Auckland team for a Ranfurly Shield defence against East Coast. It was the only occasion the three of them were in the same starting fifteen, although they were to operate together regularly for New Zealand Maori.

Because of Shelford's presence at No. 8, Brooke would have problems getting important games with the All Blacks through until 1990 when he eventually displaced him. The problem was circumvented in Japan with Brooke being used as a blindside flanker in the two unofficial internationals (in the second of which, won 106-4, he scored four tries).

But in Australia in 1988 (when five of his seven outings were as a flanker) and on the tour of Wales and Ireland in 1989 he was essentially a midweeker, operating in the broad, dark shadow of Shelford, the inspiring leader whose teams never lost. His brief moment of glory came at Twickenham in the '89 tour finale when he scored a stunning try against the Barbarians only minutes after coming on as Shelford's replacement.

His staggering tryscoring exploits for Auckland during these two years – he bagged 17 in 1988 and 18 the next season – didn't count for anything when it came to choosing test line-ups. By the time the 1990 season rolled around, Brooke had played 20 games for his country only two of which were test appearances, one of them as a replacement against Argentina. Which explains why he was almost lured away to league in Sydney.

Although many people had been championing Brooke as a test No. 8, his selection ahead of Shelford, when it came, was an absolute bombshell and didn't do Brooke any favours. Shelford was discarded after the Scottish tests early in the '90 season and Brooke introduced for the Bledisloe Cup series. "It was the worst thing that could have happened to me," says Brooke. "What should have been a source of great satisfaction became a nightmare. There were endless unpleasant phone calls and the talkback callers on radio seemed to be two hundred per cent in favour of Buck. It was as if I had personally engineered Buck's demise. I was lumped in with the selectors whose unexpected announcement had shocked me as much as the public."

In his biography, Brooke says that "what should have been an occasion for brief jubilation became a long, long funeral service." Shelford was the first test captain to be dropped from a team since Pat Vincent in 1956!

The furore settled, a little, by the time Brooke ran on to Lancaster Park in late July wearing the No. 8 jersey. With the captaincy transferred to Gary Whetton, the All Blacks carried on as if nothing untoward had happened. Playing bold, attacking rugby, they whipped Bob Dwyer's Wallabies 21-6. And although they weren't as convincing, another solid victory at Eden Park a fortnight later, helped by a Brooke try, clinched the trophy and extended to 50 the All Blacks' winning sequence.

Who needs to bring back Buck? Well, the Buck chorus instantly re-surfaced when New Zealand's three-year era of invincibility under Grizz Wyllie was shattered by the Wallabies in the third test at Athletic Park. The Wallabies would repeat the achievement, equally as convincingly, in Sydney 12 months later, and again, in a result that would plunge New Zealand rugby into a state of depression, in the World Cup semi-final in Dublin. Brooke would participate in all three losses and, like so many others, would struggle to explain away the downfall of a team which had so recently set itself a quantum leap ahead of the rest of the rugby world.

Brooke was in Rome in early 1992 when the new All Black coach Laurie Mains telephoned. But it wasn't Zinzan that Mains wanted to speak to – it was his brother Robin, who was urged to return for the trials. "Laurie didn't even talk to me, which indicated that I didn't feature strongly in the new panel's planning," says Zinzan. "However, if Robin was returning, I was going back, too."

Like skipper Gary Whetton, Brooke found himself on the scrapheap. He wasn't wanted for the centenary tests against the World XV or for the series against Ireland when Robin was introduced. And it seemed he would even miss selection in the 30-strong party to tour Australia and South Africa, Arran Pene and Richard Turner being the new panel's preferred No. 8s.

The revival of Brooke's career owes everything to Sean Fitzpatrick.

Zinzan Brooke

Mains conceded in his biography that Brooke didn't feature in his tour planning. "He spent too much time being an extra back. A hard-working number eight was important to me." Fitzpatrick was able to convince the new coach of Brooke's worth. "He should tour," he told Mains. "He's a great player who will play whatever game you ask of him. The reason he's been so loose is because he's had no direction in playing for Auckland. He's a hell of a good team man."

Brooke did tour, got a lucky break before the second test when Pene broke a bone in his hand . . . and went on to stardom. Mains, who was initially sceptical of his worth, was to become one of his greatest fans. And he was to admire the audacity that produced a seven-pointer for the All Blacks at a critical stage of the Springbok international at Ellis Park, Brooke tapping a penalty and charging through a startled defence to score. "Don't ask me to explain why I did that," says Brooke. "We needed points on the board, but my action remains a blur. It was totally instinctive. I had often backed myself against the opposition and against the odds, and this was one of those occasions."

It would be nice to record that Brooke has been an automatic choice at No. 8 since that tour, but in 1993 there was a serious hiccup, in the form of a rogue sciatic nerve which so afflicted him he had difficulty even getting out of bed. Yet he kept playing because he didn't want Pene to reclaim his test position. "I should have declared the injury and rested it," admits Brooke now. "But I had blinkered vision at the time."

Brooke dropped out for the third test against the Lions, and would not recapture the test No. 8 position until the second international in 1994. Throughout the tour of England and Scotland he would operate as a flanker, mostly on the openside (in the unexpected absence of Michael Jones who had broken his jaw in training in Auckland), with Pene ensconsed at No. 8.

In the foreword to Brooke's autobiography, Buck Shelford wrote that the sadness of Zinzan's career was that New Zealand audiences saw too little of the genius of the player at top level. "It wasn't really until 1994, for the domestic series against the Boks, that the best of Zinzan was produced consistently at test level."

Brooke was awesome against the Boks which secured his place for

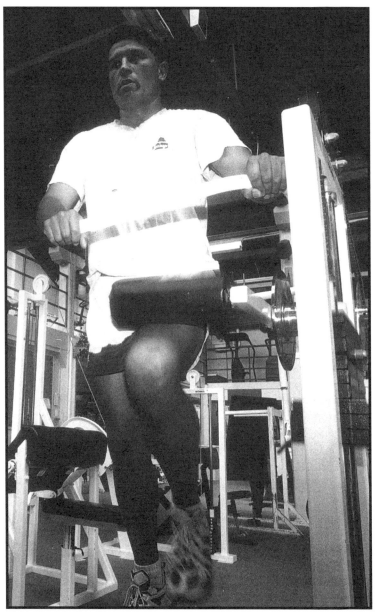

Zinzan Brooke working out at the gym and enjoying life as a professional rugby player.
Ross Land *(Fotopress)*

the third World Cup tournament. But there was to be another crisis in his career, a shattering injury to the Achilles tendon in Hamilton in April '95 that threatened to make the World Cup a non-event for him. That Brooke got to South Africa was a triumph for the All Blacks' medical team and modern sports medicine treatments. They even put him in the decompression chamber at the Devonport Naval Base in Auckland, the theory being that pure oxygen hastens the mending process.

It was all worth it. Brooke made South Africa, the leg still feeling alarmingly tender, and after not a few anxieties returned to action in the final pool match against Japan. Once into the play-offs, Brooke recaptured his finest form, providing one of the tournament's magic moments with a 45-metre dropped goal in the semi-final rout of England at Newlands.

He was one of a sprinkling of individuals to avoid the poisoning that flattened almost the entire All Black squad 48 hours before the final at Ellis Park. He alone, though, couldn't overcome the Springbok challenge and when the final whistle blew, the sense of disappointment he experienced was total. But when all the drama of the day was over, and he had time to reflect, he knew he'd be back. There was that unfinished business to attend to!

Brooke was overwhelmed by the ticker tape parade given the All Blacks back in Auckland. "You're not aware at the time of what victories mean to the people back home," he says. "Danyon Loader broke down in tears at the civic reception he received in Dunedin. He hadn't realised just what he'd achieved at the Olympics. It was the same with us."

By the time the 1997 season rolled around, Brooke, approaching his 50th test, and his 150th game for Auckland, was enjoying life as a professional rugby player. "You can become stressed out if you're thinking scrums and lineouts all the time," he says. "I'm into property development, building a couple of houses a year. It allows me to switch off from rugby, to maintain a balance."

Olo Brown

L eisure time is treasured by international rugby players when they're on overseas assignment. Some like to unwind playing golf, others are compulsive shoppers and every team has its video addicts while there are those who value afternoon naps.

If you were trying to locate Olo Brown, All Black, between training sessions, you wouldn't bother with any of those options. The most likely place to encounter the quietly-spoken powerhouse prop would be at a nearby cafe or coffee shop.

Very likely he'd be in the company of his captain and fellow front-rower Sean Fitzpatrick. And almost certainly they would be sipping coffee or tea and concentrating intently on a game of backgammon. Conversation would be minimal.

"It's just our way of relaxing," says Brown, the player who in recent seasons has been the popular choice as the strongest and best tighthead prop in the world. "At training and in matches, we're full on," he says, "so when the opportunity comes to relax, Sean and I prefer to unwind over a board game. I prefer chess but Fitzy can't play it, so it's usually backgammon we settle for. I must say, he's boosted my pocket money substantially over the years!"

Opponents who've been bent and buckled by Brown, the anchor man of the Auckland, Auckland Blues and All Black scrums, might have difficulty associating such a tranquil pastime as backgammon with the player they've encountered on the rugby field.

But Brown's coaches and fellow players will all tell you that away from the rugby field he's a gentle giant. To which the media

Olo Brown

Olo Brown finds a path through the Springbok forwards during the first test of the 1996 series at Durban. Others, from left, are Kobus Wiese (19), Ian Jones, Mark Andrews and Marius Hurter.   John Selkirk

would add . . . 'and an uncommunicative one too.' Since his arrival on the first-class scene, Brown has consistently declined media exposure preferring to remain in the background, the further back the better.

Following his exploits in 1995, *Rugby News* had this to say: "If the All Blacks to Italy and France were rated on personality, quotability and willingness to be interviewed, the finalists would probably have been Richard Fromont, Andrew Mehrtens (while he was involved), Josh Kronfeld, Eric Rush, Bull Allen and Liam Barry. Trailing the field would have been Olo Brown. But if awards were for commitment at training, achievement on the field and impact on the opposition, the 28-year-old Auckland accountant would have graduated with honours. From the Joe Stanley school of I Don't Give Interviews, Brown prefers to let his achievements on the field do his talking for him."

Ironical, therefore, that Brown's international debut should have come at La Rochelle in 1990, on the only occasion Joe Stanley captained the All Blacks and had to give aftermatch interviews. Smokin' Joe's reluctance to deal with the media was directly related to two incidents early in his career when he considered he was seriously misquoted. In Brown's case, though, it's simply an intense desire to keep out of the limelight.

To finally corner him for an interview for this chapter was no mean achievement. "Are you sure you really want me in there?" he asked. "There must be a lot of players more deserving of a chapter." Only when assured that the All Black coaches since 1982 had determined the 25 subjects for the book, and that he had polled better than any other prop, would he consent.

The Olo Brown story varies from most of the other subjects in this book in that he didn't play rugby until he was well into his teens. Apart from a couple of runs at first-five (repeat, first-five) while at Ponsonby Primary School, all Brown's early football was with the league code. The All Blacks meant nothing to him and it wasn't till he was 15, had bulked up and was eligible for the first XV at Mt Albert Grammar School that rugby took on any special significance.

He had been born in Apia, the middle of five children produced by Sola and Toesulu Brown. When Olo was an infant, the family moved to Auckland where his father worked at a variety of jobs, including running a pool room and as a travel agent specialising in Pacific Islands travel. His mother Toesulu became a teacher (and presently holds a position at Auckland Girls' Grammar School).

Rugby held no status in the Brown household and Olo, whose early interests were league and basketball, doubts he could have named an All Black at the time he enrolled at Mt Albert Grammar.

Invited to join the first XV squad when he was 15, Brown accepted, and so launched a career that would take him rapidly to the top. He was instantly sited in the front row because of his squat build and obvious strength. "I don't remember anyone bothering too much about the intricacies of my position," says Brown. "Basically, it was put your head down and push!"

Livening up the backline, particularly in 1985 when Mt Albert won the Auckland schools championship, was Matthew Ridge. He only sometimes played fullback, having to share the position with John Akurangi, who, when he broke into representative rugby with Auckland nine years later, was a member of the front row club along with Brown.

For someone involved in the game for barely 12 months, Brown made spectacular progress in 1985. The Auckland under-18 selector snapped him up, next he was chosen for North Island under-18 (whose pack also featured Ian Jones, Steve Gordon and Errol Brain) and then he was off to Australia with the New Zealand secondary schools team.

For what would be the first of several times in his career he found himself, on that Australia expedition, being coached by Graham Henry. Henry and Brown found the New Zealand forwards seriously disadvantaged because, back home, they had been forced to operate in depowered scrums. Taking a hiding up front, they lost their international 20-9. While the loss was disappointing, Brown's first overseas rugby trip made a lasting impression. He was, he acknowledges now, eager for more.

Academically, he did well at college, gaining an A Bursary which gave him a good start at University where he studied for, and achieved in three years, a Bachelor of Commerce degree. Considering the distractions that rugby presented, this was no mean achievement.

As a student, he might have been tempted to play for University but having grown up in Ponsonby he felt there was only one club he could realistically join. Ponsonby welcomed him and soon had him anchoring its strong under-21 team, a side which, for a part of the season, also featured the ubiquitous Ridge. For about the seventh time in ten years, all involving Trevor Paterson as coach, the club won the title.

Brown wore the Auckland jersey at under-19 level that year and in 1987 became an Auckland Colt, once more under the expert tuition of Graham Henry. It was around this time that Brown came to occupy the tighthead role regularly. "I was pretty casual about it," he says, "but because the team had a specialist loosehead, I was asked to take the other side. I've been there ever since."

Success seemed to associate itself with Brown. Having participated in championship wins at school and in the under-21 grade, he found himself sharing in Ponsonby's Gallaher Shield triumph in his first season of senior rugby in 1988. Not many 20-year-olds make their mark propping at senior club level in Auckland but Brown managed it. It was obvious he was a footballer destined for the top.

Auckland coaches Maurice Trapp and Bryan Williams didn't hesitate to harness his talents. Throughout 1988, the Auckland front row had been unchanged, props Peter Fatialofa and Steve McDowell and hooker Sean Fitzpatrick remarkably packing down in all 17 matches. But when McDowell decided to return to Rotorua prior to the new season, it created a vacancy at prop which Brown filled. He came in at tighthead, with Fatialofa switching across to the loosehead side.

Brown played the first 11 matches, including a unique appearance, against Argentina, at hooker. It was one of the extremely rare occasions that Fitzpatrick was unavailable for Auckland through injury and coach Trapp asked Brown if he could hook. "I said I'd done it a couple of times at club level," says Brown, "and suddenly I had the job. The hooking wasn't a problem but throwing to the lineout was a worry. We won the game by about sixty points notwithstanding my throwing in."

Then out of the blue, McDowell, a test regular, returned to Auckland and was immediately reinstated in the front row, at Brown's expense, Fatialofa reverting to the tighthead role. "I didn't mind," says Brown. "I was only twenty-one and delighted to be involved at all. I sat out the season on the reserves' bench with Robin Brooke. He was dirty on me because my eleven outings were more than he'd managed in three seasons with Auckland. He was a reserve bench regular!"

Brown had made sufficient impact to be included in a New Zealand Development squad to attend a coaching school in March, 1990. Before the year was out, he would be an All Black.

With McDowell still around in 1990 it was Fatialofa, by now heavily committed to the Western Samoan cause, who was sacrificed, Brown establishing himself as Auckland's tighthead specialist. He appeared in the early All Black trial at Palmerston North in May, winning praise for his excellent all-purpose display.

Brown shared in Auckland's victory over the Wallabies, marking Tony Daly, but the match he most vividly remembers from that season, for all the wrong reasons, is the no-try Ranfurly Shield clash against Canterbury.

The game ended up as something resembling touch football after Canterbury's hooker John Buchan was ordered off in only the fourth minute. Even though Canterbury's replacement player Phil Cropper had represented New Zealand Colts as a hooker, he was now officially a loose forward, so Canterbury, invoking the NZRFU's rules governing player safety, declined to play scrums. From that moment, tap penalties were substituted for scrums. "It was the craziest game I've ever played in," says Brown. "I came off not feeling I'd played a game of rugby at all. We told the Canterbury guys what we thought of them, but they were acting within their rights. It was a farcical situation." The game became a drop-kicker's delight and 45 points were posted before a try was scored, Auckland eventually winning 33-30.

Brown faced a demanding schedule after the domestic season concluded, for he had been named in both the New Zealand Development team to tour Canada and the Auckland Development team to tour Argentina. What wasn't in his diary at that point was a match for the All Blacks in between!

He'd thoroughly enjoyed his trek across Canada with the Lane Penn coached national side, appearing at St Johns and Winnipeg. He was preparing for the team's 'test' against British Columbia in Vancouver when manager Graham Atkin called him aside and said he'd received a call from the NZRFU in Wellington, and Brown was needed as a replacement player for the All Blacks in France.

"I couldn't believe it," says Brown. "Me . . . wanted for the All Blacks! I didn't know who was injured or whether I was required as a player or just on standby, but once the game against British Columbia was over, I was on my way."

As his teammates were preparing to fly back to Auckland, Brown boarded a flight for Paris, from where he flew across to Nantes and was then driven through to La Rochelle. It could have been a thoroughly overwhelming experience for a newcomer, but for Brown meeting the All Blacks was almost like a Ponsonby club reunion. Already on tour were Joe Stanley, Inga Tuigamala and Craig Innes and there were another 11 Aucklanders in the side. "In fact," says Brown, "there weren't too many All Blacks there I didn't know."

Brown found the injured player he was replacing was Graham Purvis. He also found, to his intrigue, that Stanley was the captain and that the opposition was France B. "The actual game was a bit of a blur," he says. "I was pretty jetlagged and concerned that I wouldn't measure up. But things went well. Inga produced a blinder, we won, Joe made a speech . . . it was a great day."

After watching the All Blacks crush France in Paris, Brown the jet-

Olo Brown . . . as formidable an opponent at backgammon as he is on the rugby field.   *Andrew Cornaga (Photosport)*

age prop was on a flight through to Buenos Aires, to link with Graham Henry's Auckland Development team. "My body clock went berserk for a while," says Brown. "But it was an enjoyable few weeks, playing in all those exotic countries. None of the teams lost." Not only that, but Brown was now an All Black.

The 1991 season was, as things turned out, probably a good one not to be involved with the All Blacks who were on the slippery slope. Richard Loe and Steve McDowell were the props as the team stumbled against Australia in Sydney in August, a portent of what was to happen at the World Cup two months later.

Brown didn't miss out altogether on international rugby that year. He featured in a couple of games with a difference, for a New Zealand XV against Romania at Eden Park and the Soviet Union in Hamilton. Prepared by John Hart, the New Zealanders ran up 115 points in the two unofficial test matches, proving that technique and good old rugby savvy will always win out against bulk and raw enthusiasm. Brown's teammates included Robin Brooke, Bull Allen, Eroni Clarke and, as captain, the incomparable Buck Shelford.

In September, following the World Cup squad's assembly, he experienced a rare NPC defeat, against Otago at Carisbrook. "We had fourteen players out," recalls Brown. "There were shades of the Baby Blacks of '86 but our patched-up team (featuring a few notable survivors such as Joe Stanley and Peter Fatialofa) wasn't good enough on the day." Otago's victory put it a point ahead of Auckland, an advantage it clung to, to claim its first NPC title.

Brown admits that he is not a keen follower of sport when not directly involved. So he wasn't setting the alarm clock while the '91 World Cup tournament was unfolding. He was content to monitor the All Blacks' progress on the radio the morning after. When they crashed out against Australia in Dublin, he mused that changes would probably follow, but he didn't believe they would involve him.

One of new coach Laurie Mains' immediate objectives was to improve the players' fitness. So when they assembled in Napier in April for the trials, he exposed them all to the Beep Test, an exhausting exercise that determines a player's precise level of fitness. Worst of the lot was Inga Tuigamala. Brown concedes that he rated "in the bottom bracket, but not as bad as Inga." Down there with them was Steve McDowell.

For the first time, Brown appeared in a main trial, packing down against Laurence Hullena who had toured Argentina as an All Black in 1991. He opposed him again three days later when the Saracens took on a shadow test fifteen in what became a perplexing afternoon for the selectors – not only was their shadow test line-up defeated but their captain-to-be Mike Brewer suffered a serious leg injury.

Brown's powerful scrummaging had been a factor in the Saracens' unexpected success, but the selectors didn't consider he was quite ready to make the step-up to test rugby. So they stuck with the trio of props who had gone to the World Cup, Loe, McDowell and Graham Purvis, plus Hullena. The loser in the next few months would be Hullena, a loosehead. He didn't get on to the field for any of the centenary tests, wasn't needed for the Irish series and was abandoned when the 30-strong touring party for Australia and South Africa was announced.

Mains recorded in his biography that Brown wasn't involved in the centenary tests simply because he wasn't fit enough. "He was one of many individuals who arrived in Napier with their aerobic fitness levels seriously deficient," Mains wrote.

Brown acknowledges that at the time he thought turning up at the gym and doing 20 minutes on an exercycle was "good enough" for his aerobic levels. Compared with what fitness trainer Martin Toomey and coach Mains would have him doing from midway through 1992, he admits that his training then was grossly inadequate.

Brown's call-up followed the All Blacks' lack-lustre showing against Ireland at Carisbrook. Sweeping changes were made for the rematch in Wellington. Out went Greg Cooper, Tuigamala, Paul Henderson, Jamie Joseph, Blair Larsen and Richard Loe. In came Matthew Cooper, John Timu, Michael Jones, Mike Brewer, Robin Brooke and Brown. Apart from Cooper, who would remain on the fringes, the others would all become vital members of Mains' team.

Being matched against Nick Popplewell, acknowledged as one of the strongest and best props in the world, didn't faze Brown. "I'd opposed him in the Auckland game a couple of weeks earlier, and he hadn't caused any problems." The Auckland front row (McDowell, Fitzpatrick and Brown) was now the test front row.

The bonus for whipping Ireland by a record 50 points was having Mains announce to the players in the dressing room afterwards that

Olo Brown

they were all starters for the tour of Australia and South Africa. "That was pretty heartening," says Brown. "We had a test victory and tour selection to celebrate all in one evening."

Mains identified exciting potential in Brown. "In his years with Auckland, he was *just* a prop," says Mains. "I could see at trainings that he was a player who had speed and great ball skills, so we developed a lot of play for Olo specifically to get him running with the ball. Of course, that motivated and excited him, as well as allowing us to use a big, strong body to put pressure on the opposition."

Brown found training sessions in Australia under Mains' guidance unlike anything he had ever experienced. Although Mains' specialties, the 150m sprints and the down-and-ups, were exhausting, Brown undertook them enthusiastically. "Being new to the All Blacks, I thought this was what they did all the time. Training sessions under Laurie and Martin (Toomey) were hard, but good for the team. I finished up fitter than I had ever been."

Although defeating the Springboks on Ellis Park represented an enormous achievement, Brown took greater satisfaction from the three-test series against Australia. While the Bledisloe Cup was lost (by the narrowest possible margin), Brown found it stimulating to be part of an All Black team that was developing a bold, new attacking concept, one designed to run opposition teams ragged. "It took us three tests in Australia to put it together properly," says Brown. "But we dealt to them in Sydney. Considering they were the reigning world champions, we were pretty thrilled."

The super-fit Brown returned to help Auckland retain the Ranfurly Shield and was named one of the five players of the year by the *Rugby Almanack*. Sharing the honour with him was his backgammon partner Fitzpatrick.

Brown's most remarkable achievement in 1993 was completing the Bledisloe Cup game in Dunedin after seriously damaging his neck in training. Driven awkwardly into a tackle bag by one of his teammates, he suffered compression of the C5 and C6 joints in the neck. Bearing the discomfort stoically, he not only survived 80 minutes on the field, he turned in a rousing performance, responding to Mains' request that he should run with the ball more. The injury would sideline him for six weeks and force him to miss the Western Samoan international at Eden Park.

Rugby Greats

He gave another eye-catching performance that year, against Scotland at Murrayfield, but the All Blacks' amazing 50-point effort there was seriously overshadowed seven days later by the loss to England at Twickenham. Brown did his bit, scrummaging well and providing a snappy pass to John Timu that almost yielded a winning try, but the defeat took the gloss off an otherwise successful season.

The 1994 season was a strange mix for the All Blacks. Winning the series against the Springboks was a thrill. For Brown and his fellow front rowers the greatest single moment was managing a pushover try against them at Athletic Park, a notable first in tests against the great foe dating back to the 1920s. "The Springboks try and dominate you mentally through their scrummaging," says Brown, "so to score a pushover try represented a significant victory to us." The victories at Dunedin and Wellington, however, were offset by a draw at Eden Park and the losses to France and Australia.

It was apparent that the fitness levels of the All Blacks were substantially down on what they had been in 1992 and, to a lesser extent, 1993. Mains says of Brown that he was "bloody awful in 1994 because he wasn't fit."

All that would be remedied at the summer training camps leading into the World Cup in 1995. Mains set out to make the All Blacks 20 per cent fitter than any other team in the world – and succeeded.

Brown relished the challenge. "What the camps at Taupo and Christchurch taught me," he says, "is that you can push yourself further than you ever thought possible. What it achieved was to build a confidence so that you knew you could outlast the opposition."

Those fitness levels would carry through into the 1996 season and allow the All Blacks to pull off a couple of sensational comeback victories when all appeared lost.

Brown, who regarded the World Cup as "fantastic until the final", took no satisfaction from being a runner-up. "Finishing second was no better than coming in third or fourth or fifth," he says. "The biggest disappointment was that we didn't play as well as we could have. Sure, the poisoning affected our preparation, but the final was lost because South Africa shut us down. They'd worked out how to disrupt our game plan and we didn't adapt accordingly. We were too loose, made too many mistakes and didn't take our opportunities."

Revenge is sweet, and the All Blacks got their own back in 1996,

Olo Brown

Reduced to a spectator after tearing a calf muscle, Olo Brown watches his Auckland Blues team during the 1997 Super 12 campaign. John Selkirk

creating history by winning a series on South African soil for the first time. Brown says that identifying problems in the first Tri-Nations test against the Springboks in Christchurch was critical to winning in South Africa. "We weren't as aggressive as we should have been," he says, "but the South Africans unsettled us by coming fast into the scrums and getting a big hit. We weren't ready for that, but we were in South Africa. If you can neutralise the Springboks in the scrum, you're half way to winning."

Brown had had a personal trainer in 1995 but was content to organise his own training schedules in '96. "I had a friend I worked out with," he says. "We kept each other up to the mark. For me, the most important aspects to concentrate on were aerobic fitness and weights." We would regularly run from forty to sixty minutes, adding in an occasional bit of hill work.

The hard work paid off, particularly in the third test at Pretoria when the All Blacks had to call on all their reserves to hold out a desperate South African team during the final stages. "There were a few moments of anxiety towards the finish as the Springboks kept taking tap penalties and charging towards us, but we managed to hold on. The sweetest sound I've heard in a long time was the final whistle.

Though we were elated at the time, I don't think that what we had achieved really sank in until the next day."

Brown celebrated his 50th outing for the All Blacks at Ellis Park while back home he registered his 100th game for Auckland as he helped the Awesome Auks to a fourth straight NPC title.

The manager of audit and business services with Price Waterhouse, Brown was obliged to step down to a part-time role in 1996 because of his heavy commitment to rugby.

Frank Bunce

Frank Bunce not only merits his place in *Rugby Greats*, he would also qualify for a prominent chapter in a rugby believe-it-or-not publication.

This is the player who after taking four years to win his Auckland blazer threw his lot in with Western Samoa after abandoning hopes of ever representing New Zealand.

But at the advanced age of 30, when many players are contemplating retirement, he was catapaulted into the All Blacks where he has been a permanent fixture ever since. By the end of the 1996 season he had supplanted the great Bruce Robertson as New Zealand's most capped centre and was approaching his 50th test.

If his remarkable survival qualities keep him involved until the All Black tour of Wales and England in November, 1997, he will become, at 35 years and more than 290 days, New Zealand's second oldest player of all time.

The man who ranks with the best centres in the world takes it all philosophically. "I don't feel any different from seven or eight years ago when I wasn't being selected for rep teams," he says, "except that I'm a lot wiser now, a lot more contented and a lot better paid."

Bunce's career may have languished but for the persistence of his good friend Peter Fatialofa who kept imploring him to play for Western Samoa. Bunce consistently rejected him because he wanted more than anything to represent the All Blacks. And, anyway, he knew he had more Niuean than Samoan blood in him.

But Peter Fats isn't easily dissuaded, not when the good of Western

Rugby Greats

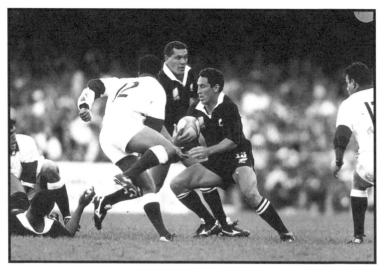

Frank Bunce has his midfield mate Walter Little in support as he wrongfoots Jeremy Guscott during the All Black rout of England at Cape Town during the 1995 World Cup tournament.   John Selkirk

Samoan rugby is involved. He kept hounding Bunce until finally his great drinking buddy from the Auckland B team gave in. "Once we had Buncey," says Fatialofa, "I knew we were going to perform strongly at the World Cup – I knew how good a player he was and how he could influence a whole team. He was our trump card."

The Western Samoans were a sensation at the World Cup in 1991, reaching the quarter-finals. Frank Bunce was a sensation too, with a number of highly regarded rugby writers naming him in their tournament teams, ahead of such established international stars as Philippe Sella and Jeremy Guscott.

One who took particular interest in Bunce's performances, through television for he followed the event from his Dunedin home, was new All Black coach Laurie Mains. He immediately identified the then 29-year-old as the strong man he needed in midfield, albeit initially as a second-five.

The rest, as they say, is history, although Bunce had some important decisions to make when he returned from the World Cup. Not only was Mains after him, but so were the Australian league scouts. And Fatialofa dearly wanted him to continue with Western Samoa.

Frank Bunce

The three-year stand down qualification didn't apply then, or Bunce, at his age, would undoubtedly have stayed with Western Samoa. And while the money being offered by league was appealing, deep down, more than anything, Bunce wanted to play for the All Blacks.

That had been his burning ambition all along. But after a sensational call-up for North Island in 1986, ahead of Joe Stanley, he was consistently rejected by the Auckland and All Black selectors. He never abandoned hope. But when his name wasn't among the trialists in 1991, well . . . that's when he decided to give Peter Fatialofa a call.

"You still want me for Western Samoa?" he asked.

"Yeah, man," said Fatialofa.

"I've made a decision – I want to play for you guys."

There were several times when Bunce's promising rugby career almost ground to a stop, through selectors' indifference to him, the lure of the league dollar and his own waywardness.

After he had been 'discovered' by Manukau club officials playing loose forward in their odd-ball fifth grade side – a team comprised mostly of bikies who were strongly anti-establishment and who had a dreadful reputation for getting into scraps – his entry into senior ranks had to be put on hold for 12 months while he was on periodic detention.

He had been twice caught driving intoxicated, the second time while disqualified. The judge who sentenced him to nine months' periodic detention, which involved labouring for the Justice Department every Saturday throughout the 1981 rugby season, said he was fortunate not to be going to prison.

Every Saturday, he and the other mostly petty criminals would build stone walls or cut scrub. The routine never varied. Bunce branded the others "a bunch of losers" and he resolved never to get himself in that situation again.

When he resumed his rugby career in 1982 it was as a centre. That was the position the Manukau senior coach Alby Pryor, who had made a name for himself as a bruising forward with Auckland and New Zealand Maori, had chosen for him. "Frank always wanted to be a loose forward, because he liked to be totally involved," says Pryor, "but he was such a great playmaker, he was wasted there."

An end-of-year tour to the United States with Manukau fired

Bunce with enthusiasm. He revelled in the experience which took him to such exotic destinations as Las Vegas, San Francisco, San Diego, Disneyland, Arizona (where Manukau claimed second place in a tournament) and Hawaii. "If through rugby I could get to places like this, than I knew rugby was my game," says Bunce. Before the team returned home, Pryor called Bunce aside. "You see what you can get out of the game," he told Bunce. "My advice is, stop mucking around when you get home. Give rugby one hundred per cent and it will reward you ten times over." Bunce would agree, except that he might adjust that figure of Pryor's to one thousand times!

Bunce made modest progress as a footballer with Manukau, getting an outing for Auckland C in 1983 (in a team that also included Terry Wright and Lindsay Harris) and making his first-class debut the next season for Auckland B against King Country at Eden Park. The player he marked was Murray Kidd, later to become coach of Ireland but that afternoon making his 109th appearance for King Country. Bunce's awesome display hastened his retirement. "I decided to step down after what Frank did to me that day," says Kidd. "He may not have been the most skilful player I ever marked but he was undoubtedly one of the most physical. It surprised me he took so long to become established at top level."

Although Bunce turned in consistently high quality performances for Auckland B, he failed to convince the Auckland selector-coach, John Hart, of his worth, Hart being more than satisfied with the player then wearing the No 13 jersey, Joe Stanley.

Fortunately, there was one selector about prepared to champion Bunce – Bryan Craies, Hart's predecessor with Auckland and in 1986 a North Island selector. He'd observed Bunce's progress at senior club level and regarded him as 'the complete centre'. "He had pace and all the skills," says Craies, "and was one of the few guys around who could make a clean break. The only thing he couldn't do was kick."

Now 1986 was a most unusual season, and with the Cavaliers away in South Africa it meant the inter-island selectors were obliged to introduce a lot of fresh talent. The 'fresh' midfield combination Craies went for was John Schuster and Frank Bunce, which naturally drew protests from Stanley's supporters.

Good fortune was not to be on Bunce's side. He arrived in Oamaru for the game carrying an ankle injury, having damaged the ligaments in a club match. He prayed it would respond to physiotherapy treatment but when it did not, he contemplated withdrawing from the North Island side. Fatialofa, a prop in the team, would not hear of it. "Hey, man," he said, "you didn't come all this way for nothing – go for it!"

He hoped the adrenalin rush would disguise the injury, but it didn't, and after 30 minutes he came off, to be joined a short while later by lock Mata'afa Keenan, also injured. They sat there, feeling sorry for themselves, aware their careers had suffered serious setbacks. Five years on, they would be at the World Cup together, representing Western Samoa.

It wasn't Bunce, or *any* of the centres who had participated at Oamaru or in the subsequent trial in Blenheim, who got to wear the No 13 jersey for the Baby Blacks against France and Australia. It was Stanley, aged 29. And he wouldn't yield his All Black jersey until 1990.

Stanley also commanded the centre position with Auckland but when he was away on test duty in August, Bunce got to make his Auckland debut, in a Ranfurly Shield defence at Eden Park.

Under Hart, Bunce would make only that one appearance for Auckland. Hart acknowledges that he possibly underestimated the Manukau centre. "I questioned his discipline and commitment to the game at the time and I wondered whether he could take the outside break," he says. "I suspect Frank is one of those rare individuals who gets better with every step they take up the rugby ladder. Many players get found out as they advance but Frank blossomed the further he went."

If Bunce thought his prospects at representative level would improve when Maurice Trapp and Bryan Williams took over the Auckland team, he was further disillusioned. They chanced him only once in 1987, again when the leading personalities were away on national duty. Bunce was resigning himself to a lifetime of playing for Auckland B.

Things improved marginally in 1988 when he appeared eight times for Auckland. If that sounds impressive, note that only one outing was at centre (against Manawatu when he scored three tries and was named man of the match). He was three times used as a winger and the other four appearances were as a replacement.

Although they sighted him infrequently, the national selectors

Rugby Greats

They should excel in that all black outfit! Bloemfontein schoolboys receive coaching advice from Frank Bunce during the 1995 World Cup visit to South Africa.   *John Selkirk*

Frank Bunce

obviously sensed that he was a footballer with potential because in '88 they called him to a trial match in Palmerston North, arranged for players not involved in the South Pacific championship series. Marking him was Craig Innes, a teenager who'd bounded on to the scene and who was threatening to displace Bunce from the Auckland squad. Here was a second chance for Bunce to prove himself at national level.

Murphy's Law would intervene again. Almost unbelievably, three days before the trial Bunce was injured. He'd run on for Auckland late in the Southpac game against Wellington at Eden Park and in sprinting to support speedster Terry Wright had torn his hamstring.

Having blown his great opportunity two years earlier, he was now heading for an All Black trial with a damaged hamstring. "There was no opportunity of getting myself right in three days," he says. "I shouldn't have played, but I did, and I performed hopelessly. Richard Becht, writing in the (now defunct) *Auckland Sun*, gave me a three out of ten. I thought that was generous!"

Late in the game, after he'd been tackled ball and all by the opposition fullback Lindsay Raki when he should have passed, as they lay on the ground in a tangle, Raki said, "Shit, Frank, you're having a shocker!"

While the national selectors probably put a big cross through Bunce's name, back in Auckland he would emerge as a hero before season's end. Because it was his tackle on Otago winger Noel Pilcher which saved the Ranfurly Shield for the blue and whites.

As usual, he started the day on the reserves bench but became involved when Terry Wright was concussed. Pilcher put Otago ahead with an intercept try and looked to be heading for another try, which would have given the challenger an almost unassailable advantage, when Bunce lowered him a metre from the goalline with a copybook tackle. Auckland was able to regroup and hit back with two late tries.

Such heroics failed to improve his status when the 1989 season rolled around. Bernie McCahill and Joe Stanley had the midfield sewn up and Wright, Inga Tuigamala and Craig Innes were the preferred wingers. The only spot available to Bunce again was on the reserves bench.

So he gave league serious consideration, accepting an invitation to check out, and train with, the Newcastle club in Australia. "They had an excellent set-up," he says. "If that had been what I'd wanted, I would have signed up. But I knew in my heart I was still a rugby person. It's not easy to explain, when your bank balance is nil, why you're rejecting money to stay with a game that is completely amateur. But I did."

By the end of 1990, Bunce had played only 18 games for Auckland, a third of these as a replacement, and was understandably disenchanted. Yet he never abandoned hope of becoming an All Black and although now under intense pressure from Fatialofa to play for Western Samoa, he didn't make his decision until after the 1991 trial teams had been named. "I still naively believed, even at the age of 29, that the selectors might want me," he says.

Once aboard the Western Samoan train, it was full speed ahead to the World Cup. Fatialofa's men had swept aside Japan, Tonga and Korea in a tournament in Tokyo to qualify, a source of great satisfaction after Fiji and Tonga had participated in the inaugural event in 1987 at Western Samoa's expense.

Fatialofa had continued to recruit players who had a minimum of one-sixteenth Samoan blood. Bunce was his best signing yet. By October, assembly time, he would also have Stephen Bachop, Pat Lam and Mata'afa Keenan aboard.

Bunce excelled in the trials in Apia and made his debut as a Western Samoan representative on a four-match tour of New Zealand. There would be a couple of outings in Australia to complete the team's preparation. Their accommodation for a game in Sydney was at a backpackers hotel at Manly. "What the hell's this place?" Bunce asked Fatialofa. "I thought we were supposed to be an international team." "We are," replied Fatialofa, "but we're broke!"

The Western Samoan union had debts approaching half a million dollars by mid-1991, so to fund the World Cup campaign, the players embarked on a novel fundraising exercise, pushing a wheelbarrow around Upolu, the main island. It took them two and a half days and they raised almost $NZ150,000 which ensured that Fatialofa's men were worthily outfitted, although by comparison with the All Blacks they received only the bare essentials. The contrast was further emphasised when they flew to London with Air New Zealand, the All Blacks in business class, the Samoan boys down the back in economy.

Following their matches in New Zealand in April, coach Peter

Frank Bunce

Schuster told Bunce he wanted him to be playing top-level rugby through until October. Which meant the time had come for him to choose a new union. He selected North Harbour, joined the Helensville club and was pretty soon a regular performer at first-class level. In fact, by October he had made eight NPC appearances, one more than he'd managed in five seasons with Auckland!

Western Samoa's entry into World Cup rugby was a daunting one. First up, they'd drawn Wales at Cardiff Arms Park. The ground would be packed to capacity and only a handful would not be cheering for the men in scarlet. Bunce was named at second-five. The player whose test position he took, Keneti Sio, came to him and said, "If your heart is not fully there, take my heart." Bunce's heart was there all right. At the age of 29, the boy from Manukau was about to make his international debut, on the ground he considered the most famous in the whole world.

Bunce was so uptight he took the field with his boot laces undone but was soon immersed in an enthralling encounter in which Western Samoa's punishing tackling seriously unsettled the Welsh. With Apollo 'Terminator' Perelini and Sila Vaifale leading the way, the Welsh lost three players injured. "Some of the tackling was phenomenal," says Bunce. "You could sense the Welsh backs were passing the ball earlier than they should have, not wanting to draw the tackler."

Western Samoa survived a desperate late Welsh revival to achieve a stunning 16-13 victory, its first over an IRB nation. Coach Peter Schuster hailed it as the greatest moment in his country's rugby history. On the other side of the world, 15,000 people had watched the game live on giant screens at Apia Park.

Overnight, the Western Samoans had become the darlings of the tournament. And their support only increased as they held World Cup favourite Australia to 9-3 and then ran Argentina ragged, to set up a quarter-final clash with Scotland at Murrayfield.

Wind blasts straight off the Arctic didn't help the south sea islanders' preparations in Edinburgh but they were ready for Scotland. Unfortunately, the guile and experience of seasoned veterans like Gavin Hastings, Finlay Calder and John Jeffrey proved too much. Attacking until the finish, they were given a standing ovation by the Murrayfield crowd.

If they were disappointed at failing to reach the semi-finals, that was instantly forgotten when a huge crowd welcomed them upon their arrival back at Auckland Airport. And the celebrations continued in Apia where a national holiday was declared.

No one enhanced his reputation at the '91 World Cup more than Bunce. Upon his return he was almost overwhelmed with offers for his services. The Canterbury Bankstown League Club in Sydney was looking for a midfield partner for Jarrod McCracken, Western Samoa naturally wanted to retain him and Laurie Mains telephoned expressing interest in him as a midfielder.

He didn't rush his decision. He went to Sydney to check out the league scene and he discussed his allegiance to Western Samoa with people whose opinions he respected. But when it came to the crunch, he knew what he most wanted was to be an All Black. Phase Two of the Bunce career began that moment in February of 1992 when he declared his allegiance to New Zealand.

Bunce was delighted to be teamed with Stephen Bachop in the main trial at Napier because they had developed an excellent understanding during the World Cup. He was even more delighted when his team won 44-17 and he was named in the shadow test fifteen to play the final trial where his main concern was the presence in the opposition of Marc Ellis, a youngster with a huge reputation. Bunce was 30, Ellis 20. "With youth on his side, I didn't want him squeezing through ahead of me," he says. "I tried a bit harder because he was there."

In the event, both Bunce and Ellis were in Mains' first All Black squad, a squad that would be reshaped several times in the ensuing seasons before Mains felt he had the ideal line-up to take on the world in South Africa in 1995.

Bunce made his All Black test debut (against the World XV) at second-five, the position in which he had represented Western Samoa with such distinction. Initially, Walter Little was outside him but following the disastrous first-up loss in Christchurch, Grant Fox was dropped, Little switched to first-five and Bunce stationed at centre (which is where he would play 42 of the All Blacks' next 43 tests).

Coach Mains says that the selectors' initial thinking was to use Bunce at second-five "because he was a strong man who could take the ball up and allow Walter, from centre, to use his flair. It quickly became apparent they were a more effective combination the other way round."

Frank Bunce

The All Blacks salvaged their reputations by winning at Wellington and Auckland but they almost came unstuck against Ireland at Carisbrook a month later, which would have been hugely embarrassing after Auckland had defeated the tourists 62-7 the previous weekend. Bunce could take the credit for saving them, his two tries allowing them to escape with a 24-21 win. In the rematch at Athletic Park, he scored another two tries (and indeed holds the individual test record for most tries against Ireland).

Those matches provided an important boost to his career. It was then he first sensed he was genuinely worthy of the All Blacks. "It had taken me a while to adjust to the greater pace and demands of All Black test rugby," he says.

Walter Little didn't need any convincing of Bunce's value. "As we had discovered at North Harbour," says Little, "he was an excellent reader of a game, and a motivator. His other great strength was his ability to bring off awesome tackles, ones that would give the team a huge lift."

It was in Australia and South Africa over the next two months that Bunce and Little's midfield liaison found full expression. They were linked together eight times, including all the major games, and claimed that by tour's end they each instinctively knew what the other was going to do.

Bunce was determined to make a big impression in the tour's first big game, against New South Wales. He did more than that – he caused mayhem! He charged 20 metres into a maul to dispose of Michael Brial whom he considered offside. He careered into him with such force, he left him concussed, and in the process sparked a major brawl in which two All Blacks, Paul Henderson and Arran Pene, broke bones in their hands. Bunce later left fullback Marty Roebuck with a badly lacerated mouth from one of his crash tackles. Altogether, five New South Wales players went off injured, prompting the *Sydney Morning Herald* to produce their classic headline: ALL BLACKS DEFEAT NSW – NOT MANY DEAD.

Although the All Blacks lost the series 2-1 to the Wallabies, yielding the Bledisloe Cup, they were amazingly even contests, as the scorelines of 15-16, 17-19 and 26-23 suggest. Each team scored six tries.

The series pitted Bunce and Little against Jason Little and Tim Horan in the rugby heavyweight midfield championship of the world.

Rugby Greats

In Mains' view, the All Black pair achieved a clear edge on their illustrious opponents. "In fact," says Mains, "in my time as coach, there was not a combination in the world better than Bunce and Little. No one ever outplayed them."

They arrived in South Africa to find Springbok coach John Williams labelling them "extremely dangerous players – the team's main weapon". He went on to describe them as "explosive players with lots of skills and imagination. They not only shut out the Aussies but were on top of them all the time."

A tough billing to live up to, but the *Midfield Liaison* combination did themselves proud, both producing big games in the test at Ellis Park, won so impressively by Mains' men. The game's most spectacular try was achieved through Bunce running laterally across the Springbok 22 and linking with John Kirwan who dotted down between the posts.

It had been a marvellous year of international rugby for Bunce and at the conclusion of it he was named one of the five players of the year in both the *Rugby Annual* and the *Rugby Almanack*. Not bad for a 30-year-old who'd alternated between Auckland B and the Auckland A reserves bench for six years!

Throughout his term as All Black coach, that is, from 1992 through to the end of the 1995 season, Mains never considered another player for the centre role. Bunce was his man. He thought so much of him, he eventually involved him in team selections and regularly sought his expert opinion. In Mains' view, Bunce was the toughest centre in the world – "a rugged, gifted footballer". Bunce was there providing the midfield steel against the Lions, the French, the Springboks, the Wallabies, the Brits and throughout the '95 World Cup. Mains says that on only three occasions in four years did he have to get tough with him because he'd let his attitude soften. "Frank responded on each occasion." The only test Bunce missed (out of 34) during Mains' era was the World Cup pool match against Japan at Bloemfontein when the All Black selectors took the opportunity to give the second-tier players an outing.

Because he was 34 when John Hart took over as coach in 1996, many expected Bunce would be phased out, and his indifferent early-season displays for the Waikato Chiefs gave credence to this line of thinking. According to Bunce, his poor form was directly related to an

84

Frank Bunce

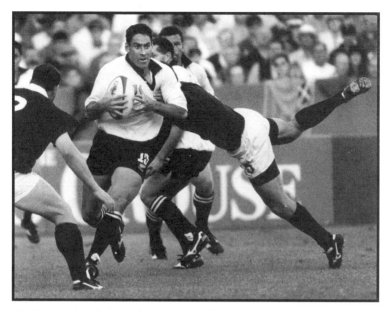

Frank Bunce has the Scottish defence on full alert during the World Cup quarter-final at Pretoria in 1995. The tackler is Gavin Hastings, in his final appearance for Scotland.   John Selkirk

ongoing groin injury. "It was something I couldn't shrug off," he says. "It flared up whenever I sprinted."

He had a discussion with Hart who commented that his fitness was obviously not what it should be. "John assured me I was still in the frame and that as long as I could show him I *wanted* to be there, he was interested. He told me he wanted me keen, eager and fit, and I was given till the All Black trial in Napier to come right. After the trial, he said I had kept my share of the bargain, and selected me. Once I was back, I realised I did not want to be away from the All Blacks."

Bunce appeared in all 10 tests in 1996, extending his test appearances to 43. He concedes that he was operating at about 80 per cent efficiency against Western Samoa and didn't recapture his best form and fitness till he reached South Africa.

He scored only one try in '96, but it was a matchwinner, against the Australians at Ballymore. He was a major participant in the daring last-gasp move called by Andrew Mehrtens. "We'd practised the move many times and never used it," he says. "We've got a host of moves like that. It's a case of finding the ideal time to use them."

The greatest thrill for Bunce was being part of a team that finally achieved a series victory over the Springboks on their soil, although he concedes his greatest personal achievement was surviving the 80 minutes of the Pretoria test. "I remember looking at the clock and realising there were seventy minutes to go," he says. "Mark Andrews had trodden on me and cut my lip which was bleeding, and we'd started the game so furiously I was gasping for breath."

He recalls that after Jeff Wilson's first try, Zinzan Brooke collapsed from lightheadedness while running back. "That altitude affected everyone at some stage, but the guys showed great fortitude to hang in. Once we got the sniff of victory, we were able to lift ourselves. We knew what an incredible prize awaited us if we could hang on."

Andy Dalton

Suggest to Andy Dalton that his illustrious rugby career deserved a more satisfactory ending and he laconically passes it off as "character building". The son of an All Black and grandson of a Rhodes Scholar prefers to remember all the good times he experienced in rugby.

"Life has taught me never to waste time worrying about the might have beens," says Dalton, who rates as one of the most successful All Black captains. Just as well, because the might have beens were substantial in Dalton's case.

He might have helped the Cavaliers square or win their series in South Africa in 1986 had not a Northern Transvaal forward busted his jaw at the start of the tour; and at the age of 35 he might have been a star of New Zealand's first World Cup campaign had he not torn his hamstring in training.

Fate denied him active participation in both of these historic events. And so the Bledisloe Cup thriller at Eden Park in mid-1995, which the All Blacks won by a single point, unexpectedly became Dalton's farewell to international rugby.

He had recovered well enough to sit on the reserves bench for the semi-final of the World Cup against Wales and the final against France. "I kind of hoped Sean Fitzpatrick might limp off towards the finish of one of those games," says Dalton, "but as we've seen he's probably the most resilient footballer in the world, and he was too smart to let me get a foot back in the door!"

One of the lasting memories of the All Blacks' triumph in 1987 is

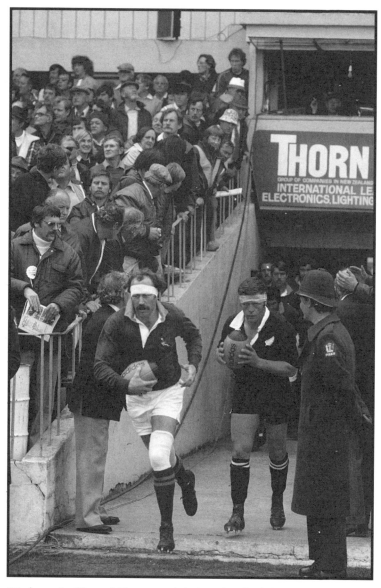

Rival captains Wynand Claassen and Andy Dalton lead their teams on to Eden Park for the decider of the 1981 series. Notwithstanding the pilot who dropped flour bombs throughout, the game was played to a conclusion, New Zealand winning 25-22.

Photosport

Andy Dalton

of David Kirk and Dalton in the front of the grandstand at Eden Park jointly holding the Webb Ellis Trophy aloft. Dalton confesses that he was a most reluctant participant in that ceremony. "I never felt I was part of the All Black performance," he says, "having never got on the field. I wanted to stay in the changing room and let those who'd played share the limelight, but I was forcibly escorted up into the grandstand!"

All Black coach Brian Lochore invited Dalton to remain part of the team for the Bledisloe Cup contest in Sydney a month later, but Dalton declined. "The leg still wasn't a hundred per cent and after the frustrations of the previous two seasons, I decided to ease out of the game altogether. I didn't make any dramatic announcement, just faded into the background."

Dalton retired as the most capped All Black hooker, although his mark of 35 tests has since been well and truly eclipsed by the remarkable Sean Fitzpatrick who has gone on to become the most capped forward in the history of the game and also an outstanding leader. "I hope he appreciates the break my torn hamstring gave him back in 1987," says Dalton with a smile.

Unlike Fitzpatrick, who captained New Zealand Colts, Dalton was a late developer as representative rugby players go. He failed to make the first XV at Lincoln College where he studied for a Bachelor of Agricultural Science degree and was 23 before he began playing senior club rugby.

An examination of his family background suggested he was always likely to succeed at the sport, particularly as a leader. His father Ray, who represented Wellington and Otago as a prop, was vice-captain of the 1949 All Blacks to South Africa while his uncle George (Ray's brother) was a Rhodes Scholar (who died aged 45 while working as the chief engineer of the Atomic Research Establishment in Sydney).Not many All Black captains come out of the Auckland senior B competition, but that was where Peter Wahlstrom, selector-coach of the Auckland under-23 team (and brother of nationally ranked referee Glen Wahlstrom) 'discovered' Dalton in 1974. "I spent most of my time watching the senior A sides," says Wahlstrom, "but I had a call from someone who advised me that the Eastern senior B team had a damned good hooker. I checked him out, and he was outstanding, all right, a player with a future."

Rugby Greats

That future would happen not in Auckland but in Counties. Dalton had joined Eastern while working with the Ministry of Agriculture at Warkworth, but the next year when he began working as a farm adviser based in Pukekohe he joined the Bombay club. Well, he actually turned up for trials at the Pukekohe club but finding the hooking berth well secured by Brian Cochrane, an All Black trialist, he took himself down the road to the less fashionable Bombay club.

He made an instant impact and was quickly snapped up by Counties' enterprising coach Barry Bracewell, who used him against North Auckland at Whangarei on Queen's Birthday. His opponent was Peter Sloane who would become his rival at national level for many years. He played all 12 matches for Counties that season, the Almanack's editor Arthur Carman thinking enough of him to make him one of his five most promising players.

Dalton singles out Bracewell as one of the most influential coaches during his career. "He was the first to explain the game's intricacies to me," says Dalton. "He was a tactician and a strategist who had made a thorough study of the game. We played thrilling counter-attacking rugby under Barry. He made Counties one of the glamour teams in New Zealand. People still talk about those daring days."

Counties continued to flourish when Hiwi Tauroa took over in 1976. The success of the team naturally brought them national recognition, and it was no surprise when Dalton, who had taken over the captaincy, was selected for the North Island, although Bracewell's presence on the panel probably had a lot to do with that. Dalton didn't immediately win over the New Zealand selectors, however. Tane Norton and Graeme Crossman were the hookers with the main All Black squad in South Africa while Peter Sloane and an outsider, John Black (plucked from the New Zealand Universities team) went to Argentina with Graham Mourie's team.

He wasn't among the four hookers called to the All Black trials in Wanganui in May of 1977 – those ranking above him being Tane Norton (who would captain New Zealand against the Lions), Sloane, Black and Ken Bloxham. Dalton, 25 at the time, consequently gave little thought to international status. But the three tightheads he claimed off Bobby Windsor in Counties-Thames Valley's game against the Lions and the consistently top-class performances he turned in at NPC level for Counties meant he leapfrogged most of his rivals when

Andy Dalton

the All Black team to tour Italy and France was named at season's end. He and Black were the preferred hookers, Norton having declared himself unavailable.

Two other new players were Gary Knight and John Ashworth with whom Dalton would form a powerful front row liaison in the years ahead. Intriguingly, all three of them made their All Black debuts in the tour opener at Padua, a game the All Blacks were in serious danger of losing until captain Graham Mourie came on as a replacement (and promptly scored two tries).

Black was used in the first test at Toulouse but after the French outmuscled the New Zealanders changes were made for the rematch in Paris, Dalton coming in for his test debut. Although injuries had seriously depleted the touring party, a combination of masterly scheming and fortitude saw them decisively outplay the French. The tactics were masterminded by Bruce Robertson and coach Jack Gleeson who had been outraged at the French forwards' lineout obstruction the previous Saturday. They devised two-man lineouts involving only Dalton as the thrower and Andy Haden and Lawrie Knight as the jumpers.

"The biggest problem," says Dalton, "was finding somewhere to practise away from the prying eyes of the French camp. We found a park which suited us, but not the gendarmes who kept shooing us away. They didn't appreciate rugby players on their patch!"

The younger, fitter All Blacks played the game at breakneck speed, to the exasperation of the crusty French forwards, to pull off one of the great tactical victories. "Bruce Robertson was the individual who convinced us the way to overcome them was to take tap penalties, quick lineouts and run at them for eighty minutes."

That tour was Dalton's introduction to the player who would dominate the lineout scene in world rugby through until the mid 1980s, Andy Haden. Dalton quickly appreciated that Haden was a perfectionist who would not accept second best from his throwers-in. "The throw-in was his lifeline which was why he demanded accuracy," says Dalton. "It was pretty daunting in those early days to have him toss the ball straight back to you at training and bark 'No!' or 'Again, but where I want it this time!'"

Dalton became the first All Black hooker to throw to the lineouts, that duty previously being the prerogative of the wingers. It might have remained thus, but Brian Ford, the Marlborough speedster on that tour, found memorising lineout calls somewhat taxing and willingly stepped aside for Dalton.

There were seven tests in 1978, and Dalton played the lot, stamping himself the best hooker in New Zealand. Only one of those tests was lost, the third against the Wallabies at Eden Park, the day Greg Cornelsen claimed four tries (an extraordinary achievement considering they were the only tries he scored in a lengthy international career).

There were to be no such setbacks in the UK. Well, not in the tests, the four victories against Ireland, Wales, England and Scotland constituting the first (and to this day, the only) Grand Slam achieved by New Zealand on their soil.

But there was a loss, a famous victory being achieved by the men of Munster at Limerick. In the more than 90 years of rivalry between New Zealand and Ireland, this remains the only occasion an Irish side has triumphed. They succeeded through what All Black coach Jack Gleeson branded "kamikaze tackling".

Dalton has no doubts that New Zealand's Grand Slam owed everything to Munster. "If they'd been easybeats, I've no doubt we would have lost the test to Ireland four days later. It was a great lesson to us, just when we were thinking we could cruise through the tour undefeated they tackled their hearts out and proved there's always a place for the underdog."

It was Dalton's try three minutes from time – one of only three in 35 tests – that allowed the All Blacks to escape from the Irish test with a victory. Until he dived across in the corner, after an untidy lineout tapdown had forced Mark Donaldson to probe the blindside instead of setting his backs alight, the game had been deadlocked at 6-all.

Dalton brands the Scottish test – another desperately tight one – the most physically draining he ever played in. Ian 'Mighty Mouse' McLauchlan, the Scottish prop, exerted enormous pressure in the scrum, leaving Dalton physically shattered. It was also the darkest test he ever played in. "It was like a night game, without lights," he says.

The easiest of the Grand Slam wins was against England because, Dalton says, the England selectors didn't choose the best team available. "In seeking mobility, they foolishly selected two specialist looseheads," he says, "which suited us fine. In the other games in

Andy Dalton

As the successful All Black captain, Andy Dalton receives the congratulations of NZRFU chairman Ces Blazey following the series victory over the Springboks in 1981. John Ashworth looks on.   Ross Wiggins (NZ Herald)

Britain the scrummaging exhaused us. Against England we had reserve power to do our share in the loose."

Save for Andy Haden's audacious dive out of the lineout at Cardiff, an act which scandalised the Welsh, the All Blacks were model tourists in '78 – until Ashworth put a sprig through J.P.R. Williams' cheek in the penultimate encounter at Bridgend. That gave the London tabloids, who'd almost lost interest in the tour, all the incentive they needed. They attacked like frenzied sharks. Ashworth became a villain and was subjected to intense booing when he took the field as a replacement in the tour finale against the Barbarians in Cardiff.

Dalton had mixed emotions about the 1979 season. On the credit side, Counties won the national championship – the only occasion it has been New Zealand's premier union – and his fellow front-rowers John Spiers and Rod Ketels were elevated to international status for the end-of-year tour of England and Scotland. But Dalton's own career stuttered. After appearing in the domestic tests against France, the second of which was lost, he was replaced by Black for the Bledisloe Cup encounter in Sydney. Reinstated for the Scottish test at Murrayfield, he was back on the reserves bench at Twickenham when coach Eric Watson introduced Sloane as his test hooker.

Four hookers represented the All Blacks in Australia and Fiji in 1980, and none of them was Dalton (or Sloane). Hika Reid, who would make electrifying progress and win the test spot, and Black were the first choices but when both suffered serious injuries, Ken Bloxham and Grant Perry came in as replacements.

Dalton had made himself unavailable for the eight-week tour of Australia and Fiji, for personal reasons. He was establishing his farm at Bombay and his wife, Pip, was expecting their first child. He considered criticism that he was "letting the side down" – Colin Meads being one who said players should not pick and choose tours – to be unreasonable. "There were so many tours at that time," he says, "and as an amateur, I simply could not afford the time away, not on a daily allowance of $18." Ashworth and Knight had been unavailable for the tour of Scotland and England the previous year because of their farming commitments.

Dalton was back for the tour of Wales at the end of 1980 but found himself in the shadow of Reid, who had recovered from a broken leg. It was Reid who not only hooked in the centennial test in Cardiff but who scored a spectacular try.

There will, hopefully, never be another rugby year quite like 1981. Although some of Dalton's favourite memories emanate from those times, he concedes that the extraneous pressures associated with the Springbok tour, which thrust unreasonable pressures on himself and his wife, are something he could have done without. Dalton was not only the All Blacks' premier hooker throughout '81, he assumed the captaincy for the South African series after Graham Mourie declared himself unavailable on moral grounds.

Dalton resented the invasion of his privacy by many of those protesting against the tour. "It was a trying time for families," he says. "There was a lot of pressure from crank calls and from the media who wouldn't leave it alone." Dalton says that while aware of the divisions caused by the Springboks' presence, he weighed all the issues and was satisfied that playing against them was a just thing to do."

A graphic example of the tensions that existed at the time came when Dalton was working away in a remote corner of his farm when suddenly a helicopter landed nearby. "There were stories of players possibly being hijacked," he says. "The adrenalin really started pumping. I had a hammer behind my back as these two blokes got out, but it turned out they were genuinely lost and looking for another farm. But it gave me a hell of a fright."

Because the Springboks possessed such awesome power among the forwards – with prop Flippie van der Merwe weighing in at a staggering 130kg – the New Zealand selectors knew they needed strong, experienced players among the tight five. And so they turned to the front row trio who would become known as the Geriatrics – Dalton, the youngest at 29, Knight and Ashworth – to anchor the scrum.

Notwithstanding the presence of barbed wire within the stadiums and angry, protesting hordes, who regularly confronted squads of police, outside, '81 developed into a classic series, in the great tradition of New Zealand-South Africa meetings.

Dalton's men claimed a stirring victory at Lancaster Park, Dalton contributing massively with a telling tighthead at a critical point 25 minutes into the game. The Springboks had great attacking options when a scrum formed near the All Black posts, but they never received the ball. A timely heave by the New Zealand forwards unsettled the Bok scrum, Dalton stole the tighthead and the All Blacks cleared. It rates as one of the most valuable scrums Dalton ever won, giving his team an important psychological advantage over the tourists who until that moment considered their pack all-powerful.

The Springboks levelled the series at windswept Athletic Park. Although acknowledging that the tourists were the better team that day, Dalton says the All Blacks' chances weren't helped by "a totally unsatisfactory" preparation. "Our build-up was dreadful," he says, "the worst for any first-class match in my entire career. The dungeon-like dressing rooms where we were quartered (for security reasons) from early morning were a disgrace. "God, it was cold," says Dalton. "I was huddled under three blankets and I still couldn't get warm."

The All Blacks had to move out of their hotel at 8.30am on the day of the third test at Eden Park because of concerns that protestors might block off the Harbour Bridge. While that was disruptive, at least the facilities at Eden Park were comfortable. And warm.

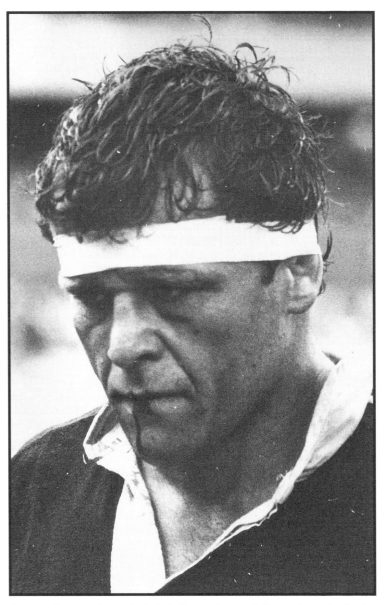

A jaw and a tour shattered. Andy Dalton a picture of abject misery after having his jaw broken by a Northern Transvaal player at the start of the Cavaliers tour in 1986. Wessel Oosthuizen

Andy Dalton

Dalton, however, was back delivering winning test speeches the next season, two of them against France and two in Australia. For a long time in Australia, though, the news was all grim. The Wallabies not only took the first international in Sydney, they opened up a commanding 12-nil advantage in the second at Ballymore. Never had the All Blacks come back from such a deficit in a test. Fortunately, they had Dalton to guide them. The Rugby Annual captured the drama at Brisbane thus: "Comparing them in terms of pure human dynamism, Hika Reid should have been the All Black hooker in Australia, ahead of Andy Dalton. But Dalton possesses exceptional qualities of leadership which have never been better exemplified than in this dramatic international. Some skippers would have been frantically desperate at 0-12 but Dalton quietly emphasised to his troops the need to achieve control up front and implement the battle plan they had devised. In supervising his players and ensuring that the plan did indeed work, Dalton stamped himself one of New Zealand's outstanding captains."

The All Blacks came back to win 19-15 and clinched the series 25-24 in a penalty-marred third test in Sydney. Dalton's outstanding leadership was recognised when he was presented with the 1984 New Zealand player of the year award.

He was at the peak of his form and after further successful performances, as hooker and captain, against England and in the one-off test against the Wallabies in 1985, it seemed Dalton had a lot more to offer New Zealand rugby.

But fate would intervene in the cruellest manner possible. The High Court injunction denied Dalton and his fellow All Blacks the opportunity of a lifetime, to play the Springboks in South Africa, an event described by Dalton as "psychologically and mentally destroying". He is critical of the NZRFU in the wake of the High Court ruling. "It had no contingency plans and the union's lawyers were out-thought. In many respects, it was found wanting."

Attempts to get to South Africa as individuals were blocked at the time but the players, determined to engage the Springboks in combat – for many of the senior players this was a last oppportunity – assembled in the republic in April, 1976, as the Cavaliers to undertake an abbreviated (12-match) itinerary.

Dalton survived less than 40 minutes of the tour, Northern

Transvaal flanker Burger Geldenhuys breaking his jaw with a punch from behind. "There was this enormous whack," he recalls, "and blood was gushing out. Our physiotherapist, Malcolm Hood, took one look at it and said, 'You're off'." They did such a bad repair job on the jaw first up that it had to be re-set.

Geldenhuys, who did not come near Dalton during the tour, wrote to him five years later offering an apology. "He was pretty slow to say sorry," says Dalton. "I felt no desire to make contact."

Disappointed in the extreme (because the injury prevented him taking any further part in the tour, and the Cavaliers lost the series), Dalton played no further rugby that year, instead concentrating on getting himself into peak shape for the inaugural World Cup early in the 1987 season. He was in shape, and he was appointed captain. But then came the hamstring injury that shattered his last remaining ambition. The Dalton career, spanning almost a full decade as an All Black and embracing 35 tests plus 122 games for Counties, was at an end.

He went on to coach Counties from 1989 to 1991 but found the experience challenging and frustrating. "They were a very young team who didn't have the level of commitment I presumed they would have," he says. At the end of '91, the team was relegated to second division. "I know few would agree with me, but in hindsight it was probably a good thing – it allowed them time to regroup. Ross Cooper picked them up and brought them through strongly. My satisfaction is in seeing so many of the youngsters I introduced mature into quality representative players."

Dalton, who still farms 920 acres at Bombay, became the manager of a waste business, Hazardous Wastes in 1989. When the company was sold to Nuplex Industries in 1996, he was retained as the general manager and a director. He is also chairman of the Counties-Manukau Sports Foundation. He and his wife Pip have two children, Kate and Hamish.

Sean Fitzpatrick

Everyone was depressed after New Zealand bombed out of the 1991 World Cup, Sean Fitzpatrick included. In fact, he'd been deriving so little satisfaction from his rugby that he decided to retire.

When he arrived home, he threw his boots away, advising his wife Bronwyn that at the age of 28, a veteran of 40 tests, he was giving up. He'd had a gutsful. Bronwyn didn't over-react to the announcement. "Give it time," she said. "See how you feel after the holidays."

As the summer sun soothed his body, and matters far removed from rugby relaxed his mind, Fitzpatrick began re-assessing his future. "I didn't like the prospect of becoming a former All Black," he says. "That didn't sit easily with me.

"And a few things started to niggle away at me, such as the Wallabies being endlessly referred to as the world champions and Phil Kearns being dubbed the best hooker in the world. That really started to grate. I knew I wouldn't rest easily unless I had a crack at claiming that title back from Phil Kearns."

By the time the new All Black coach telephoned Fitzpatrick in late January, he'd made his mind up. Yes, he assured Laurie Mains, he would be playing again. "Laurie sounded very positive but warned me that I would need to get a lot fitter and be prepared to play a more expansive game than in 1991."

Get fitter, eh? Old Fitzy could manage that. If fitness was going to be an important factor, he'd be ready. "I started getting up early and running, running greater distances than ever before," says Fitzpatrick.

Rugby Greats

Did you ever see a happier Sean Fitzpatrick? New Zealand had just won the first World Cup and Murray Pierce, Fitzpatrick and Buck Shelford had plenty to smile about.   John Selkirk

"Whenever I started to slacken, I would remind myself that Phil Kearns was number one in the world, and that would spur me on."

Looking back on that important phase of his career now – after extending his test appearances from 40 to 83 *and* reclaiming the No 1 hooker's rating – Fitzpatrick relates it to the philosophy of the international giant he works for, Coca-Cola. "At Coke, we prepare for any challenge as if we are number two, wanting to become number one. We never take our position in the market for granted. In 1992, I *knew* I was number two, if that, and I desperately wanted to become number one again. It's the philosophy that has motivated me over the past several seasons."

Although Mains' first preference for captain was Mike Brewer, who was removed from the equation through injury, the rejuvenation of All Black rugby commencing in 1992 owed an enormous amount to the Mains-Fitzpatrick partnership. As a coach and captain they immediately jelled and, notwithstanding a few disappointing results along the way, they guided the All Blacks into a new rugby strata by

Sean Fitzpatrick

the time of the third World Cup in 1995.

Fitzpatrick admired Mains' honesty and was excited from the start by his vision for a daringly different high-action game. He appreciated the manner in which Mains confronted his problems, which his predecessor Alex Wyllie had never done.

Mains, in turn, soon recognised that in Fitzpatrick he possessed a leader of exceptional qualities. "Following the tour of Australia and South Africa in 1992," he says, "it was obvious he was something special. He possessed that almost indefinable X Factor of which great All Black captains are made."

Being the son of an All Black could have placed unreasonable pressures on Sean as a youngster and perhaps even forced him to make his way in another sport. His father Brian, often known by his initials of BBJ, had been a strong personality in the All Black teams he represented in the early 1950s. Renowned as a hard-running, strong-tackling midfielder, he appeared in three tests, against Wales, Ireland and France on the 1953-54 tour with Bob Stuart's team.

But Sean speaks glowingly of his father's attitude when he was growing up. "There was absolutely no pressure on me to make it as a rugby player," he says. "If I'd been hopeless, it wouldn't have mattered. As long as I was happy."

Young Fitzpatrick was a dead keen rugby enthusiast from day one, however, and when one of his sisters brought home the autographs of Bryan Williams and Andy Haden he can remember being hugely impressed.

His first coach (at College Rifles) was Jim Anderton who would make a greater impact in life as a politician than a rugby coach. If he remembers Sean as a player, it's probably more for his bulk than his skills. "I was a pretty big kid at school," he says. "I was drop-kicked out of the Roller Mills primary school trial because I was two stone overweight. I was never in the same teams as my friends because I was so heavy. I was always trying to lose weight."

There was no suggestion that Sean Brian Thomas Fitzpatrick, weighing in at almost 11st at the age of 12, was destined for a distinguished rugby career when he was placed in the 3D team in his first year at Sacred Heart College. A weight-restricted team, it comprised the worst players at the school.

He wouldn't make it into the Sacred Heart first XV until his sixth

Rugby Greats

form year when he came in as a hooker. In his final year, he was used at prop where his bulk was considered to be of greater benefit to the team. He immediately started making an impression. Although his own memories are totally hazy – "I only worry about the next match, not what happened years ago," he says – he was good enough to represent Auckland at under-16 and under-18 level and to make reserve for the North Island under-16 team. The hooker who kept him out, Tony Flay, would go on to play international rugby for the United States.

Bernie McCahill, who would be a fellow All Black at the 1991 World Cup, remembers Fitzpatrick at Sacred Heart as a player everyone knew. "He was one of the feared ones – a player with a big reputation." His impact in 1981 was recognised when he was awarded the trophy as the Auckland secondary schools personality of the year. The handover was made by the 1980 winner, Grant Fox.

After a year playing third grade with the Auckland University club (from where he captained the Auckland third grade representative side) Fitzpatrick became a contender, at the age of 19, for the seniors. The coach, Graham Henry, with whom he would have a lot more to do, assessed him during pre-season training. "He arrived as a prop, but I suggested to him he could struggle in that position," recalls Henry. "I thought he was better equipped to play at hooker. He was a bit apprehensive at first, but the conversion was completed during a pre-season trip to Australia."

Henry remembers the 19-year-old as a player with considerable physical presence on the field. "He needed monitoring, because he was overly aggressive. But if you haven't got aggression as a rugby player, you've got nothing, have you? Fitzy's aggression just needed channelling."

He was snapped up by the New Zealand selectors for the colts, an event which brought him great satisfaction. "Being selected for the test at Pukekohe was the greatest feeling I'd ever known," he says. Unfortunately, he couldn't celebrate his arrival in the black jersey with a victory, an awesomely strong Australian under-21 team (featuring David Campese, Brett Papworth, Michael Lynagh, Steve Tuynman, Jeff Miller, Troy Coker and Tom Lawton) winning 26-18.

Fitzpatrick's career was coming along nicely. It was about to take off . . . or so he thought. In February of 1984 he found himself

Sean Fitzpatrick

winging his way to Europe with the Auckland team. "It came out of the blue," he says. "John Hart telephoned one day and invited me to join the team on its pre-season tour. Naturally, I accepted." The tour embraced two games in France, three in Britain and one in the United States.

"Considering I was a bit of a joke with the University seniors about how badly I threw the ball to the lineout," says Fitzpatrick, "my selection for Auckland came as a shock. Precision lineout throwing is so crucial and I didn't see the warning signs until I was overseas."

Fitzpatrick says that he came to hate training because of the pressures placed upon him by Auckland's lineout king Andy Haden who, the 20-year-old hooker soon discovered, was an absolute perfectionist. "Andy was really hard on me," he says. "If I threw in poorly, he was at me. He'd stop training and say, 'No, that's not right'. Sometimes he drew a sketch of what he wanted in front of the whole team. I felt so small. It was one hell of a learning curve. I now regard it as a lesson in how not to treat young players, but it was how the old brigade operated in those days."

The final humiliation for Fitzpatrick, whose two outings had been against La Rochelle and West Hartlepool, came in training at San Diego before the final match against the Grizzlies. Fitzpatrick had been selected but after three poor throws, Haden stopped the practice. 'Get out of here,' he said. Iain Abercrombie stepped forward, took over at training and played the match.

And that was end of Fitzpatrick's involvement with Auckland for 1984. Hart, reflecting on those events, says that Fitzpatrick was a pathetic thrower-in of the ball. "It was the first time he'd come into contact with professional rugby people who didn't tolerate sloppiness."

Demoralised, but not totally defeated, Fitzpatrick realised he had to improve his throwing in, and quickly. So he contacted Kevin Boyle who had been Auckland's hooker in 1983 and asked if he would help. "I rated Kevin from club play," says Fitzpatrick. "Initially, he was wary because he perceived me as a rival. But he rang back and agreed to assist. We practised a couple of times a week, and gradually I improved. When I'd built my confidence, I tempted fate by ringing Andy Haden and asking him for assistance. To my delight, he agreed to join me at the Auckland Domain. I don't know why he did that, maybe he saw some potential in me."

While Auckland's coach had gone cold on him, the national selectors still regarded Fitzpatrick as the best under-21 hooker in the country. And for the 1984 colts visit to Australia, they made him captain. The coach was Brian Lochore.

Fitzpatrick had an exciting start to 1985, touring England, Ireland, France and Italy with a New Zealand Universities team captained by David Kirk and, within days of returning, popping across to Australia for a couple of outings with the Barbarians. But on the Auckland scene, the news was all glum. Hart's preferred hooker was Abercrombie, and that was that. It concerned Fitzpatrick that Hika Reid had moved to Auckland, joining the queue behind Abercrombie and himself and new All Black John Mills.

At one stage, he approached Hart who told him he still wasn't throwing the ball in well enough and that he was sick and tired of watching him play for University and give away penalties through over aggressive play. "By 1985," says Hart, "he was probably a better player than Abercrombie but not as professional. If I'd put Sean in the team then he would never have been a great player – good, but not great. I use him as an example in speeches." Abercrombie made 17 appearances for Auckland in 1985; Fitzpatrick played the non-championship game against South Canterbury in Timaru and came on as a replacement against Wanganui.

Nothing changed when the 1986 season kicked off, Abercrombie being the hooker for Auckland's opening games. But suddenly New Zealand rugby was pitched into turmoil by the dramatic departure for South Africa of the Cavaliers, leaving All Black coach Lochore with a lengthy shopping list for the test coming up against France.

Bruce Hemara and John Buchan were the hookers in the inter-island fixture in Oamaru while Auckland rivals Abercrombie and Fitzpatrick opposed each other in foul conditions in the trial match in Blenheim. It was Hemara who won selection, with Fitzpatrick the surprise reserve. After all, he'd played only three times for Auckland (at La Rochelle, West Hartlepool and Timaru) and come on twice as a replacement while Abercrombie, six years his senior, boasted more than 50 rep appearances.

"I guess I was lucky," says Fitzpatrick, "although Brian Lochore knew me from the Colts tour in 1984." If making the squad was

Sean Fitzpatrick

lucky, what were the odds on Hemara dropping out injured at training? He had arrived in Christchurch with damaged rib cartilage that became too painful to continue. Lochore approached Fitzpatrick after training and told him he would be playing.

"It was incredible, the fulfilment of a boyhood dream," says Fitzpatrick. "Thirty of the best players might have been overseas, but we were going to run on to Lancaster Park as All Blacks. I was really apprehensive about whether I could perform. After all, I couldn't even make the Auckland A team."

Fitzpatrick did perform. The All Blacks performed. Against all expectations, the Baby Blacks demonstrated what spirit and youthful determination, particularly when embodied in an All Black jersey, can achieve. The French, Five Nations co-champions, and boasting such international superstars as Serge Blanco and Philippe Sella, were kept tryless and lost 18-9.

Fitzpatrick threw accurately to the lineouts where the All Blacks matched the French. The scrums were a different story. "Every scrum

Sean Fitzpatrick has made a specialty of scoring tries at international level. This is the first one he ever dotted down for the All Blacks, against Australia in Sydney in 1987. Riding on his back is Brett Papworth. John Selkirk

was a disaster," says Fitzpatrick. "I was under such pressure I could hardly breathe. They were so much heavier and Jean-Pierre Garuet, their prop, exerted intense pressure on me. Every scrum was a nightmare. Sometimes they marched right over the top of us."

The fairytale didn't stretch to two victories for the Baby Blacks. Though they did well, with so little international experience, to hold Alan Jones' Wallabies to 13-12 in the opening encounter of the Bledisloe Cup series, once the Cavaliers were eligible it was inevitable changes would be made. The extent of those changes – 10, in total, including the entire pack – surprised many. Fitzpatrick was relegated to the reserves' bench behind Hika Reid.

"Things were suddenly different," says Fitzpatrick. "We weren't a particularly happy team. The return of the Cavaliers brought seniority and hierarchy into the set-up. The Baby Blacks had their place, and it was at the bottom. I think Lochore later felt he should have kept the younger team together but apparently Colin Meads, his fellow selector, wanted the Cavaliers back in. Their compromise didn't work. One who really suffered was David Kirk, who was retained as the captain. He bore the brunt of the Cavaliers' hostility. In the team meeting before the second test Jock Hobbs said, 'Right, let's show these young pricks we're still the best,' which summed up the attitude."

With Fitzpatrick now an All Black, and one who'd proven he could throw in straight, Hart could no longer ignore his claims. From the Counties match in late July, Fitzpatrick took over the Auckland No 2 jersey, leaving the hapless Abercrombie to move to the reserves' bench. A loss at Athletic Park meant Auckland yielded the NPC title to Wellington for 1986, but the Ranfurly Shield was retained, notwithstanding a monumental effort by Alex Wyllie's men to claim it back at season's end.

In October, Fitzpatrick headed for France with the All Blacks and had the satisfaction of being chosen ahead of Reid for the internationals at Toulouse (won well) and Nantes (lost horribly).

With the curtain falling on one of the most controversial and fractured seasons ever in New Zealand rugby, with test losses matching wins, who could have foreseen the glorious days that lay ahead. The All Blacks would not bow to any opponent in the next 50 games (stretching almost four years). And the young hooker

Sean Fitzpatrick

Fitzpatrick would display unbelievable resilience, and form, by playing a world record 63 tests in succession in constructing an international career that would span three World Cups.

The contrast between the first and second World Cup campaigns would be vast. Of course, it took another lucky break for Fitzpatrick to even participate in the inaugural event after Andy Dalton, a veteran of 35 tests (who'd been unavailable for the tour of France) was named hooker and captain. Logically, Dalton would have played five, perhaps all six, of New Zealand's matches. But when he first strained and then tore his hamstring in training, Fitzpatrick took over, being one of seven players (John Kirwan, Joe Stanley, Grant Fox, David Kirk, Alan Whetton and Gary Whetton were the others) to play in all six games.

With Lochore (so ably assisted by his new partners Hart and Wyllie) rebuilding team spirit and introducing a highly mobile game that caught most opponents by surprise, the All Blacks were in a class of their own at that first World Cup, scoring 43 tries while conceding only four. The team put 70 points on Italy and Fiji, blitzed Wales 49-6 in the semi-final at Ballymore and roared clear of France in the second half of the final at Eden Park. The 1987 All Blacks were a freak team, in Fitzpatrick's opinion. "What made them great was their unbelievable natural ability. In my career, I've never seen another team approach it."

Their World Cup triumph happened in June, 1987. Four years and four months later, with six of the same players involved, the All Blacks crashed out of the second World Cup, beaten comprehensively by the Wallabies at Dublin. What would produce serious repercussions back home was not simply the fact the All Blacks lost to an extremely talented and well-prepared Australian team, which would go on to claim the Webb Ellis Trophy and dominate international rugby for several years, but that so many things had been going so seriously wrong, obviously for some time, with the once great All Black machine.

In Fitzpatrick's view, by the time the All Blacks were touring Argentina six months out from the World Cup, coach Wyllie was struggling. "As a coach he seemed to have run out of fresh ideas," says Fitzpatrick. "Everything that could go wrong was going wrong. When our form dropped off, he let things slide.

A Steinlager spray for captain Sean Fitzpatrick and coach John Hart to celebrate a famous first series victory over the Springboks in South Africa in 1996.

John Selkirk

"We'd been so great for so long, it was inevitable complacency would develop. Probably there should have been more changes. There was only one – the dropping of Buck Shelford, which sent shock waves through the All Blacks. Buck had been a magnificent leader. He led by example in every game and so we naturally followed. In hindsight, the dropping of Buck coincided with the wheels falling off the All Blacks. But his absence wasn't the reason for the team's subsequent failures."

The NZRFU wanted Wyllie to take an assistant coach to France in 1990 but he refused. Then when his team began to stumble in the year of the World Cup, the council decided to introduce Hart, not as a deputy, but as co-coach. "Grizz seemed shellshocked by Hart's appointment," says Fitzpatrick. "At the World Cup they played out a private game in public. In press conferences, they'd contradict each other. The tension between them unsettled the team, and because we weren't playing well, and the media was getting stuck into us, we weren't happy. No wonder we weren't a PR hit – the contrast with 1987 could not have been more noticeable."

The All Blacks didn't fire at any stage of the second World Cup.

Sean Fitzpatrick

While their victory first up over England was convincing enough, they played muddled rugby against the United States and had only 10 points to spare against Italy. By the time they arrived in Dublin for the semi-final, they were a mere shadow of the side which had dominated world rugby in the late 1980s. The Wallabies, meanwhile, were at the peak of their powers and had the semi-final well in control by halftime. Having to play off for third against Scotland in Cardiff only prolonged the players' agony, and Fitzpatrick, for one, couldn't wait to get across to Italy and John Kirwan's wedding. "I just wanted to get my mind right off rugby," he says. "I'd had a gutsful."

An exciting new era of All Black rugby commenced in 1992 with Mains at the helm. He'd approached Fitzpatrick at Napier, asking him if he was prepared to captain the All Blacks in some of the midweek games on the tour of Australia and South Africa. Mike Brewer would be the Saturday captain. Fitzpatrick having agreed, he was the logical person to take charge when Brewer came to grief in the final trial.

Fitzpatrick had the feeling the new selection panel (Mains, Earle Kirton and Peter Thorburn) had cut too many of the old brigade adrift as they sought to rebuild New Zealand rugby. Gary Whetton was one the new captain felt should still be there, but plainly Mains wanted a complete break with the old team.

Following a disastrous start against the star-studded World team in Christchurch and extensive adjustments in personnel, the All Blacks, responding strongly to Mains' new-age policies and Fitzpatrick's leadership, developed into a very fine side indeed. They rebounded from two narrow losses in Sydney and Brisbane, and a midweek shocker against Sydney at Penrith, to outgun the world champions in the final test of the series before sweeping undefeated through South Africa.

During the next two seasons Mains and Fitzpatrick, who developed a strong bond, sought to build on their achievements of '92. But a fall-off in fitness levels, some offbeat selections at times, the loss of important individuals such as Grant Fox and Inga Tuigamala and luck that didn't always run their way, meant the All Blacks weaved an erratic path towards the third World Cup.

They hit their nadir at Athletic Park in 1993, losing badly to the British Lions, after sneaking home through a late Fox penalty goal in Christchurch. Fitzpatrick turned in his worst performance as an All

Black at Wellington. "It was an absolute shocker," he says. "I don't think I could have done worse if I'd deliberately set out to. I gave away two penalties which Gavin Hastings kicked and, at a crucial stage, I knocked-on, creating the tryscoring chance that Rory Underwood was looking for."

The nation's rugby followers weren't content to criticise an obviously sub-standard performance by the national team. They demanded the captain be axed. "Everywhere we turned, we were slammed," recalls Fitzpatrick. "It was open season on me and I hated it. I suppose I'd been lucky until that point. Now I was washed up and Norm Hewitt (who played a blinder in Hawke's Bay's win over the Lions) was wanted."

Mains was angry. "A great player like Sean should not be subjected to such vitriol," he says. "After all the great rugby he had played, how could you condemn him on one performance? I attacked the critics for being so fickle."

Adversity brings out the best in champions. Mains as a coach, Fitzpatrick as a captain and the All Blacks as a team answered their critics in magnificent style, sweeping the Lions aside in the decider on Eden Park. That got the public and the critics off their backs, and within a few weeks they were heroes again with memorable victories over Australia (at Carisbrook) and Western Samoa.

There were serious hiccups against England at Twickenham, the French (twice) and the Wallabies under lights in Sydney – and Mains had to survive a strong challenge as coach from Hart – before the All Blacks were ready to seek to recapture their title at the third World Cup tournament in South Africa.

"The summer training camps were a huge success," says Fitzpatrick. "In fact, they are something the NZRFU should look at introducing on a regular basis. We indulged in the most intense training at Taupo. What that achieved was to identify the test pack from the rest.

"It was exciting to see our game plan unfold. It was as if a switch had been turned on. The All Blacks had never played that daring, all-attack game before. It wasn't really in our make-up to do so. But now we had the confidence to take quick taps and run the ball from our own line. Although winning obviously is everything at that level, the team of '95 developed an attitude of not worrying about losing.

Sean Fitzpatrick

Sean Fitzpatrick leads the All Blacks on to the field at Durban for the second test of the 1996 series in South Africa.   *John Selkirk*

"Laurie Mains' openness and honesty bred a positive attitude within the team, as a result of which the players were a lot more open with each other. Players spoke out about what they saw as good and bad. On top of everything else, we were superbly fit, certainly fitter than any of our opponents. We were one of the smaller sides, but we were so competitive and fired up, and mentally we were at our peak."

Before the semi-final against England, Fitzpatrick observed a sense of confidence within his team. "When we left the shed, I knew we could beat anyone that day." Sadly, after the disruption caused by food poisoning in the days leading up to the final, he didn't have that same sense of reassurance as the players ran out against South Africa in the final. "I don't linger on the poisoning issue," he says. "The South Africans worked us out. They were so hungry for victory and determined to stop us. Maybe the result wouldn't have been any different if we'd had an untroubled run to the final."

At the dinner following the final, Fitzpatrick said in his speech that although the All Blacks had disappointed that day, he believed they would probably go on to become one of the great teams. And as he winged his way back to New Zealand, he decided he would like to be part of it, if Mains' successor wanted him.

Hart told him if he was the best hooker then he would lead the All Blacks in 1996. "It was up to me, therefore," says Fitzpatrick. "I had a contract with the NZRFU and Coca-Cola okayed my playing for another year. I had to meet my side of the bargain."

In the year in which he turned 33, Fitzpatrick produced some of the finest rugby of his career while sharing in endless successes. The Auckland Blues won the Super 12, Auckland regained the Ranfurly Shield and took out a fourth NPC and the All Blacks not only claimed the Bledisloe Cup and the Tri-Nations title but achieved the most elusive goal in rugby, a series victory on South African soil.

After then taking out the New Zealand player of the year award, Fitzpatrick reflected on a job incredibly well done in South Africa. "Perhaps," he said, "it may have been a blessing not winning the World Cup. Most of our team were very young, and the responsibility of being world champions may have limited their development. It was apparent that the pressure had got to the South Africans."

Grant Fox

Grant Fox was never one to prevaricate. When he flew to Wellington at the beginning of June, 1992, to assemble with the All Blacks for the second Irish international, he had a message to deliver to coach Laurie Mains.

He had discussed it with his wife Adele, and she understood. In fact, she was delighted at the prospect of having her husband around for the rest of the winter.

Because Fox, the greatest pointscorer in the history of the game, was going to tell Mains not to consider him for the tour of Australia and South Africa. He was ready to step aside for a younger man.

It wasn't that he was piqued at not being in the starting fifteen, even though the Wellington test would be the fourth international in a row at which he had warmed the reserves bench watching Walter Little in the No 10 jersey.

No, he just didn't see the point in taking a 29-year-old along on a tour of Australia and South Africa as an understudy. "There was nothing in it for me as a midweeker," he says. "The selectors were better off blooding a young player."

Fox didn't allow himself to become melodramatic. He'd had a marvellous innings at international level, been on the losing side only four times in 36 tests, scored 531 test points and, starting with the World Cup of 1987, had participated in the greatest winning sequence in the entire history of the game.

He had one unfulfilled ambition, to play against the British Lions, but that tour was still a year away. He had achieved every other goal.

Grant Fox . . . record pointscorer who wanted to pull out of the All Blacks in 1992.   Fotopacific

Grant Fox

He could step aside contentedly.

It was the Friday before he got Laurie Mains alone in Wellington. "There's something I'd like to talk to you about, my involvement in the tour of Australia," he said. "Well, there's something I want to talk to you about, too," came back Mains, before Fox had a chance to get to the nitty gritty. "When we play the Wallabies in the first test in Sydney on July 14, you'll be playing."

"I got the shock of my life," says Fox. "I expected Laurie to tell me he hadn't sorted out what would happen in Australia. As it transpired, he told me I would be playing. He said he had been happy to let me rest because he didn't consider the pelvic injury I had suffered at the World Cup had fully healed. And from the reserves bench, he wanted me to fully absorb the style of game the All Blacks were developing. It was all part of Laurie's master plan that I knew nothing of!"

Foxy went straight from Mains' room and telephoned Adele. "I have a problem," he said. "I'm going to be touring Australia and South Africa for nine weeks. Laurie wants me back in the test team."

"You sure?" asked Adele.

"I can trust this guy," replied Fox.

The rest, as they say, is history. Not only did Fox take his place in the No 10 jersey at the Sydney Football Stadium on July 14, he featured in every test on tour, and went on to fulfil his dream of playing a series against the Lions.

When he finally stepped down, before the tour of England and Scotland at the conclusion of the 1993 domestic season, aged 31, he had accumulated 1067 points for the All Blacks (including 645 in tests) at the remarkable average of 13.6 points a game.

Fox had emerged from the unsuccessful 1991 World Cup venture intact but with his body and his ego bruised. A serious pelvic injury had caught up with him in the semi-final against the Wallabies and took all of the summer to mend. Meanwhile, his unkindest critics were pointing the finger for many of the All Black backline's ills at him.

Fox, always one to confront issues, requested a meeting with the new selection panel (Laurie Mains, Earle Kirton and one of his sternest critics, Peter Thorburn) when he arrived in Napier in April, 1992, for the trials. "I was open with them," says Fox. "I basically asked them what they wanted. They explained. I told them my groin still wasn't one hundred per cent but I believed I could offer what they wanted. Laurie gave me the chance. He was great. During those early tests when he was using Walter Little at first-five, he was always explaining to me what he wanted."

Fox relished the fresh challenge under Mains and although the Bledisloe Cup tests of '92 would be the only losing series he participated in, he describes those tests as amongst the most enjoyable he ever experienced.

They say you can't teach an old dog new tricks. Well, Mains blew that theory apart, teaching the terrier Foxy a whole host of new tricks.

In his biography, Mains said he couldn't speak highly enough of Fox. "What we needed (for the tour of Australia and South Africa in 1992) was a competent, accurate punter who was also a good tactician. Once he made the necessary adjustments, that player was Fox. He became an integral and vital part of our backline and midway through the tour of Australia, he was playing as good a rugby as ever."

So how did Mains change the world's most accomplished goalkicker as a footballer? Fox explains: "I'd always stood flatfooted, in a protective position. Laurie wanted me to take the ball wide and start to run, thus committing opposition defences. He also wanted me to hit the blindside . . . things I felt I was never particularly good at. He demanded more backing-up. He was happy with my kicking game but basically wanted me to be more of a threat to the opposition when I received the ball."

Fox survived. Others who had been a vital part of the world champion side of the late 1980s but who, like Fox, had come crashing down at the second World Cup, didn't. One of them was the captain Gary Whetton, another his brother Alan. They weren't even invited to the trials in 1992.

Fox believes they should have confronted Mains as he did. "I encouraged Gary to talk to Laurie, but he never did. If he had, I believe his All Black career would have been extended. While I understood where the new selection panel was coming from, I personally believe they culled the old team too hard, got rid of one or two players too many."

Fox concedes that he, and probably a few others, came out of 1991 expecting things to be the same. "Some of us, perhaps arrogantly, felt as of right that we should be there. We'd come through a fabulous period with the All Blacks, fifty games without a loss, before things started going wrong. Clearly, things were not right, but it's hard for those in the forest to see the trees at times."

The player who would rewrite the record books so comprehensively – it would take almost two pages of his autobiography to list all the record-breaking achievements – and who would twice be crowned international player of the year, has an amazing story to tell about how he became a goalkicker and why he wore the lightest possible boots.

Growing up on a farm at Waotu near Putaruru, young Grant, taking inspiration from his father who played fullback and goalkicked for South Waikato in Peace Cup matches, was into kicking at goal from an early age. Early, like six or seven. And always barefooted.

Barefooted when he let fly at the sticks that made do for goalposts on the farm, barefooted when he played for the Putaruru Athletic club on frosty Saturday mornings. He didn't wear boots until he was 13. By then his feet were incredibly tough and he could kick proficiently with both of them.

"You play a season barefooted in nine degree frosts and it's amazing how tough your feet become," says Fox. Because kicking barefooted became so natural, when Fox matured and goalkicking began to matter he took to wearing the lightest available boots, eventually settling for calf skin. "I liked the feel of leather on my foot," he says, "so I went for the lightest, tightest boots I could buy, the closest I could get to kicking barefooted."

Fox was fortunate to have narrow feet because most (wide-fitting) New Zealand boots were heavier than he wanted. But his narrow (size 8) feet slid easily into Japanese and Italian made boots. "Initially, I used kangaroo hide but finished up with calf skin. Light as can be and do 'em up tight. The next best thing to kicking barefooted!"

Fox's bruised, and often sprained, toes owed much to Barry John, who toured New Zealand with the British Lions in 1971 when Fox was nine. "My father had toe-kicked," says Fox. "Don Clarke had toe-kicked, Bryan Williams had toe-kicked, most New Zealanders toe-kicked. Suddenly, here was someone kicking round-corner, and kicking fantastically well. I was fascinated. His style impacted on me and I began practising his way. I've been kicking like that ever since.

Rugby Greats

And it hasn't half saved my toes!"

Progressing promisingly through the schoolboy ranks, which included representing Waikato schools against Auckland at Eden Park, Fox began to emerge as a footballer of uncommon talent at Auckland Grammar School where he played for Graham Henry's first fifteen for three years.

Henry took him to Fiji as a fourth former and says he was a sensation. "For the match against one of the outer islands, everyone played in bare feet," he says. "That didn't stop Foxy from kicking a penalty goal from halfway. Our final outing was our test match, against Combined Suva Schools. Foxy was carrying a hamstring but even on one leg he played and controlled the game."

The first XV Fox captained in 1980 included no less a personality than Martin Crowe, who would achieve greatness in cricket but who was a dashing winger in those days with a penchant for scoring tries. He and Fox, who were intense competitors at school, formed a close and lasting friendship. Fox himself was a better than average cricketer, featuring in the first XI at college and going on to represent Bay of Plenty in a Hawke Cup challenge against Nelson as a No 3 batsman.

But it was rugby that would consume Fox. And although he became an astute tactician who directed games masterfully from first-five, with such effectiveness that he was hardly ever on the losing side, it was as a goalkicker that he would achieve world renown.

If he wasn't born to goalkick, he perfected the art from such a young age that no one else ever got to be the kicker in a team featuring Grant Fox. "I chose at a young age to be a goalkicker," he says. "Right from the start I enjoyed the craft. It was never a burden. My philosophy as a kid was that if I was the best goalkicker, they would have to play me!"

He remembers being asked to share the goalkicking with Greg Cooper for Auckland in one match in 1986. "David Kirk, our captain, tried to take me off and I spat the dummy. I said, 'I do the kicking in this team!' I got ticked off by John Hart later!"

Fox's first year of club rugby, with Auckland University (bringing him under the influence again of Graham Henry), coincided with the Springbok tour of 1981. He actually played at Eden Park the day of the Flour Bomb test, for Auckland Colts against Counties in the curtainraiser. He watched the light plane that buzzed the ground with

Grant Fox

Grant Fox lines up another kick on his favourite piece of turf, Eden Park. He accumulated 1067 for the All Blacks and 2746 for Auckland. John Selkirk

some horror, praying nothing would go wrong.

A year later he was back on the ground, as one of the new lads in new coach John Hart's Auckland team, at 19 the first-five and the goalkicker. He was in awe of the great footballers with whom he was sharing the dressing room, All Black legends like Bryan Williams and Andy Haden and emerging stars like Gary Whetton and John Drake.

Hart was endeavouring to rebuild Auckland after some forgettable seasons, and Fox was pivotal to his plans. After a couple of early losses to Counties and Canterbury, however, Fox's confidence was shaky. He fronted Hart, which was always his way when things weren't going right. "I poured it all out to him," says Fox. "I always set high standards and knew I wasn't achieving them. I asked John what I needed to do.

"What he gave me was reassurance. He told me I wasn't a one-off, that he believed in me as an investment. I think I probably bought myself a few extra games at the time, and the rest is history."

Speaking of setting high standards, Fox immediately came under the influence of Haden, an All Black of 10 years standing.

"Andy was a revelation to me," says Fox. "He was first to training – and was still getting there first at thirty-five when he was no longer an All Black – and worked so diligently on the basics. His standards started rubbing off on me, particularly with restarts. 'Come on, son,' he'd say, 'get it right!' At secondary school, I had demanded high standards of myself but I'd never had any feedback. Suddenly, Andy was giving me feedback, and more. I'd suggest the ball should drop in a particular spot. Andy would say, 'No, I want it here.' And you didn't argue with Andy. Well, a pipsqueak first-five wasn't going to argue with a seventeen stone lock!

"Thanks to Andy's demands, I began dropping my kick-offs and drop-outs on a sixpence, to the point where they became an important attacking weapon for Auckland. I never felt the public or the media cottoned on to this until around 1987. If you win the ball from a restart, you immediately build pressure and you're in an ideal situation to launch an assault."

Fox made significant progress in that first season as a representative player, scoring 154 points in all matches, sharing NPC success with Auckland, representing New Zealand Universities (in two internationals against Japan) and New Zealand Colts (in Australia). It wasn't all success, the Colts getting a hiding in their test in Sydney, against an Aussie side featuring such up-and-comers as David Campese, Michael Lynagh, Steve Tuynman, Peter FitzSimons (was he ever that young?), Jeff Miller and Tom Lawton.

Fox was the hero of Auckland's thrilling one-point victory over the British Lions in 1983 with a late dropped goal, achieved after he ignored his fellow backs' call for a tryscoring move. That win seemed to point to another season of success for the Auks, but they came crashing down at Lancaster Park in September, whipped by Grizz Wyllie's Canterbury men who would deny them the NPC title and the

Grant Fox

Ranfurly Shield. The Auks would gain revenge two years later.

Fox played for the North Island at Blenheim, which would be an important step in his advancement to the All Blacks, although perhaps not quite as important as in 1994 when North Island's coach Colin Meads appointed him the backline leader and asked him to kick the goals at Rotorua. This was the game that convinced national coach Bryce Rope that young Fox (who had a dream afternoon) was international material. Until then, he had considered Fox's passing to be laboured and his kicking skills to outweigh his attacking qualities.

By the time Auckland had dazzled their way to NPC glory in '94, averaging an astonishing 46 points a game, he could no longer be ignored by the national selection panel. In late September he was named in the All Black team to make a brief, four-match tour of Fiji under the captaincy of Jock Hobbs. It wasn't a major event as All Black tours go. But that didn't matter. Foxy was there as a first-five, along with Wayne Smith. He was on the way.

His debut came at the national stadium in Suva, against a President's XV. He marked it appropriately by scoring 19 points, taking him past 400 in first-class play for the year. Not surprisingly, both the Rugby Almanack and the Rugby Annual made him a player of the year.

Auckland's fitness trainer Jim Blair made an important adjustment to Fox's goalkicking technique in 1984 after he'd performed poorly against Sydney at Eden Park. "I kicked the difficult goals that day and missed the easy ones," says Fox. "Obviously, I was tensing up on kicks I was expected to land. Jim witnessed this and offered to introduce me to breathing exercises that would relax me. The exercises don't rid you of nerves but they help you focus and build an image of the ball sailing between the uprights."

Fox says he never thought about his run-up on the field. "All that was done at training. Through repetition, your body knew where to go. It was a bit like riding a bike – what you needed to focus on was the end result."

Fox is amused when he watches present day goalkickers emulating his style, down to the deep breathing and shaking of the hands. "They're welcome to copy my mannerisms," he says. "I just hope they appreciate they have nothing to do with getting the ball between the posts. They're simply about relaxing and achieving positive reinforcement. Successful goalkicking relates to technical efficiency and practice routines. If a kicker is not technically correct, all the deep breathing in the world won't help."

Events beyond Fox's control, all New Zealand rugby players' control, in fact, meant his career didn't follow its predestined path through 1985 and 1986 when he might well have overtaken Wayne Smith and established himself permanently in the All Black test line-up. Instead, he would make just a solitary test appearance in those two years, opposite the incomparable Hugo Porta in Buenos Aires.

Buenos Aires? The All Blacks shouldn't have been anywhere near there. They should have been playing internationals at Durban and Cape Town and Pretoria. But, of course, people outside rugby made critical decisions for people inside rugby in 1985, causing the long-awaited tour of South Africa to be abandoned.

So the All Blacks went to Argentina instead and Foxy got the first test. He drop-kicked a goal but, for the only occasion in his test career, he was not the goalkicker, that duty falling to Kieran Crowley. For the second test, he was supplanted by Smith.

He did finally get to tour South Africa, in 1986, not as an All Black but with the unauthorised Cavaliers team which boldly tackled the Springboks in four tests on successive Saturdays. Fox played the first three, with skill and authority, against another of the game's celebrities Naas Botha, whose magic touches had a major influence on the outcome of the series. A heavy defeat in the third test forced the Cavaliers to seek greater attacking options and Smith was introduced for the finale at Ellis Park. But that test was lost, too, and the series conceded 3-1.

Fox's involvement with the Cavaliers, and subsequent two-test ban, allowed Frano Botica to slip through and secure the All Black test first-five berth. He performed so effectively he was to win the New Zealand player of the year award for 1986. And any hopes Fox had of displacing Botica during the end-of-year tour of France disappeared when he was hospitalised in Toulouse with a collapsed lung caused by a broken rib, sustained six months earlier but which had gone undetected.

With the defeat by France at Nantes at the conclusion of that tour, an era ended. A glorious new one would be ushered in at the commencement of the 1987 season. Brian Lochore survived as coach but almost everything else was changed. New selectors (Alex Wyllie and John Hart), exciting new test players (Michael Jones, John Gallagher and Alan Whetton), a bold new game plan. And Foxy at first-five. The immediate goal? To win the first World Cup.

The mission was accomplished in the most emphatic manner, the All Blacks sweeping aside opponents mercilessly in pool play, clinically dissecting in the quarter-finals a Scottish team that fancied its chances and humbling the old foe Wales at Ballymore before completing the job handsomely in the final against France at Eden Park.

Playing a highly mobile, 15-man game, the All Blacks left most opponents gasping. There were several individual heroes, notably Gallagher, who electrified the backline from fullback, Buck Shelford, unstoppable from No. 8, John Kirwan, the consummate finisher and, of course, Fox.

Fox's contribution as a tactician and setter-up of movements tended to be overlooked because of his staggering goalkicking exploits. His hauls in the six matches make incredible reading: 22, 26, 22, 22, 17, 17 for a total of 126 points, an aggregate that may never be bettered.

The victory against Scotland at Lancaster Park is nominated by Fox as, without question, the outstanding display by the All Blacks, even though in most other games they scored substantially more points. "It was a brand of rugby which was to carry the All Blacks into perhaps the greatest era in New Zealand rugby history."

Fox would be an essential component throughout that era. He became such a heartbreaker for overseas opponents and so inseparable from the test No 10 jersey that finally Frano Botica, himself a world-class performer, abandoned hope of ever participating in a rugby test again and went off to play league in the UK.

Including the World Cup performances, the All Blacks went more than three years and 23 tests against most of the world's leading nations without defeat, until finally Bob Dwyer's men lowered their colours in stormy conditions at Athletic Park in 1990. The solitary hiccup in all that time was the 19-all draw with the Wallabies at Ballymore in 1988. Fox could have won that encounter, too, but he missed the late, wide-angled conversion attempt of John Kirwan's try. He finds a certain irony in that fact that he failed to land that goal because it was, he says, the only genuine pressure kick he faced in

Wallaby centre Tim Horan fails to rattle super-cool Grant Fox during the 1993 Bledisloe Cup test at Carisbrook, Dunedin.   Andrew Cornaga, Photosport

those 23 internationals. "The All Blacks (who averaged 37 points a game in that period, of which 16 were Fox's) were always so far in front," he says.

It wasn't until his 21st test, against Scotland at Carisbrook in 1990, that Fox managed a try. He'd scored a beauty at Dublin the previous November, but Scottish touch judge Jim Fleming, pedantic in the extreme, was responsible for it being erased. Claiming Sean Fitzpatrick had stepped into touch while throwing into a lineout, Fleming blissfully stood with his flag raised for fully three minutes before Fox scored. Referee Sandy MacNeill wouldn't have been aware of Fleming's flag yet if the ball boy hadn't sprinted 40 metres to bring it to his attention! Fox, who Buck Shelford reckons used unprintable language at the time, describes Fleming's flagging of Fitzy as "Victorian primness".

"The only test try I was awarded wasn't half as memorable," says Fox. "Scottish winger Iwan Tukalo took a horrible flykick at the ball over the goalline, missed, and I fell on it."

At the time he ran out on to Athletic Park on August 18, 1990, Fox was the Invincible All Black. He had by then represented his country on 46 occasions (of which 24 were tests) over six years without experiencing defeat. The Wellington loss was the first indication that the wheels on the mighty All Black wagon were beginning to loosen. There followed a couple of setbacks in provincial matches in France in late 1990, brilliantly retrieved in the internationals where Fox twice won the Golden Talent award handed out by French television viewers. Those losses weren't considered of concern, but the 21-12 battering by the Wallabies in Sydney, two months out from the World Cup, was.

It followed a drawn-out tour of Argentina where Fox suffered what seemed to be a minor abdominal strain but which turned out to be osteitis pubis, more commonly known as Kicker's Disease. With constant treatment the complaint was well enough disguised to allow Fox to take his place at the World Cup but in trying to stop David Campese in the semi-final the groin tightened up like a vice.

Fox was confronted with one of the most difficult decisions of his career to stay or go? "How do you walk away when your team is down in such an important game?" he says. "In the heat of battle, I chose to stay on. With the benefit of hindsight, I would have rested the injury after the tour of Argentina and got it right before I played again."

Fox was as devastated as anyone at the defeat in Dublin which put Australia into the final against England. "I guess," he concedes, "the All Black machine had been creaking for a while. Some of us were too close to notice."

New Zealanders are intolerant of losing All Black teams, whatever the circumstances. So the level of condemnation of a team which had gone off to the UK expecting to win but which failed to reach the final can be imagined. And high on the list of those under fire was Fox. The talkback shows ran red hot with irate rugby followers venting their spleens.

Fox did seriously consider retirement, especially with his pelvic region causing him so much pain. But he always held to the belief that decisions about retirement were made at the beginning of a season, not the end. And by the time 1992 rolled around, the urge to get out and play rugby was as strong as ever. Which is where Laurie Mains came powerfully into his life.

When Fox did decide to retire it was after the 1993 test against Western Samoa (in which he kicked a record seven penalty goals). "It was the right time to step aside," he says. "Business and family commitments were starting to mean more to me than rugby. You know when you start turning up for matches with a brief case and a cell phone, your time has come!"

His father Ian had been a role model. "He retired from rugby at 28 and missed only three of the sixty matches I played for the Auckland Grammar first fifteen. I hope I can be as devoted a father to my children, Ryan (who is 10) and Kendall (seven)."

Fox is the managing director of Carnegie Sports International New Zealand Ltd, a company specialising in signage at sports events, corporate hospitality and sponsorship. He's also Television New Zealand's rugby comments person. For relaxation, he plays golf, off a handicap of five.

John Gallagher

It's a long flight from London Heathrow to Wellington. More than 24 hours, in fact. Long enough, when you're flying on your own, to do a lot of thinking. And worrying.

When John Gallagher made the journey in March, 1984, at the age of 20, he spent most of the journey thinking. And worrying. Thinking about what he'd let himself in for in agreeing to play a season with the Oriental-Rongotai club in Wellington. Worrying that he would be 'exposed' as a fraud. You see, he'd jumped at the opportunity to play rugby in New Zealand as a goalkicking fullback. But there were two problems – he didn't play fullback and he didn't kick goals.

Gallagher hardly slept on the flight because of his anxieties. What if he didn't fulfil the expectations of the club inviting him to New Zealand? He was committed to a six months stay. He could finish up with no friends and no family.

As the flight droned on, he reflected on the incredible sequence of events that now had him winging his way to New Zealand to play rugby.

It all happened really because the previous Easter he'd gone on a trip to Dublin with the London Irish under-21 side where he'd played a couple of curtainraisers to the club's senior team, the second one at fullback, a position unfamiliar to him. As he was leaving the field after a game against Clontarf the senior team's manager approached him.

"He had a major problem," recalls Gallagher. "His fullback had gone missing. Would I play for them? After two matches in forty-eight

A young John Gallagher placekicking for Wellington against Auckland at Eden Park in 1985.   Trevor Coppock

hours on soft fields, my legs were saying no, but my mouth said yes. So twenty minutes later I was in action again. I managed to get through without making any mistakes, and we won. But I was so fatigued that on the ferry trip home, while the others partied, I slept all the way."

A few weeks later the Askeans club made contact. They'd heard Gallagher had played for London Irish. They had a few injury problems. Would he mind helping out on the subs bench against Kent? Love to, said Gallagher.

"Similar scenario," says Gallagher. "This time a winger got injured, and I was in the action. Again, I managed to do most things right. Again, the team won."

At 20, enthusiastic and looking for opportunities, Gallagher was hoping he might receive further invitations to play for the club. He wasn't prepared for what unfolded though. The player he'd replaced that day was one of the club's leading sevens exponents, and Askeans had qualified for the famous Middlesex sevens tournament at Twickenham. Was Gallagher available to take his place?

"I couldn't believe my luck," he says. "On the strength of one lucky outing for London Irish, I'd got a game for Askeans. Now I was heading for Twickenham."

Gallagher says he was fine until he ran on to the pitch and found himself surrounded by 50,000 spectators. "I was totally overawed," he says, "and played the whole game in a dream. We lost twelve-nil to Waterloo and spent the rest of the afternoon watching the action from the grandstand. I'd had my big chance, and blown it!"

It was the following October that he encountered a fellow called Tony O'Malley, whom he played rugby with at college, at a party in London.

"He'd not long returned from a trip to New Zealand where he'd played for the Oriental-Rongotai club in Wellington," says Gallagher. "He'd scored 189 points in the season, and the club was naturally eager for him to return, but he wasn't available.

"So I said, 'Well, put my name down for next year, if you don't change your mind.' To my surprise, he said he would, because he'd heard I'd played for London Irish on tour and represented Askeans at the Middlesex sevens. I couldn't be bothered explaining the circumstances of those outings!"

Rugby Greats

Gallagher had been feeling disillusioned about the game and was seriously considering a break, but after his discussion with O'Malley he thought he'd better start playing again. He resumed with the Askean fourths and progressed swiftly through the thirds and seconds to the first team where he occasionally appeared at wing or centre.

He'd almost given up on the New Zealand option when he fielded a phone call the morning after his birthday (January 29) from Clive Currie, the senior team coach for Oriental-Rongotai, in Wellington. "I was horribly hungover," says Gallagher. "Clive's voice was faint but I could just make out the words. He said he was looking for a goalkicking fullback to go to New Zealand in March, and was I interested? I said I was.

"A few weeks later a short letter of confirmation arrived. It was only at this point I worried that I didn't know how to play fullback and I didn't kick goals. Oh well, there were a couple of months before I had to travel. I would spend most of that on the practice ground."

This is the player who would not only make an immediate impact with Oriental-Rongotai, but who would soon become a star of the Wellington representative team, would break into the All Blacks in 1986 and, five years after his intrepid journey Down Under, would win an award as the most outstanding rugby player in the world.

New Zealand rugby players are, almost without exception, immersed in the game from birth. They're usually playing competitively from the age of five, their role models the All Blacks. Not John Gallagher. Of Irish parentage (his mother was from Limerick, his father from Derry), he grew up in south London in a soccer environment, and was "soccer mad" as a youngster, an Arsenal supporter who scored 31 goals in his final year at primary school. The second youngest in a family of five, at every opportunity he played soccer. The only time he stopped, as he recalls, was to watch soccer on television! His idol was George Best.

He didn't know what a rugby ball was until he began attending St Joseph's Academy College from the age of 11. When he went home one evening and told his mother he'd scored a try, she asked what a try was. "I don't know," he replied, "but I got one!"

His sporting future was determined the day he started at St Joseph's, a non-fee-paying catholic school. It was a traditional rugby school with no soccer played at all. Because most of his friends were attending, Gallagher didn't mind having to sacrifice his favourite sport. But, like 99 per cent of the first year students (who'd all been raised on a diet of soccer), he was totally bemused at his first outing with the oval ball. "Only one boy had played rugby and knew what to do," says Gallagher. "The rest basically ran after him and indulged in what these days would be called pile-ups."

Once the rudiments of the game became apparent and Gallagher developed a level of enthusiasm for it, he was placed at flyhalf in the first-year team. His team won most games because the No. 8, a giant named Martin Quin, picked every ball out of the scrum and ran at the opposition, scoring a phenomenal number of tries. He also kicked the goals. "As the flyhalf, I hardly ever touched the ball because Quinny ran the whole game. The rest of us didn't mind because he won every match for us. But the next year the coach dropped him and wouldn't allow him back until he learnt to share the ball with his teammates. A salutary lesson for selfish rugby players!"

Because he was so small, Gallagher didn't command a position in the first XV until his lower sixth form year. He was at flyhalf, with Tony O'Malley, who would create the opportunity for him to play in New Zealand, at fullback. St Joseph's developed into a formidable team and surprised everyone by defeating Sevenoaks, who had the Kent selector as coach, four national schoolboys and several county representatives in the side, were unbeaten and had just returned from a world tour. "Although we lost the final, we had proven to ourselves that we could live with the best."

Although St Joseph's defeated Sevenoaks twice more in the next 15 months – Gallagher's exceptional pace being a valuable asset – the school found itself dropped from Sevenoaks' fixture list. "It was typical of the attitude that pervaded English rugby at the time," says Gallagher. "As a comprehensive school, we didn't fit into their public school set. The whole affair served to turn off our coach and most of the players, myself included. Not surprising, many of our players afterwards decided to revert to soccer where they weren't exposed to such attitudes. That 'who you know' attitude was prevalent throughout English rugby. Unfortunately, to be accepted, you had to have money. After I became an All Black, people often asked me if I thought I would have made it with England or Ireland if I'd stayed in the UK. The answer is a definite no, not as a St Joseph's student. I would probably have finished up as a spectator at Highbury, watching Arsenal play."

Gallagher had wanted to become a physical education teacher, and had applied to attend St Mary's College in London to study for a degree in Human Movement. But that plan was scuttled when he failed his exams. Devastated initially, he eventually decided to follow his father into the police force. He was accepted, after a series of interviews, and was scheduled to start at Hendon Police College in March, 1984.

But in March, 1984, he was on a plane instead, heading for Wellington, and something completely different. Notwithstanding the Sevenoaks experience, he was totally hooked on rugby at this stage. During London Irish's visit to Dublin, he'd met the great Irish flyhalf Ollie Campbell and his arch rival Tony Ward. He was encouraged to find them no bigger than himself. "Because I'd been so small as a kid, I had a bit of a complex about my size," says Gallagher. "I think I felt you needed size to succeed in rugby."

All that Gallagher knew about New Zealand was what he'd culled from following the 1983 British Lions tour on television. "We sent our best team out and were whitewashed in the series, losing the final test 38-3. I remember thinking, 'Blimey, what have I let myself in for'."

He was met at Wellington Airport by Oriental-Rongotai's coach Clive Currie, who'd been a fullback with the Grand Slam-winning All Black team of 1978, the secretary Dave Thurlow, with whose family he would board, and Don Bond, who would look after any problems Gallagher had with immigration.

Thanks to Tony O'Malley's goalkicking, Ories had won the bottom section of the Wellington competition in 1983. Currie was hoping they could improve and qualify for the top eight. Obviously, they had high hopes for their new 'Pom'. O'Malley had told him he would undoubtedly be the quickest player in the team.

At the first training Gallagher was introduced to his new teammates. "I was immediately struck by the different ethnic mix," he says. "There were Maoris, Western Samoans, Tongans, Rarotongans and Pakehas. Even the pakehas were tanned and my lily white skin stood out a mile!"

His debut for Ories was a friendly against Red Star at Masterton. Barely surviving the tortuous drive over the Rimutaka Hill, which left

John Gallagher

him paler than ever, he scored with his first touch of the ball, having raced up wide and taken the winger's pass. With his great acceleration, the ability to cruise effortlessly outside wingers would quickly become his trademark. Another try that afternoon left the Oriental-Rongotai officials believing that their new Pom might be something special.

When he then scored 18 points (of 22) in the first championship game against Porirua, coach Currie sensed Ories had struck the jackpot with their import. Currie passed on the not inconsiderable knowledge he'd gained from playing at representative and international level. "He taught me the basics of fullback play," says Gallagher. "It was well into the season before I confessed to him that the position was almost completely foreign to me when I arrived in Wellington."

Currie's first impression of Gallagher was that he was "pale, gangly and somewhat awkward". "However," says Currie, "as the season unfolded, his raw natural ability, exceptional pace and flair for rugby became evident. He showed qualities that would take him to the top – the ability to change pace and swerve past opponents and an exciting capacity for counter-attack."

A couple of months into the season Gallagher was given a job by the Wellington Rugby Union which entailed visiting schools and coaching. As a spanking new stationwagon went with the role, he was also mobile. That was encouraging enough but he then found himself included in Ian Upston's Wellington squad, as a utility back, for matches in the deep south against Southland and Otago. "I was fortunate because the All Blacks were touring Australia (which took Allan Hewson, Mike Clamp and Bernie Fraser out of the reckoning)," he says. "That let me get my foot in the door."

When work commitments prevented Allan Pollock from getting to Invercargill for the first game, Gallagher took his spot on the wing. As the goalkicker, his two conversions helped Wellington complete its first win in Invercargill since 1970.

Before the Otago game, coach Upston called Gallagher aside and questioned him about his future, saying he was no use to him if he was going to return to the UK at season's end. Gallagher replied that he had "fallen in love" with New Zealand and was, through Don Bond, making the necessary arrangements that would allow him to remain in the country.

Rugby Greats

On the strength of that reply – Bond had already arranged for a two month extension of his visa, through till the end of the representative season – Upston installed Gallagher at centre for the entire NPC campaign, even using him as the goalkicker ahead of Hewson in several matches.

Oriental-Rongotai got its money's worth out of him. It qualified (in fifth place) for the championship round, a rare achievement indeed for the club. And Gallagher finished with 205 points (out of 309 scored by the team), a record for the Wellington senior club competition.

Before he returned to the UK for a break, there were two important developments. He sat, and passed, an entrance exam for the Wellington Police, and the resourceful Don Bond had his passport stamped with a multiple entry/exit visa. Things had worked out so well in his newly adopted country that, upon his return, he'd decided, he would apply for permanent residency.

His family didn't regard these developments with great enthusiasm. They had understood he was returning to live and to launch into a career with the police. The local Chief Superintendent, who was involved with the police rugby team, clouded the issue by calling on him, and taking him to Scotland Yard where he was assured he would have a good future with the police. When Gallagher then started socialising with all his old mates, and readjusting to the London scene, he decided the security of life back home was the way to go. He told his parents he was staying and in November he signed on at the Hendon Police College.

He began playing his rugby for the Metropolitan Police but found it totally uninspiring. One match turned out to be against a visiting team from the Wellington club. And in the side, as a ring-in, was Steve Cox, his best mate from Ories. After the final whistle, 'Coxy' crash tackled him into a mud puddle where they proceeded to splash about mock wrestling. Later they went out drinking and Cox declared he was on a mission from Ories. "I've got to take you back, Pom," he said.

"Meeting Coxy made me yearn for New Zealand," says Gallagher. "My mind automatically associated him with good times and a happy lifestyle. I wasn't enjoying the police college and every Monday I dreaded turning up there. It was early in January when my mother, identifying my mood, said, 'You still want to go back, don't you?' I

John Gallagher

Australian fullback Greg Martin can't stop John Gallagher from scoring a try in the 1989 Bledisloe Cup international at Eden Park.   John Selkirk

nodded. 'Well, why don't you?'"

It took Gallagher one week to reach a final decision. He telephoned his closest friends seeking their guidance. Half said go, half said stay. "I knew if I didn't return, I would never know what I could have achieved," said Gallagher. "I would give myself three years, and hope to make it in rugby and in a career."

As he flew back into Wellington, on a beautiful summer's evening, Gallagher observed the open spaces and clean streets he adored. "All of a sudden the stresses and worries of the previous few weeks just evaporated," he says.

Although he soon graduated as a policeman and continued performing heroics for Oriental-Rongotai, the 1985 season didn't quite work out the way Gallagher had planned. In September, in his 11th outing for Wellington (all of them at centre), he suffered an ugly injury playing against Counties at Athletic Park. He dislocated his ankle and broke his fibula and was encased in plaster up to his thigh. It was six weeks before the plaster came off. It took most of the summer, with a lot of swimming and running in the surf, before he was back to normal.

Things were happening in 1986. The Cavaliers, denied their authorised tour the previous season, were off to South Africa, and Wellington had a new coach, Earle Kirton. It was a while before Gallagher and Kirton were on the same wave length. Kirton began using him at fullback when his preferred position was centre. Then when he was switched to the wing, Gallagher protested. "Play me at centre or play me at fullback," he told his coach, "but not both – and definitely not on the wing."

Whichever position Kirton believed was the ideal for Gallagher mattered not when, shortly thereafter, Allan Hewson decided to retire from representative play. That settled it, Gallagher was Wellington's fullback. *And* the goalkicker.

He was optimistic of getting a run at the trials with the Cavaliers away. "There were thirty players out of the country and another forty needed for the trials," he says. "I figured I had to rate among New Zealand's top seventy players. When my name was missing I was quite disconsolate. It was obviously because I was English, I decided. But later I realised I was more concerned with the consequences of every game than playing rugby. I refocused on my technique and my play improved markedly. Being ignored in 1986 was probably the best thing that could have happened to me."

Wellington went on to win the NPC, the clincher being its victory over Auckland at Athletic Park, with Gallagher accumulating 185 points for the season, only five short of Hewson's record. Then when the All Black team to tour France was announced at the end of September, Gallagher was in it, named as a fullback along with Kieran Crowley.

Ories gave him a huge send-off because he was the club's first All Black in more than 100 years. Clive Currie was an honorary international, but he'd been selected for New Zealand from the Christchurch HSOB club.

Learning the haka was a challenge for a Pom, but eventually Gallagher got the hang of it. Performing as an All Black was straightforward by comparison. He was given four outings (at Strasbourg, Toulon, Bayonne and La Rochelle), two at fullback and two at centre, and was on the winning side each time. But the tourists

John Gallagher

wouldn't remain invincible, the test side taking a hiding at Nantes. It was a notable occasion – there would not be another loss in Gallagher's time as an All Black.

It was to Gallagher's advantage that John Hart and Alex Wyllie, the hugely successful coaches of Auckland and Canterbury, were introduced to the New Zealand selection panel for 1987. They encouraged coach Lochore to develop a fast-moving, wide-ranging game for the inaugural World Cup. One essential requirement was backline pace. Which, naturally, gave Gallagher a head start over Crowley. Before Gallagher took the field in the final trial at Whangarei, Lochore approached him, stabbing his finger into his chest. "Kipper," he said, "don't do anything bloody stupid today, just play a safe game and don't take on the whole world."

Although they were both named in the 26-strong World Cup squad, Gallagher was the man the selectors wanted. He would wear the No 15 jersey in all except the pool match against Argentina, equal the New Zealand test record with four tries against Fiji and emerge as one of the superstars of the tournament. In the opening match the All Blacks scored 12 tries against Italy and Gallagher was somewhat miffed that he'd missed out. In fact, at that stage he'd played five games for the All Blacks and hadn't got on the scoresheet. He certainly made amends at Lancaster Park.

He became a prime target for the British media who naturally wanted to know, with such marvellous skills, why he wasn't playing his rugby in England or Ireland. "In the euphoria of winning the World Cup, I couldn't be bothered trying to explain why I'd become disenchanted with the rugby scene over there," says Gallagher.

Not the least of Gallagher's achievements was to defeat the ultra competitive Zinzan Brooke in a hamburger eating competition in Brisbane prior to the semi-final. Brooke was a sprinter, Gallagher a stayer. By the time that Kipper had demolished his ninth burger, Zinzan conceded defeat.

It wasn't just in hamburger-eating terms that Gallagher was supreme. Over the next two and half years, he electrified the All Black backline from fullback, complementing the attacking skills of footballers like John Kirwan, Joe Stanley, Terry Wright and John Schuster (with whom he became great mates) perfectly. He really was the ideal modern-age fullback.

Rugby Greats

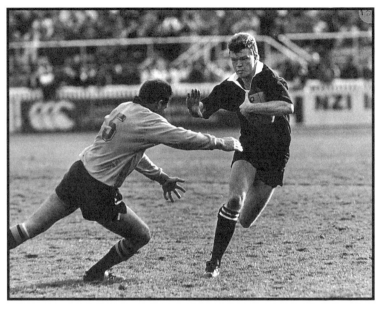

The attacking style of John Gallagher well demonstrated here against Australia at Eden Park in 1989. The tackler is Greg Martin.   John Selkirk

Of the 35 tries he scored for the All Blacks, in 41 outings, the finest was unquestionably that against Ireland at Lansdowne Road in November, 1989. Wright had a reputation as one of the swiftest wingers in rugby, yet Gallagher effortlessly cruised up outside him to take his pass and race into the clear. Only the Irish fullback Philip Rainey threatened his progress to the goalline. Rainey, renowned for his defence, obviously calculated that anyone travelling as fast as Gallagher had to take the outside option. Wrong. Gallagher propped off his left foot, with no obvious loss of speed, and hurtled on for a fabulous try. No one appreciated it at the time – not even the great player himself – but this was to be his last All Black test appearance.

As he soaked in the bath following the Barbarians match a week later, he reflected that he had done everything he wanted in rugby. He'd represented the All Blacks, shared in a World Cup victory, toured Australia, the UK and France, played in the Hong Kong sevens and won the New Zealand player of the year award.

So when early in the 1990 season he received a phone call from the Leeds League Club, he acknowledged his interest. They wanted to fly

John Gallagher

him to England but he said that wouldn't be necessary because he was already journeying there to receive the International Player of the Year trophy. That ceremony completed, he called in at Leeds before returning to Wellington (where he had been appointed captain for the season).

"I'd watched league on television often enough and it looked like a fast, physical and entertaining game," says Gallagher. "I thought it would provide me with the challenge I was looking for."

To cut a long story short, Gallagher accepted Leeds' offer. The only problem was where and when the announcement would be made. Ironically, the day he arrived back in New Zealand, Matthew Ridge, Gallagher's understudy on the tour of Wales and Ireland in 1989, was featuring on television, having signed to play league with Manly. "One of the reasons he gave," says Gallagher, "was that he couldn't see himself getting into the test side for a few years. I wonder what might have happened if I'd been able to let him know of my plans."

After a great deal of subterfuge, it was finally made public that Gallagher had signed with Leeds and by mid-year he had severed his connections with rugby and was working out at Headingly.

His first season in the new code went reasonably satisfactorily, until injuries became a problem. The greater problem, though, was the the appointment at season's end of Doug Laughton as Leeds' coach. He plainly didn't rate Gallagher as a fullback which was obvious when he signed Morven Edwards and Alan Tait, two international fullbacks.

Gallagher got only 16 outings in two seasons under Laughton, playing most of his league with the reserve team. "Irrespective of how I played, Laughton didn't want me," he says, "so I looked for somewhere else to go. Warrington and Halifax were interested but when Tony Gordon became coach of the London Crusaders (later taken over by the Broncos), it was arranged for me to play there."

In a team that wanted him, Gallagher prospered, scoring 386 points (including 19 tries) in the 1993-94 season, placing him second only behind Wigan's Frano Botica. The team got through to the play-offs, losing to Workington in the final at Old Trafford.

Finding the travel excessive after taking a job at a local private boys' school in London, Gallagher, then 31, decided to retire, although he was lured back by the Broncos early in 1995, playing nine more games for them, as a goalkicker, before retiring again.

Rugby Greats

The advent of professionalism rekindled Gallagher's interest in rugby. Dick Best, the former England coach, first got him involved with Harlequins. Then he appeared in Ieuan Evans' testimonial match at Stradey Park (operating in the same team as Jonah Lomu) and after a few appearances for the Irish Exiles he was chosen to play for Ireland A against Scotland A. "The coach congratulated me afterwards," he says, "and asked if I was available for the following games. I said yes, and I never heard from him again!"

That really was the end of John Gallagher's international career.

In recent times he's helped out with the Blackheath seniors, whose coach is the former All Black hooker Hika Reid and whose halfback is another ex-All Black Dean Kenny. But rugby holds a much lower profile for John Gallagher now. Away from schoolteaching he concentrates most of his spare time on his wife Anita and sons Alex, 4, and Matthew, who'll be one in October.

Craig Green

It was a bitingly cold mid-winter's morning in Christchurch in late July 1987. Craig Green was sitting on his tool bag on the roadside waiting for the pick-up to take him to the site where he would put in a day's toil as a roofing contractor. Not yet 7am, it was pitch black.

"What am I doing here?" thought Green. "I've just helped the All Blacks become the best rugby team in the world. I was a celebrity then. Now I'm just Craig Green, labourer, wondering how I can pay my bills."

His tax return for the previous year had recorded an income of $6000, less than a quarter of the national average wage. In April he had approached Alex Wyllie, one of the All Black selectors, asking if he could be excused from a zonal fixture in New Plymouth.

"Why?" asked Wyllie.

"Because I'm operating as a contractor and I need to put in a few days work to get some money – I've got nothing in the bank."

"Well, if you pull out, you'll probably miss the World Cup, because we're regarding them as trials."

"All right, I'll be there."

"Why don't you approach your club – I'm sure they'd help."

"I'm never there, that's why."

"Well, what about the Canterbury Rugby Union, can't they do something?"

"Not likely."

Green, scorer of 110 tries in first-class matches, was only 26, with a lot of rugby still to be played. But he couldn't see how he could

Rugby Greats

Craig Green is crunched by Laurent Rodriguez and Jean-Patrick Lescarboura in the first test against France at Toulouse in 1986.   *Peter Bush*

continue to make the sacrifices necessary to sustain his career at the highest level. Rugby, Green realised, was as frustratingly amateur as when he'd first started playing it as a five-year-old.

"It was pretty disappointing to realise there was nothing for the players in the wake of the World Cup triumph," says Green. "No bonus, not even a celebration dinner. It was a case of, 'Thanks, fellas, now get back to work – we'll call you again when we need you!'"

Green was envious of John Kirwan who was cashing in on his high profile and obviously supplementing his income with promotional work. "That sort of thing wasn't happening down here in Christchurch," he says. "What else could I do?"

It was the very same John Kirwan who provided the answer. Unfortunately, JK's solution didn't allow the extremely talented Green to extend his record of 75 appearances for Canterbury and 39 for the All Blacks beyond that 1987 season which had ground to a halt for Green when he suffered a fractured bone in the face during the

Craig Green

Bledisloe Cup match in Sydney.

Because what Kirwan did was recommend Green to the Benetton Treviso club in Italy, initiating a relationship that would flourish for seven seasons, boost Green's sagging coffers and win him an Italian wife.

He settled back in Christchurch in 1994, two years before the professionalism he had craved at the time of the first World Cup engulfed rugby. When it came, it was total with players probably less talented than Green commanding salaries of up to $200,000.

Green salutes them. "Good luck to them," he says. "They won't be needing to be picked up at 7am for a day's labouring a few days after playing an international. Their futures should all be secure, which is marvellous. What a shame the revolution didn't happen in 1986 instead of 1996!"

Green was a footballer who after finishing up on the wing almost by default became one of the most elusive runners and tryscorers in the game, developing a trait of running on different angles to bewilder opponents. "If you could come at different angles, I found that often it took your opponents a good ten metres to work out what was happening," he says, "and most wingers don't like tackling anyway!"

The position of wing was a long way away when Green first started playing rugby. The player who would take his place in the first World Cup at the modest weight of 78kg was big for his age at primary school and started out as a lock, winning representative honours for the first time as a hooker. From there, he moved to the side of the scrum, later became a halfback, broke into representative play as a five-eighth, was used by the All Blacks as a centre and finished up on the wing. "Thank goodness for wing," he says. "They couldn't push me any further out!"

Green, who grew up in Shirley and attended the local intermediate and high schools, inherited his speed from his father Bill who had been a sprint champion. Craig's sister Carol was pretty swift also, representing Canterbury as a sprinter in the early 1970s.

Green had three years in the Shirley Boys' High first XV, the team's competition play being in the union's open under-19 grade where Craig came up against his elder brother Phillip who was playing for the Shirley club. "What a grudge match," says Craig. "He was totally obstructive and when I scored, I remember him berating his teammates.

Rugby Greats

'What the hell did you let him score for!' he shouted at them."

By the seventh form he was making a big impression as a first-five and was not only selected for the Canterbury under-18 team, he was named captain. The vice-captain was an ugly-looking front-rower named Richard Loe and also in the side were Bruce Deans and Albert Anderson.

Green's qualities were recognised by the South Island under-18 selectors who placed him at first-five in the big clash with the North Island at New Plymouth, a game dominated by North's big forwards.

Upon leaving college Green decided to pursue a Diploma in Agriculture which required him to gain practical experience in farm work. It took him to Rakaia where he moved in with Alistair Riddell, a young farmer who was setting up a low budget farm. Green recalls that they worked well together and had a common interest in rugby.

Although Green's parents lived in Christchurch, they had a strong rural background, having farmed at Amberley, not far from the Ashworths to whom they were related. Green and John Ashworth, his first cousin, would later play together for Canterbury.

Green loved Rakaia, an area famous for salmon fishing and jetboating. As good fortune would have it, it was also the champion rugby town of Mid-Canterbury. In fact, the club had completed a hat-trick of championship victories, so Green was privileged to step into such an accomplished side. Although he had only just turned 18, he was swiftly snapped up by the senior team (which claimed the title again in 1979) and, in turn, by the Mid-Canterbury selectors, Nev Goodwin and Brian Sampson.

It is a period of Green's career (and life) that he cherishes, epitomising all that is good about the country scene in New Zealand. "Everyone knew everyone, everyone played against everyone – it was great," says Green. "Guys you were playing against on Saturdays you were involved with at stock sales during the week. The club teams were chock full of farmers, stock agents and truckies, who all socialised together after the games."

While Messrs Goodwin and Sampson recognised the enormous potential of Green, they protected him in his debut season, not risking him (as a second-five) against Canterbury and Otago. "They really looked after me," says Green. "They told me I was too young to have to tangle with those teams." From the grandstand, Green watched the

Craig Green

Mighty Mids, as they became known, defeat Canterbury at Ashburton. "It was," he recalls, "a trip the Canterbury guys never looked forward to. Canterbury always used the Ashburton game as a build-up fixture while Mid-Canterbury played it like a test match!"

The nine wins Mid-Canterbury achieved in 1979 was the best in its history, a record which lasted only 12 months. The next season, it recorded 14 wins from 17 games, narrowly failing to win promotion to the first division of the NPC. The now 19-year-old second-five, sporting a beard and combining brilliantly with Murray Roulston, headed the tryscoring table with 10. Among the Mighty Mids' victims (both at Ashburton) were Canterbury (again) and New South Wales.

Mid-Canterbury developed a move called Harry which yielded an astonishing number of tries. It was, recalls Green (the chief benefactor), a simple ploy but a good one. At a scrum 30 to 40 metres from the goalline, the Mid-Canterbury halfback would take off acrossfield on a dummy run, leaving the ball in the scrum. The No. 8 would promptly pick it up and pass on the blindside to the second-five (Green) or fullback who would be racing through at full pace. "Normally, it would leave the defending winger in no man's land," says Green, "and if I didn't score, our fullback or left winger did."

Opposition teams eventually got wise to the Harry move, forcing Mid-Canterbury to improvise. And then eventually it was outlawed, it becoming illegal for a halfback to take off on a dummy run. 'Harry' served its purpose though, bringing Mid-Canterbury a generous number of tries and helping thrust Green into the national limelight.

Green encountered a wonderful camaraderie within the side, a quality which would be seriously absent when he joined Canterbury the next season. "The coaches and manager created a fantastic spirit within the side," he says. "We had guitar players and we sang a lot. Our trips were all memorable events."

At the beginning of 1981, Roulston (sadly) bade Rakaia farewell and headed for Lincoln College. At club level, it would turn out to be a magic year, Lincoln celebrating its centenary in the nicest possible way by winning the Chrstchurch senior title. Green remembers the final, in which Lincoln disposed of Marist, as a gala occasion. "The support was incredible," he says. "Rugby Park was crammed with students singing and chanting. It was one of the most memorable occasions of my career."

Rugby Greats

By comparison, the Canterbury team was in the doldrums, lacking direction and spirit. When he was added to the squad, Green found the whole show a shambles. "I couldn't believe what it was like," he says, "especially after my experiences with Mid-Canterbury where the team was like one big family.

"I was genuinely shocked at what was going on. I remember thinking, no wonder they never win. They used to meet upstairs before matches in a dingy old room at the Cantabrian Hotel. They finished third to last in the NPC that season, which, all things considered, was where they deserved to be."

Green was given only two outings, one at second-five against West Coast in Greymouth, the other, interestingly, against Mid-Canterbury at Ashburton where Canterbury ended its losing sequence by drawing 15-all!

Something drastic was needed to salvage Canterbury rugby and it arrived, in 1982, in the form of Alex 'Grizz' Wyllie who'd coached the Country team the season before. "He just took over," says Green, "and terrorised everyone, doing what he wanted to do. He could see, from his days, what had to be done. He had a free hand, really, because everyone realised that another season like 1981 could result in the unthinkable – Canterbury being relegated."

Once Wyllie got the team up and running and began sorting out his best fifteen for the important matches ahead, it was apparent he had a logistical problem in the backline: He had three talented individuals (Warwick Taylor, Vic Simpson and Craig Green) for two midfield positions. One would have to switch to the wing.

Simpson was offered the post and declined in terms that would not grace a family publication like this. "Vic wouldn't have a bar of wing," says Green. "To be honest, it wasn't a position that suited his personality. He didn't have the patience to operate there. Vic was a player who liked to be involved perpetually and on the odd occasions he was played on the wing, he would go walkabout, leave his man to spot tackle the centre and create all sorts of problems.

"So Alex asked me if I was interested in playing on the wing, a position which at that stage was completely foreign to me. I could see that Warwick had the inside running for second-five, so eventually I said to Alex, 'If I agree, do I get a regular spot?' He said, 'Yeah'. So I agreed."

Craig Green

Look out, here comes Cowboy! Craig Green (South Zone) is chased by Mark Shaw (Central Zone) during the George Nepia Trophy match at New Plymouth in 1987.   Fotopacific

Green struck up a strong relationship, on and off the field, with Bruce Deans who was also attending Lincoln College. Like Green, Deans had had a couple of outings in the woeful Canterbury side of '81 but Wyllie made him his first-choice halfback, ahead of Steve Scott who'd been an All Black in 1980. Green and Deans developed a potent move called Lefto which always stretched the defence and produced many valuable tries.

The rejuvenation of Canterbury rugby under Wyllie was complete when the side lifted the Ranfurly Shield from Wellington in a thriller at Athletic Park. Green should have had a try but Wayne Smith threw him a forward pass. "I was shocked at the time," says Green. "It could have cost us the game, but Smithy made amends with a stunning try later in the spell. I followed him all the way to the goalline but he didn't risk a pass the second time!"

Rugby Greats

The next Saturday, Canterbury defended the shield against Countics before a near full house. "The contrast with '81 was unbelievable," recalls Green. "A year earlier, the team that was a shambles and virtually coaching itself was playing, and usually losing, in front of deserted terraces. Now here was Grizz's side defending the shield in front of forty thousand fans. Having said that, we almost blew it against Counties. We took that first challenge too casually and needed a late penalty goal from Robbie Deans to escape with a draw."

The shield era was a stimulating time for Canterbury rugby. It focused media, and obviously New Zealand selector, attention on events at Lancaster Park and undoubtedly provided an important stepping stone into the All Blacks for several of Wyllie's men. Green made significant advancement in 1982 when he was chosen to captain a New Zealand Colts team featuring Grant Fox, Kieran Crowley, Steve McDowell and Andy Earl, on a five-match tour. Everything went well until they encountered David Campese in their 'test' at Sydney. He shredded them, sparking the Australians to a 36-12 victory.

Within the Canterbury team an amazing culture developed, largely through Wyllie's influence. "He transformed everything," says Green. "He was a country man, and he used the country spirit to build unity and camaraderie within the team. Present day coaches would probably be shocked by some of Grizz's methods and his enthusiasm for alcohol. While he created a powerful team spirit and togetherness, the married guys must have had their relationships stretched to the limits. It was a great time to be single. After every training, we'd be back in the bar! We trained hard and played hard, which was why it was so enjoyable."

Grizz Wyllie stories are legend. Green offers one more, to illustrate the exceptional 'culture' that existed within the Canterbury shield team. The setting was the referees' room at Lancaster Park, following a heavy night and the final Sunday morning workout of the season. Wyllie had arranged for a keg of beer to be opened and ordered the players into a circle. As they passed the keg, they filled their glass, which had to be empty by the time they returned to the keg. Wyllie enlivened proceedings by occasionally ordering the circle to "about turn". A huge amount of KFC was produced for lunch, but Wyllie wouldn't let anyone touch the chicken before they'd down a miniature

Craig Green

of whiskey. Green was among those who cried off at this point. "I can't handle whiskey," he says, "so I told Grizz what he could do with his chicken."

The next scene has Wyllie on the floor wrestling with about five of the rougher, tougher forwards when Garry Hooper, a lightweight winger plainly feeling the effects of the whiskey, steps forward and puts the boot into his coach. When he did it a second time, Wyllie roared like a stag, flung the five forwards aside and took off after Hooper. According to Green, they reached speeds approaching 100mph across Lancaster Park, but Wyllie was never going to catch a lightweight winger. "I hate to think what would have happened if he had!" Eventually, Wyllie returned to the party, cursing. A few minutes later, Hooper drove Wyllie's utility van up and parked it across the doorway, preventing anyone from getting in or out of the referees' room. Hooper nonchalantly stepped down from the cab and went home.

Canterbury defended the shield nine times in 1983, and Green scored tries in eight of them, including the 31-9 rout of John Hart's Auckland team, the result that brought greatest satisfaction to the team. Every member of the backline except Andrew McMaster, who would make it to the final trial in 1987, graduated to the All Blacks.

Green's call-up, as a utility back, came at the conclusion of the 1983 season, for the tour of England and Scotland, a mission that was always going to be difficult when six key members of the pack, including captain Andy Dalton, declared their unavailability. The team won only five of its eight matches, losing to Midlands and England and drawing with Scotland.

For Green, who replaced Warwick Taylor at Murrayfield and played the England international at second-five, there were many bizarre aspects to that tour. "The coach, Bryce Rope, a hell of a nice guy, should have been the manager," says Green. "The manager (Paul Mitchell) should have been left at home, and Stu Wilson should never have been given the responsibility of captaincy. Nothing against Stu, but expecting anyone to captain from the wing was stupid. Murray Mexted or Mark Shaw should have led the side."

The All Blacks were far better equipped when they toured Australia the next season. Andy Dalton was back as captain, Dick Littlejohn was an effective manager and the forwards were all available again.

Rugby Greats

Green started out as a centre but when John Kirwan wrecked his shoulder and Bruce Smith damaged his knee, he was shunted to the wing, where he would remain for the balance of his international career.

The Rugby Annual reviewed his tour thus: "The All Blacks' super handyman, who played three times at centre and twice at second-five before finishing up on the left wing. One of the tour's big success. Probably the team's most incisive runner with a rare capacity for breaking out of confined spaces."

There was better to come, for 1985 was Green's year. True, there was the frustration of a cancelled South African tour, his Shirley club team lost the championship final to Marist and Canterbury yielded the Ranfurly Shield to Auckland, after a monster of a game in front of 52,000 enthralled fans at Lancaster Park.

But Green was at the peak of his form and scored tries by the bucket-load, including the matchwinner in the Bledisloe Cup test at Eden Park. That was a score to dine out on for years to come, for the All Blacks had only a point to spare. They caught the Wallabies unawares when they tapped the ball 60 metres out and swung into a well rehearsed move. "The Aussies should have detected from our body language that something was happening," says Green. "But they didn't. Next thing we're careering down the left flank and when Jock Hobbs threw me a pass, I had a clear run to the goalline."

That score followed a brace of tries against England at Athletic Park while Green would touch down 12 times in six shield matches for Canterbury, including hauls of five against Marlborough and four against Southland. He finished the season with 21 tries, clear of the Auckland flyers Terry Wright and John Kirwan, capping a memorable season by winning the New Zealand player of the year award.

Green was intensely disappointed when the tour of South Africa was called off, for he regarded the All Blacks against the Springboks as the ultimate challenge. He resented being denied this opportunity of a lifetime and determined that if the chance to tour there came, he would grab it. He was among the first to commit himself to the rebel tour of '86.

Before assembling with the Cavaliers he helped the New Zealand sevens team scoop the pool at the New South Wales and Hong Kong tournaments. A leg injury sustained at Hong Kong meant he could not

Craig Green

train for three weeks, forcing him to miss the opening games in South Africa but he went on to become the Cavaliers' leading tryscorer and to feature in all the tests.

"The outcome was a huge disappointment," says Green. "We could have squared the series but the Springboks had that little bit extra. Their backs were bigger and stronger. Warwick Taylor and Vic Simpson broke the line often enough but we didn't have the speed to finish things off. It was a great series – a shame the public didn't get to see it."

Back home, suspended, standing on the bank at Lancaster Park watching the Baby Blacks deal to the French, Green wondered about his future as an international. He would be one of the lucky ones reinstated. However, he would find team unity seriously undermined. "It's hard for people outside to appreciate team unity," says Green. "It's something that takes time to come back when there are big changes in personnel."

The disjointed, and rather disspirited, All Blacks laboured through 1986, dropping the series to the Wallabies and a test to France at Nantes. But greater days were over the horizon

Winning the World Cup and then regaining the Bledisloe Cup in Sydney were the undoubted highlights of Green's All Black career, even more satisfying than his part in defending the Ranfurly Shield with Canterbury. "It was the start of a great era in New Zealand rugby," says Green. "The build-up and execution were perfectly managed and the spirit was back in the team after the trials. The coaching team (Brian Lochore, John Hart and Alex Wyllie) produced the edge that had been missing from the All Blacks in 1984, 1985 and 1986. Harty introduced his modern concepts, Grizz stayed with the rough and tumble, and gave you a clip around the ear if you didn't concentrate, and BJ brought it all brilliantly together." Green says that team members still talk of Wyllie's infamous 90-scrum session prior to the quarter-final against Scotland.

Green grabbed two tries in the tournament opener against Italy, then equalled the All Black test record with four against Fiji. He missed only the pool game against Argentina.

Part of the success of the World Cup campaign, he considers, was taking the team to the country, the players deriving immense satisfaction from their stays in the Wairarapa and at Napier. An

Craig Green shows his attacking skills against Italy in the opening match of the first World Cup at Eden Park in 1987. John Selkirk

afternoon's gentle horse riding at Napier produced a hilarious moment when Hart's horse bolted and galloped straight for a fence, breaking to a dead stop at the last moment, leaving a desperate rugby coach clinging to its neck. "Another day David Kirk and I did a spot of eeling in a creek near our hotel," says Green. "We saved one and took it back as a souvenir for our manager, although I don't think Richie Guy appreciated a live eel in his hand basin! He never did find out who was responsible."

Green's appearance against Australia at Concord Oval five weeks after the World Cup final was to be his last in an All Black jersey. Appropriate therefore that he should clinch the victory with the final try. When he found himself sitting on his tool bag on a raw Christchurch morning a few day's later, he decided it was time to try something different. The euphoria of the World Cup triumph and the win over Australia had pretty quickly dissipated.

That 'something different' was joining the crack Benetton team in Treviso. Well, Wales was actually where Green linked with the team, joining them on a pre-season jaunt. Although the language was initially a challenge, Green came to love his time in Italy. He returned to Christchurch briefly at the beginning of 1988, not totally convinced where his future lay, and played a few club matches for Shirley. But the prospect of labouring on roof tops so depressed him he returned to Italy. "I couldn't get back quickly enough," he says.

When John Kirwan arrived in Italy that year they took a flat together, their apartment adjoining Benetton's spanking new sporting complex. "We had access to the gymnasium, weight room, tennis courts, everything," says Green. "I eventually finished up the fittest I have ever been. I had an excellent contract with Benetton, I loved the food and country – I had everything in life I wanted."

Green had four years with Benetton, captaining them the final year. The club was always in or near the championship final. Then, because there was a feeling he was gaining too much control, he moved down the road to the smaller Casale club, helping it win promotion from second division.

He came back to New Zealand in 1994, returning briefly to Italy for his marriage to Antonella whom he had met in Treviso. They now live in Christchurch, Green selling real estate for Harcourts, his wife teaching physical education at a local school and also teaching volleyball which she played professionally in Italy. One of the NZRFU's staff coaches, Green is the coaching co-ordinator at the Belfast club.

Ian Jones

There's not a lot to Kamo, the township on the outskirts of Whangarei that you drive through if you're heading north. But the rugby club there has produced a couple of extraordinarily gifted rugby players who although their careers are separated by more than 50 years are related.

The one is Innes Finlayson, who appeared in North Auckland's first-ever match in 1920 and went on to play 36 games for his country, getting himself ordered off against Transvaal on the All Blacks' 1928 tour of South Africa. He was known by his nickname of Bunny.

The other is Ian Jones, the towering lock who since 1990 has played 58 tests for his country and won acclaim as among the world's most accomplished lineout exponents. No 'bunny' he. Since his arrival on the international scene, everyone's called him Kamo.

The link between the Finlaysons and the Jones's is a tenuous one, but it exists nonetheless. Ian was aware of it when he was growing up and indeed found fascination in one of Bunny's All Black caps which used to adorn the Jones household. His 1928 All Black blazer hung in the Kamo clubrooms.

Jones was always told he inherited his height from the Finlaysons. What he didn't inherit was any of the 1925-30 All Black's bulk.

Finlayson, a loose forward, would certainly never have had to endure taunts that he was too skinny to succeed as a rugby player at the highest level. When he took the field at Carisbrook against Great Britain in the first test of the 1930 series, he was, at 15st 8lb (almost 99kg) the heaviest All Black.

Ian Jones

Ian Jones . . . his lack of bulk counted against him in his early years. But not any more.   Andrew Cornaga (Photosport)

Rugby Greats

At an almost identical weight when he broke into test rugby as a lock in 1990, Jones found himself the third lightest member of the pack for the series against Scotland.

It was this lack of bulk, accentuated by his great height, that plagued Jones during his formative years as a footballer. Despite his exceptional talent, he never represented New Zealand at age grade level. He didn't even get invited to the colts national coaching school and trials in 1988, less than two years before he became a test lock.

"Everyone seemed to regard me as too skinny," says Jones, who sees the funny side of it now, but who was beginning to develop complexes about his leanness back then. "I personally didn't think it was a problem, but a lot of journalists were obsessed with my slenderness and some of the traditionalists tut-tutted that I lacked the bulk of former All Black locks."

Jones didn't rush off to enrol in a Charles Atlas course to meet the textbook requirements for locks. Recognising that he was slimmer than most of the second-rowers who were making their mark at international level, he put the emphasis on fitness and mobility. "I worked out with weights to develop upper body strength," he says, "but otherwise I concentrated on enhancing my natural skills."

And he's had the last laugh. Just when it seemed rugby was about to enter the age of gargantuan locks, the International Rugby Board decided to permit lifting (well, technically it's supporting) in lineouts, which has popularised lighter locks like Jones. "I'm sure the support players would rather hoist someone like me at a lineout than a man mountain like Olivier Merle of France," he says.

Lineout lifting was the third lucky break to dramatically enhance Jones' rugby career. A few years earlier he, and fellow classical jumpers like John Eales of Australia and Mark Andrews of South Africa, were major beneficiaries of the IRB's decision to insist on a metre gap down the centre of lineouts.

"Before that, lineouts were a shambles and a lottery," says Jones. "If you didn't have a couple of highly qualified minders, you were subjected to the most fearful obstruction. Although not all referees policed it correctly, that metre gap down the middle was the saviour of a lot of lineout jumpers' careers."

The first piece of great good fortune that fell Jones' way was Murray Pierce's decision in 1990 to accept an invitation to play for

Ian Jones

Natal in South Africa. The position of test lock had been the almost exclusive preserve of three players, Andy Haden, Gary Whetton and Pierce, for a full decade. But suddenly there was a vacancy and Jones, who'd served a modest apprenticeship in Wales and Ireland the previous year, when he was given just five outings, was promoted to lock the scrum with Whetton.

Slim by international locking standards he may have been, but Jones was an instant smash hit. And but for a brief hiccup in 1993 he's been an automatic test selection for New Zealand ever since.

If Jones had not made it as a rugby player, chances are he might still have represented his country – as a swimmer. As a teenager he was nationally ranked and finished third behind Paul Kingsman, who would swim for New Zealand at the Olympics, in the 100m backstroke at the national championships.

Growing up in Kamo meant Jones saw plenty of water when he was a youngster. His father Warren was a useful yachtsman and sailor and every summer the Jones family would holiday at Whangarei Heads where Ian came to grips with P Class yachts and did plenty of swimming.

There was no hint that Ian Donald Jones would become a world-class forward when he was a youngster. Until he was about 12, when he started to grow at an alarming rate, all his rugby was played (barefooted) in the backs. His first representative experience was as a winger.

Jones' first overseas rugby trip was noteworthy for the fact that he (and his teammates) were ordered to stop training because it was a sacred day, and he met David Bowie. The trip was arranged by Kamo High School when Jones was 14, the destination Rarotonga. "It was my first taste of international rugby," he says. "We raised all the money ourselves and had an enjoyable ten days there. Errol Brain was part of the team, as was Geoff Crawford who went on to play lock for North Auckland. We offended the locals by training on a Sunday which brought an abrupt finish to our session. David Bowie was there filming a movie and several of us sneaked into the Rarotongan Hotel to watch and get his autograph."

The next year essentially the same team advanced to the first XV where they came under the guidance of the schools' phys-ed teacher Tuck Waaka and long-serving North Auckland hooker Frank

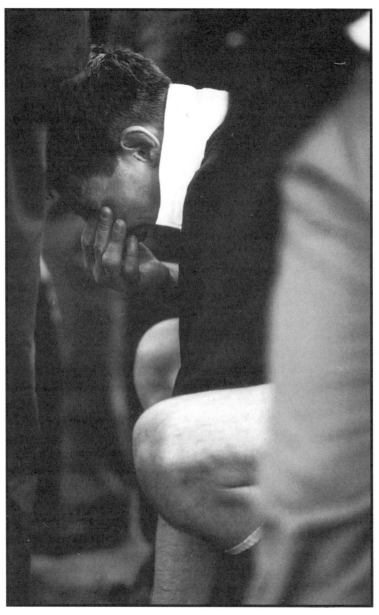

Ian Jones is reduced to tears after the All Blacks lost the World Cup final (after extra time) to the Springboks at Ellis Park in 1995.   John Selkirk

Ian Jones

Colthurst. "The first fifteen is still where most New Zealanders learn the game," says Jones, "and these guys were great. They taught us that rugby is a game of basics."

That first year in the top team Jones locked the North Auckland secondary schools scrum with Robin Brooke. One wonders if anyone watching nominated them as a future test combination. While Brooke went on to represent New Zealand at schools and under-17 level, Jones didn't advance beyond the 1985 North Island under-18 team. It was 1988 when Jones began to make his mark, although amazingly he missed the intake for the national colts coaching school. When officials of the North Auckland union protested that a future star had been overlooked, they were told that if he wasn't playing representative rugby he couldn't expect to be considered for New Zealand Colts. An interesting theory, but did the selectors want the best under-21 players in the land or not?

Within a month of the New Zealand Colts completing their tour of Australia, where they were whipped in the international at Ballymore, Jones was locking the North Auckland scrum. The team was desperately short on quality lineout jumpers so after using him as a reserve for the Bay of Plenty game (after he'd played in the curtainraiser for the Northland Colts) coach Danny O'Shea introduced him to the big-time against Counties.

He was 20, weighed less than 100kg, which was regarded as the minimum weight for a first division lock, and was certainly among the slenderest lineout forwards in the land. Which inevitably lead to cynicism among the nation's rugby writers. "I couldn't believe how negative the writers were," says Jones. "No one was prepared to accept that I might be able to compensate for my lack of bulk with athleticism. I was considered skinny and boyish which obviously didn't meet the average rugby writer's stereotype lock. Their comments only made me more determined to succeed."

That athleticism helped him score four tries as North Auckland battled through to fifth place in the NPC. His second outing was a Ranfurly Shield challenge against Auckland at Eden Park where he marked Marty Brooke. At one stage he came through the lineout into enemy territory. "Steve McDowell glowered at me and clenched his fist," says Jones. "He didn't throw the punch, just reminded me of where I should be !"

Rugby Greats

The *Rugby Annual* recorded that "fullback Warren Johnston, first-five Ian Dunn and lock Ian Jones were the spectacular successes of the (North Auckland) season".

At season's end, Jones was off to Scotland with the *Rugby News* Youth team, a nationally selected side coached by Fred Allen and Sid Going. In a notable first, the team played a curtainraiser (to the Scotland-Australia international) at Murrayfield, scoring a sensational last-minute victory against Scotland's best under-21 players, among whom were flyhalf Craig Chalmers and winger Tony Stanger. Jones was one of the heroes of the Youth team which was captained by Pat Lam and included 'Bull' Allen and Stu Forster. "It was my introduction to touring as an international, training day in, day out," says Jones. "Fred was of the old school, but taught us plenty."

Jones might have been neglected by the national selectors in 1988, but the next season, having made such a mighty impact, his progress was carefully monitored by national coach Alex Wyllie. One game 'Grizz' looked in on what was a Canz fixture against Otago at Carisbrook. "Every time the ball was thrown in, I seemed to win it," says Jones. "That game had a major influence on my career, I'm sure." It resulted in Jones appearing in the All Black trial in Hamilton where he opposed Pierce. The *Rugby Annual* noted that "the trial presented the opportunity for several in (Mike) Brewer's team to make their mark opposite the test incumbents. Several did, notably 'Inga' Tuigamala, Zinzan Brooke opposite 'Buck' Shelford and Ian Jones against Murray Pierce."

Whetton and Pierce, who had locked every All Black test scrum for three years (with the exception of one game at the 1987 World Cup), retained their mortgage on the Nos 4 and 5 jerseys throughout 1989, but obviously a couple of back-up locks were required for the end-of-season tour of Wales and Ireland.

Jones and Steve Gordon were the lucky ones. Jones had made the long journey home from Dunedin to Whangarei, following an NPC game, the day the touring party was to be announced on the 6pm television news. "All my family were in the lounge waiting," says Jones. "The tension was too much for me, so I went downstairs and watched on my own. You can imagine the joy when my name was read out."

The celebrating was done at the Kamo Rugby Club. "The reality of

Ian Jones

what I'd achieved hit me down at the clubrooms," says Jones. "I was only the third Kamo All Black (Bunny Finlayson and Bevan Holmes were the others) and I was the lone Northlander in the touring party. I wasn't going to know too many of the players!"

Jones was used sparingly on tour, getting one Saturday game, against Cardiff, and four midweekers, against Pontypool, Neath, Leinster and Connacht. He scored two tries, which was significant, because when Murray Pierce (the player he would replace the next season) dotted down against Munster it was his first try for the All Blacks in 48 appearances.

"I was more than happy to be a back-up player – observing and learning at that stage," says Jones. "That I got to play at Cardiff Arms Park and Lansdowne Road was a big thrill. As I sat in the grandstand at Twickenham watching the Barbarians game, I resolved that having become an All Black, my next goal was to become a good All Black. And deep down there was a determination to become a great All Black."

Pierce's unexpected departure for South Africa before the 1990 season kicked off meant a vacancy existed for a middle-of-the-lineout jumper. Jones obviously had the front running, having toured the UK, but he still needed to perform at the trials where he was matched up against Marty Brooke. The *Rugby Annual* recorded that "arch rivals Jones and Brooke both performed well, Jones having the edge."

And Jones it was who partnered Gary Whetton when the All Blacks ran on to Carisbrook in June for the first international against Scotland. It was a bemusing time for New Zealand rugby because since the trial a month earlier three good men, John Gallagher, Matthew Ridge and John Schuster, had defected to league.

Jones was a sensation against Scotland, completely outplaying Damian Cronin and capping a phenomenal debut performance with a try. Jones' dominance meant the All Blacks won the lineouts that afternoon by 24 to 8. While the backs were having a few problems plugging gaps left by the league raids, Jones slotted into a powerhouse All Black pack. "Steve McDowell, Sean Fitzpatrick and Richard Loe were an awesome front row, Gary Whetton was a mobile, skilled lock on whom I was modelling myself while captaining the side from number eight was the great Buck Shelford.

"Buck wielded an incredible influence," says Jones. "He was a doer, an achiever. He wouldn't ask anything of a player he wouldn't do himself. He had mana and physique and was an inspiring captain." Hyped up for his international debut, Jones could not be expected to know that this was a team on the down and that within a couple of weeks Shelford would be dropped.

Jones prepared well for his test debut and admits that he operated for most of the eighty minutes on adrenalin. That was the first of 26 consecutive test appearances for him and by the beginning of 1997 he'd packed down in 58 tests. The enthusiasm he demonstrated in Dunedin in '90 wasn't a one-off. "I prepare for every test match as if it's my first," he says. "When a test becomes just another game, it'll be time to get out."

Nothing is forever and at Athletic Park in August the All Blacks were defeated by the Wallabies, their first reversal in 51 games. Jones was shocked when the final whistle sounded and he realised the Australians had won. "It was my first loss as an All Black," he says, "something I never expected would happen. There was a sense of the invincible about the team. I was sure that Foxy (Grant Fox) or JK (John Kirwan) would rescue us, but it didn't happen. We lost."

There would be more losses in 1990 for the 'invincible' All Blacks, at Toulon and Bayonne on the tour of France. "Suddenly the All Blacks were going into a test series as the underdogs," says Jones. "The team was under intense pressure, much of it emanating from the criticism back home. New Zealanders had had too much of a good thing – they weren't used to their team losing."

With Jones performing impressively in the lineout opposite Olivier Roumat, the All Blacks re-established themselves with two clear-cut victories over the French, at Nantes and Paris. "The survivors of 1986 kept saying, 'Remember Nantes'. The boys were determined to avenge that loss; in the event, we blew them away."

The *Rugby Annual* editor thought enough of Jones' performances in his first season of international rugby to make him one of the players of the year (along with Sean Fitzpatrick, Grant Fox, Craig Innes and John Timu) and paid him this compliment: "Jones is an outstanding natural ball player who can run, pass and handle with the skill of the most accomplished loose forward."

The 1991 Bledisloe Cup series pitted Jones against John Eales for the first time. Two of a kind – slimline locks and classical lineout leapers – they would have many great contests through the 1990s. "He's virtually the only player I've opposed at international level who's got a frame like mine," says Jones, "I've always enjoyed my clashes with John because we've always contested the ball in the air. It's never been a case of who was the better cheat."

If honours between them were even after the Bledisloe Cup games, Eales was certainly in the ascendancy after Australia's stunning victory in the World Cup semi-final in Dublin, the result that represented the nadir for the All Blacks, four years after they'd been crowned champions of the world.

Jones has no doubts why the All Blacks came unstuck. "It started at the top," he says. "The management didn't function and it flowed on down. There was a feeling of uneasiness throughout the team. The two coaches (Alex Wyllie and John Hart) were operating on different agendas and the players suffered accordingly. We weren't sharp in training and we certainly weren't sharp enough against the Wallabies who gave us a good hiding."

If 1991 was a low point in Jones' career (and plenty of other All Blacks' careers), 1992 was a breath of fresh air. Laurie Mains took over as coach and brought with him a refreshing approach. "He removed all the cliques which had flourished previously," says Jones, "he brought in interesting new players like Frank Bunce, Olo Brown and Robin Brooke and he set out to achieve levels of fitness that had slipped at the World Cup.

"What Laurie made us appreciate was that the more hard work you did in January, February and March, the easier life became in July, August and September. During his term he had us pounding the roads pre-season, building our aerobic base. Then when he got us to himself overseas he was almost masochistic, ordering endless 150 sprints and down-and-ups, which are dreadful things.

"I'd have to say I enjoyed Laurie's style though. I didn't mind the hard graft which paid off in tight test matches. We didn't win the series in Australia in 1992 but the further we went, the stronger we became, and the successes in the third test at Sydney and later in Johannesburg were among the most satisfying of my career."

At Bloemfontein, Jones captained the All Blacks against a fractious Free State side. The day belonged to him. He scored an important try, won a dozen lineout throws on his own and his genial nature and positiveness probably saved the game from degenerating into a brawl. The *Johannesburg Star* would refer to Free State's "shameful display of foul play – their short tempers, ill discipline and blatant dirty play overshadowed a fine first-half showing." And who were at the cause of all the mischief? None other than the infamous Bester brothers, Andre and Johan, who would bring down Andre Markgraaff as Springbok coach five years later.

Jones, who remembers it as "no holds barred" contest, had a mission that afternoon – to get the All Blacks' midweek combination back on winning track. At their previous outing, they'd suffered a humiliating 40-17 loss to Sydney.

Jones felt privileged to be playing against the Springboks at Ellis Park. "It was a new experience for me, playing against South Africa and I thought of all the players from 1976 to 1991 who'd been denied that opportunity. I actually grew up regarding the Wallabies as the All Blacks' greatest rival." Jones had the satisfaction of sharing in a famous victory over the Springboks, his lineout supremacy an important factor. It was the first time New Zealand had won a test at Ellis Park since 1928.

Through the 1993 and 1994 seasons the All Blacks only intermittently produced the quality of play that would distinguish them at the third World Cup. "They weren't memorable years," says Jones. "The players were struggling to come to grips with Laurie's style. He was probably too inflexible at that point. Against England at Twickenham, for example, it screamed out for a change of tactics, but no one stood up and made it happen. We were robotic."

Jones was experiencing his own problems in 1993. He found the step-up from club rugby with Kamo to test action too demanding. As a Northlander, he wasn't getting the Super 10 action that was sharpening the players from Auckland, North Harbour, Waikato and Otago. "Physically, I was ready for test play," says Jones, "but mentally I was way off the pace. With Northland down in second division I took the decision at the end of '93 to move to North Harbour. Although it was sad to abandon my home territory, I knew that at that time it was the right move. Before the advent of Super 10, I would have said it didn't matter where you played your rugby. But things had changed."

The summer training camps in early 1995 prepared the All Blacks, for their World Cup campaign, like no other New Zealand team before them. "Those camps were brilliantly organised, featuring the best resources available in New Zealand," says Jones. "Taupo was the hardest weekend of my life. We were pushed beyond our normal limits. As Laurie kept reminding us, the harder we worked then, the easier it would be at the World Cup.

"Bringing Brian Lochore in as the campaign manager was a master stroke. His presence allowed Laurie to concentrate on what he did best – coach. He no longer had to worry about the media and sponsors. By the end of the summer camps we were all confident that our chosen style was the way to win in South Africa."

After demolishing opponent after opponent and going to the final a raging hot favourite, the All Blacks didn't win the World Cup in 1995. But it was no fault of Ian Jones'. Even though he'd been a victim of the poisoning which struck the team down on the Thursday, he ruled supreme in the lineouts, even claiming a number of South

Ian Jones and Liam Barry managing a spot of shopping during their tour of France with the All Blacks in 1995.   Andrew Cornaga (Photosport)

Africa's throws. "If you study videos of your opponents long enough, it's not hard to crack their combinations," he says. But no amount of fancy lineout work compensated Jones and the All Blacks for the disappointment of losing the final.

There was to be retribution, glorious retribution, a year on. With essentially the same team, but with John Hart taking over from Laurie Mains, the All Blacks would notch up four straight test victories over the Springboks and complete a historic series victory on South African soil.

"It was a tremendous year," says Jones. "The foundation had been set in 1995 and John Hart, with his excellent man management skills, took us a step further on. The comeback victory over the Wallabies at Ballymore showed that we probably possessed greater composure in '96. We went on from that victory to swamp the Springboks in similar circumstances at Cape Town."

Jones sat out the final stages of the dramatic Pretoria test after straining muscles on the outside of his leg. "In those last five minutes," he says, "there were emotions touched that only those there would truly appreciate. It was an incredible experience to be part of it."

One player Jones singles out for special mention is All Black skipper Sean Fitzpatrick. Of Jones' 58 tests, 57 have been in partnership with Fitzpatrick (the exception being the Bledisloe Cup test at Carisbrook in 1993 when he was injured). "Sean's rise as a captain has been one of the highlights of my time in the All Blacks. As his confidence has grown, he's emerged as a great leader of men. He's demonstrated, as time has gone on, an ability to chance tactics during a game. He listens to his senior players and, with the challenge of professionalism, he's got himself fitter than ever. He's approachable to everyone – players, the public, the media. I don't think I've met a tougher rugby player, physically and mentally. But the thing is, he's such a nice guy with it."

Jones' own leadership qualities were given a boost when he was appointed captain of the Waikato Chiefs for the 1997 Super 12 campaign.

In November '96 he and Janine Graham married, choosing the Sheraton Hotel in Fiji for the ceremony and celebrations. From there (and a temperature of 30 deg C), Jones flew to the UK (where the

Ian Jones

temperature was 0 deg C) to link with the New Zealand Barbarians for the match against England at Twickenham. Another storming victory set the seal on a cracker year.

He then turned out for the British Barbarians against the Wallabies, the sixth time he had accepted invitations to represent that distinguished club.

An electrician by trade, Jones worked for Lion Nathan from 1991 to 1994 when he joined Philips. After a brief stint at the All Blacks Club, he returned to Philips where, when his rugby commitments permit, he fronts promotional campaigns.

Michael Jones

It was some time before Michael Jones could celebrate because the 125kg Springbok lock Kobus Wiese was lying on top of him, and was most reluctant to get off. But Jones didn't mind, because he'd just heard the sweetest sound of his entire rugby career, the referee's whistle for full time.

The scene was Loftus Versfeld, Pretoria, in late August, 1996, and the All Blacks had just completed their first series victory on South African soil after 68 years of trying. To achieve it, many had pushed themselves to the point of exhaustion, and beyond. "It was probably the most physically sapping game I had ever been involved in," says Jones, "because we had expended so much energy building a lead. I doubt I could have picked myself up for another scrum. That's why the referee's whistle for full time was such a sweet sound."

Jones had experienced similar elation nine years earlier when he shared in the All Blacks' first World Cup triumph. Then he was 22, an openside flanker with an unscarred body. Now he was 31 and a blindside specialist who had proved himself one of the game's great survivors, fighting back from an appalling knee injury that would have instantly ended most normal players' careers.

Jones had been denied the opportunity to participate in a third World Cup tournament in South Africa in 1995 when the All Blacks faced crunch quarter-final and semi-final contests on Sundays, the day he keeps sacred. It might have saved him a severe bout of food poisoning but many saw his non-involvement as probably signalling the end of a distinguished career.

Michael Jones

Michael Jones . . . the player who popularised the term 'Doing the Damage'.

Andrew Cornaga *(Photosport)*

Rugby Greats

But then (and was it the power of prayer?) came two significant happenings – the appointment as All Black coach of John Hart, who'd introduced Jones to big-time rugby more than a decade earlier, and the announcement of an All Black programme for 1996 with no Sunday commitments. Jones admits he was close to shutting down his rugby career after 1995 but Hart's involvement made him think again. "I thought if I was selected, it would be great to play under John again."

Jones went on to feature in all 10 tests, starring in the No 6 jersey, having made his reputation in the 1980s as a No 7. Hart lavished praise on him following the drama and heroics at Pretoria. "This guy was a sensation at the 1987 World Cup," said Hart, "and today he was a sensation nearly ten years later. To play like that in his forty-ninth test was special. You have seen here one of the very special individuals to have ever played rugby."

One of the very special individuals, indeed. As he was growing up, Jones and his Western Samoan colleagues had a term they popularised, relevant to whatever sport they were playing at the time – Doing the Damage. Well, Michael Niko Jones was still 'doing the damage' in South Africa in 1996, doing it as a tackler supreme probably better than any other player in his position in the world.

Through injuries and his refusal to play on Sundays, Jones hasn't racked up the phenomenal appearance records of most of his contemporaries. For example, Sean Fitzpatrick, whose career has run almost parallel, has played 70 more games for Auckland and 49 more for the All Blacks. What might Jones have achieved had he been as resilient and as prepared to play Sundays as Fitzy?

Even with his handicaps, he has still won over the rugby world. When John Reason, the often acerbic English rugby correspondent, stepped down after 40 years following the game and was asked to nominate the best player of all those who had illuminated the game in his time, he singled out Michael Jones, declaring him "the most complete player of them all".

Those inside backs who have been terrorised over the years by Michael Jones, Flanker, can blame a rogue barbed wire fence in Remuera for what they've had to endure. Because until he attended intermediate school, he was a highly promising second-five with all the necessary skills to carve a future for himself in midfield. But when he and his brother Derek went to their uncle Niko's house to play

Michael Jones

tennis, Michael snagged his leg on barbed wire while searching for a ball. The leg was ripped wide open and took some time to mend. His coach at the time, Al Kay, concluded that because the injury would impair Michael's speed, he should move into the forwards and suggested the new position of flanker.

That Jones was a sportsman above average was apparent from a young age. His Henderson High School rugby coach Owen Stunell recalls coming upon a group in the playground watching with fascination as this talented individual spun a basketball on his fingertips for an eternity. The entertainer was Michael Jones. Stunell is of the opinion that Jones could have made it to the top in basketball or cricket. He was a lively fast bowler and talented attacking batsman while on court his hand-eye co-ordination combined with athleticisim and exceptional spring distinguished him as a quality player.

It was in rugby though that he demonstrated his greatest potential. Stunell advanced him to the first XV as a fourth former, notwithstanding Jones' initial reluctance. Stunell assured him he would be looked after, which he was. The next year, even though the team was comprised mostly of sixth and seventh formers, Jones was made captain. The players voted on the appointment and were unanimous in their decision.

The superstar of the Henderson High first XV at the time was Timo Tagaloa, who would go on to represent Western Samoa and come desperately close to All Black selection. Jones regarded him as a schoolboy legend. "The feeling in our team was that if we could get the ball to Timo anywhere on the field, he would score," says Jones. Tagaloa, in turn, marvelled at the ability of Jones who played most of his college rugby at No. 8. "He didn't say much, but he was a great leader by example," says Tagaloa. "He did the most amazing things on the paddock. He always wanted to create play, not just bash up the middle. He was totally different from the other players. Few players were as gifted as Michael – he would have been excellent in the backs."

When Henderson High made a trip to Queensland in 1981, it encountered a couple of fellows in the Brisbane State High School team who would distinguish themselves in the world of sport – the halfback Peter Slattery, eventually to take over the Wallaby job from Nick Farr-Jones, and the centre Ian Healy, who would rewrite the record books as Australia's wicketkeeper.

In their final year at Henderson High, Jones and Tagaloa were invited to train with the Waitemata seniors where coach Ray Dellabarca had monitored their progress. The New Zealand secondary school selectors weren't so convinced of Jones' worth though. They selected Tagaloa as a wing for the schools test against Australia but preferred Palmerston North's Emosi Koloto at No. 8. From the crack Henderson High team which won all 11 matches in 1982 (scoring 394 points while conceding only 39), Jones and four others made the Auckland under-16 team while he and Tagaloa represented Auckland secondary schools.

Jones' involvement with the Waitemata third grade team, in his first year at university, was short and sweet. Within two months, Dellabarca, who'd coached Wellington in the 1970s, had promoted him to the seniors. Across town about the same time, another 18-year-old, John Kirwan, who'd also started the season in third grade (at Marist) was breaking into the big time with Auckland.

Jones didn't need too much encouragement to make the step up to seniors. Between seasons he'd turned out for the Moata'a village team in Western Samoa, holding his own against players of international standing. And, anyway, wherever Tagaloa was, Jones wanted to be. "Timo was up there (in the seniors) and I wanted to be there with him."

Making an immediate impact in a Waitemata team that progressed to the semi-finals, Jones was selected for the Auckland under-18 team which would be captained by Zinzan Brooke and have as its halfback Ant Strachan. From there he advanced to the North Island under-18 team where Zinzan was again a teammate. Jones scored two tries from the side of the scrum. Keeping him out of the No. 8 jersey, still, was Koloto. Following that interisland match in Palmerston North a national under-18 team was named, and although it did not take the field, it was a source of special satisfaction to Jones to hear his name read out, the first impact he had made at national level. "It was my boyhood dream to become an All Black," he says, "and selection in that team made me believe, for the first time, that that might be possible."

Jones wasn't selected for Auckland until the 1985 season when he was 20, but there were plenty of smart rugby judges about who felt he was ready to make the step up at least a year earlier. His Waitemata teammate and Auckland squad member Brian Annan believes he was ready for Auckland at 18. "He had the skills," says Annan. "He could pick up the ball in any position. He was incredibly quiet but was probably one of the most competitive people I've ever met." Former All Black coach Fred Allen was another fan. "Watching him play for Waitemata," says Allen, "he reminded me of Waka Nathan with his panther-like movements. They both had that natural, fluid motion but were lethal with it."

Being a committed Christian and general nice guy meant Jones didn't ever get involved in what rugby people like to refer to as stoush. It wasn't in him to retaliate whatever the level of provocation. If anyone riled him, he would make his point with an aggressive, physical, but always legal, tackle.

Jones was often penalised for being offside when, in the opinion of his teammates, his exceptional acceleration and anticipation deceived referees. "He'd consistently snare the second-five before he made the advantage line," says Annan. "The referee would presume he was offside because no one else ever did that."

It was in 1985, in his third season as an Auckland Colt, that Jones came into the national limelight. No thanks to the national selectors, Brian Lochore, Tiny Hill and Bryce Rope, mind you. They ignored his claims, even after he'd scored two tries in the trial in Levin, taking Zinzan Brooke and Rob Avery as their flankers for New Zealand Colts.

September 14 was the day Auckland so dramatically wrenched the Ranfurly Shield away from Canterbury in what was billed as, and lived up to the title of, *the* Provincial Match of the Century. Doing their thing for Auckland Colts in the curtainraiser were Jones (listed in the programme as Mike Jones), Bernie McCahill and a couple of Brookes, Zinzan and Robin. Their disappointment at losing was swept away when Hart's men subsequently lifted the shield.

Jones was visiting his aunt in Christchurch that evening when the Colts manager contacted him and excitedly informed him that John Hart was wanting to get in touch with him. Hart had said that if Auckland won the shield he would add two colts to the team for the subsequent matches at Timaru and Dunedin. The players he promoted were Jones and McCahill.

Michael Jones dives across for the first individual try, against Italy, at the first World Cup at Eden Park in 1987. He would also pick up the first try at the second World Cup four years later.   John Selkirk

Jones, reserved at the best of times, didn't utter a peep on the bus journey down to Timaru the next day. "I felt pretty humble among all these famous players," he says. "I expected their attitude would be, 'Who is this guy on our bus?'"

They were all well aware of 'this guy' after he'd run in a hat-trick of tries on debut against South Canterbury two days later. The opposition wasn't too formidable, but Jones, as his biographer Robin McConnell would describe so vividly, 'went after the ball carrier for 80 minutes like a fleet-footed bailiff paid only on commission'. He was the 15th Auckland player to score three tries on debut, but the first forward. He then gave Eden Park fans a glimpse of his talent in the shield defence against Waikato when he scored another try. Sean Fitzpatrick remembers him as "a panther-like creature" running around with boundless energy and an amazing range of skills. "He showed an incredible ability to anticipate where play was going," says Fitzpatrick. "They were first impressions but they have stuck with me ever since. I still see Michael like that, more than a decade later."

Auckland had returned from its shield-winning southern journey to a hero's reception and was given a ticker-tape parade down Queen Street, with Michael involved. "I felt pretty silly being part of that," he says. "I'm sure no one knew who I was. I hadn't been part of the team when they won the shield. I was embarrassed at what my university friends would think when they saw me up there!"

Jones broke into international rugby in 1986 as a 21-year-old. Not with New Zealand, but as a Western Samoan representative. He'd been approached by Peter Fatialofa, made himself available and suddenly found himself running on to Apia Park in the royal blue jersey of Western Samoa against Wales. When the players were being introduced to the Head of State by their captain, Dick Tafua, Michael was announced as Tom Jones. "Can you believe that?" he says. "And us playing Wales. I was still laughing about it as the game was about to start."

Cheered on by almost 30,000 fans, the Western Samoans established a 14-13 advantage by halftime, then collapsed, losing 32-14. Their finest rugby days were ahead of them. They wouldn't have Jones' services again, but five years on they would achieve a famous first World Cup victory over Wales at Cardiff Arms Park.

Late in the 1986 season Jones secured a regular slot at No. 8 in the Auckland team. When Hart then stepped down as coach he made the prediction, in a farewell interview, that Jones would become one of the finest loose forwards of all time, with the potential to be the greatest. He believed he was ready to make the tour of France as an All Black.

The '86 national selection panel (Lochore, Hill and Colin Meads) took a more conservative approach. They stuck with experienced Jock Hobbs and 'Baby Black' Mark Brooke-Cowden as openside flankers. Jones would have to wait until 1987, which suited Hart. He would be a selector by then, and he wanted Jones to be part of New Zealand's shock tactics at the first World Cup.

Anyone plotting Jones' progress on the New Zealand Barbarians' tour of the UK early in 1987 would have anticipated the impact he would make at the World Cup. Against Leicester he scored a try when he chipped the ball over fullback Dusty Hare's head with his left foot and regathered it on the full, leaving his experienced teammates gasping. "Who is this guy?" Mike Brewer asked of Alan Whetton.

Rugby Greats

'This guy' was Michael Jones who was about to take the world by storm, by not only scoring the first individual try of the World Cup tournament (something he would emulate at Twickenham four years later) but by producing his panther-like support of the All Black backs and by continually disrupting opposition attacks with his uncanny anticipation and deadly tackling.

Former All Black captain Graham Mourie helped hone the skills of Jones who was still inexperienced as an openside flanker. Though banned by the IRB for pocketing the royalties from his autobiography, Mourie was happy to help Jones whom he saw as his heir apparent, and willingly passed on his strategies and philosophies, which were eagerly absorbed by the young university student from Glen Eden.

Jones capped a stunningly successful tournament by scoring the first try of the final against France at Eden Park. He was identified by most critics as *the* outstanding openside flanker of the World Cup. An exciting international career had been launched, although it was significant that he stood aside from the semi-final against Wales because it was on a Sunday. His refusal, as a committed Christian, to play on the Sabbath would seriously disrupt his rugby career at representative and international level. Indeed, a lesser player may have been disregarded altogether as Sunday fixtures, including tests, became more and more common.

It cost him participation in the All Black tour of Japan at the end of 1987, although there was adequate consolation when the Hawaiian Harlequins invited him to Honolulu to participate in their annual tournament. Having become a celebrity back home, Jones found the sun, sand and surf at Honolulu the perfect way to unwind after his big year.

Jones would continue to astonish teammates and opponents alike with his achievements over the next two seasons, until he came to grief against the Pumas at Athletic Park midway through the 1989 season. It was his 13th test (no, he's not superstitious) and he was enjoying being part of a supercharged All Black team which had been averaging almost 50 points a test.

He tried to toe the ball away from Argentinian flanker Miguel Bertranou but Bertranou dived on it and contorted Jones' leg. There was a sickening crack and Jones slumped to the ground. "I thought I could click my knee into place, but then the deep pain came," he says.

Michael Jones

"The nerves were all broken in that part of my leg. There was a dull, excruciating pain. I remember thinking that it would be all right, but I found I couldn't move my leg at all."

It would be revealed that Jones had suffered an injury as severe as you would get in rugby, with complete dislocation of the knee joint. Physiotherapist David Abercrombie said the injury was similar to those incurred in major car accidents. Only one of the four ligaments essential to operate the knee was still functioning.

Any normal footballer would have called it quits there and then. But "normal' is not an adjective that has ever been associated with Michael Jones. After what amounted to a 'miracle' repair job, Jones, calling on all his faith as a Christian, resolved to resume his rugby career as soon as that was possible. His surgeon, Barry Tietjens, described the injury as "one of such severity that we would expect few people to recover sufficiently to go back to playing first-class rugby. We were optimistic he might be able to recover to play sport again . . ."

Jones was in hospital for a week, unable to walk for five weeks, unable to run for almost six months. How does he remember that period of his life? "Looking back, it was one of the best things that happened to me," he says. "I really believe that those kinds of trials and tribulations build your character. The whole experience built and strengthened my spiritual character. I really learned to put my faith and trust in God. I became wiser and more discerning in how to relate to people – I became more thoughtful and not as happy-go-lucky. I certainly learned not to take anything for granted."

Eleven days short of one year after the accident, Jones ventured gingerly on to a rugby field again, appearing for a Henderson High old boys team against the current first XV. "I approached that game as though I had never had a sore knee," says Jones. "I wore no bandage and I didn't allow myself to think about the injury. My match fitness was lacking but the knee came through just great." Jones gradually achieved match fitness with outings for Auckland C (in ankle deep mud) and Auckland B, making his comeback for Auckland A in a Ranfurly Shield defence against Southland on September 8. He celebrated with a try behind the posts, courtesy of Terry Wright. "When I scored I paused briefly under the goalposts," he says, "and offered a little prayer. I felt that the returning was a blessing from God and it emphasised that my rugby career wasn't finished."

Rugby Greats

The comeback was completed when Jones was taken on the end-of-year tour of France and was selected for both test matches. Although creaks were beginning to appear in the once invincible All Black machine, the tests at Nantes and Paris were won in convincing fashion. Before the second test coach Alex Wyllie had made an unexpected return to the dressing room shortly before kick-off. "I hope you guys are ready," he said. "They're already butting and whacking each other over the head." "It was hard to believe," says Jones, "but, sure enough, they had plaster and bandages on, and blood on their faces and collars."

The All Black selectors gambled with Jones at the second World Cup, naming him among their 26 even though they knew he was unavailable for the third pool match, the quarter-final and the semi-final, all of which were scheduled for Sundays. It was a massive reflection of the esteem in which he was held that, in such circumstances, he would be taken ahead of a player who would have been available for everything.

Jones rewarded them with the first (and, as it turned out, matchwinning) try in the tournament opener against England when he intuitively latched on to the pass that John Kirwan had lobbed into space when tackled by fullback Jonathan Webb. He was the commanding individual in the game, being described by John Mason of the *Daily Telegraph* as "the personification of athletic power".

As an interesting aside, John Hart had a handsome collect from the betting shop on Jones scoring the first try at the World Cup (again), at odds of about 16 to 1. Offered a share of the winnings, Jones opted instead for the gift of a new bible.

Jones was a forlorn spectator as the All Blacks plummeted to defeat against Australia in the semi-final in Dublin. He was devastated by the result and irked, like the other All Blacks, that the England team they'd beaten had meanwhile, by a circuitous route, qualified for the grand final. For the All Blacks, all that remained was a low-key play-off for third against Scotland, which gave Jones his third outing at the tournament.

Jones was among the survivors when the new broom, wielded by Laurie Mains, began sweeping clean in 1992. He was an automatic selection all year, although missing the second test against the World XV with a hamstring strain and the second test in Australia because it

Michael Jones

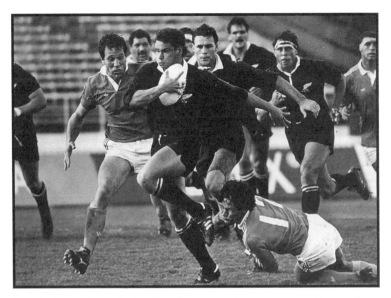

The classic running style of Michael Jones, stamping his mark as a 22-year-old on the first World Cup in 1987.　　　　　*John Selkirk*

was staged on a Sunday. But he was a major contributor in the thrilling 27-24 victory over the Springboks at Ellis Park. This test was originally scheduled for a Sunday which Grant Fox commented would have been "an all round tragedy" for Jones and his teammates. As it was, he comprehensively outjumped Ian MacDonald and Jannie Breedt at the back of the lineout and created havoc behind the South African forwards.

Jones shared in the series win over the British Lions in 1993 and the well-taken victories against Australia at Carisbrook (after which Bob Dwyer asked if Jones could be left out the next time the All Blacks played the Wallabies!) and Western Samoa at Eden Park. But he missed the tour of England and Scotland after breaking his jaw in a freak training accident.

He was naturally an absentee when the All Blacks crashed to two successive defeats against France in 1994, because both games were played on Sundays, and niggling injuries resulted in him sitting out the first two tests against the Springboks. When he came on as a replacement at Eden Park, it was like a tornado descending on to the field. He was instantly the most dynamic individual in the game. It saw him recalled to the starting fifteen for the Bledisloe Cup test in Sydney, the game in which the All Blacks gave the Wallabies a big start and almost hauled them back with a huge and spectacular second-half effort.

While he would have loved to have been among the elite few who could claim participation in all three World Cups, he accepted Mains' explanation that the selectors could not justify taking someone to South Africa in 1995 who, because of the amount of Sunday play, would be available for only 50 per cent of the games.

That would probably have been an appropriate time to lower the curtain on an illustrious career. But the arrival of John Hart as Mains' successor (and the elimination of Sunday internationals) influenced Jones, at the not extreme age of 31, to have another crack at the All Blacks. With, as it turned out, brilliant results. Jones featured in all 10 tests in 1996, scored tries against Scotland (at Auckland) and Australia (at Wellington) and produced rugby as a blindside flanker of the highest quality.

Because of an Achilles tendon injury his form in the Super 12 series had been disappointing, prompting some critics to suggest it was time to retire. Jones ignored the attacks. "At this stage of my career I'm immune to what people write and say about me," he says. "They said I wouldn't play again after my injury in 1989 and I've had another seven seasons. I look to other things, beyond the critics, for motivation, such as my being a Christian. My faith is central to any decision I make."

Before taking the field for any match, Jones takes a minute out to say a prayer. "I also take inspiration from knowing my family are supporting me and praying for me. We always manage to talk before every game I play."

Jones' outing in the 1996 series finale, at Ellis Park, was his 50th test. He doesn't consider that rugby gets easier the more experienced you are. "Unfortunately, experience equates to age. At thirty-plus, the body isn't as supple as when you're twenty, so everything is a little more demanding. Against that, you are more confident about making decisions."

The highlight of a memorable '96 season was winning the series in South Africa. What special qualities did he consider brought the All Blacks through? "They were the qualities epitomised in the last five minutes at Pretoria – discipline, character, desire and pride. We were a team of immense experience and not a little skill. We were supremely fit and we had license from our coach (John Hart) to attack from anywhere. It was a master stroke taking thirty-six players, because it allowed the test fifteen to focus totally on the four internationals."

Jones, who has a masters degree in geography and a Bachelors degree in town planning, works as the inbound tourist development manager for the Pacific Islands with Air New Zealand, when hs rugby commitments permit. He is married to Maliena.

John Kirwan

Ask New Zealand rugby's most prolific test tryscorer John Kirwan to nominate the most important decision he's made in his sporting career, and the answer comes unhesitatingly.

"Choosing to play league for the Warriors in 1995," he says. "Because it rejuvenated my career. Look, I'm still going. I'm off to Japan to play rugby for three years. I could have been two years out of sport now."

Kirwan is enormously relieved that the Warriors' chief executive, Ian Robson, chose to have a second go at convincing him to try league after he'd retired from rugby at the conclusion of the 1994 season.

"I'd had ten years at the top in rugby and when Laurie Mains made it apparent he didn't want me, I pulled the pin. I was going to concentrate on my family and my job. Rugby hadn't gone professional and I wasn't interested in league . . . I thought."

Enter Ian Robson in November 1994 with a proposal.

"He felt I had a future with the Warriors," says Kirwan. "I didn't. So I said thanks for calling, but the answer's no.

"Ian was hardly out the door before I realised I'd made a huge mistake. And every night after that I cursed and told myself I should have accepted his offer."

Fortunately for Kirwan, Robson came a-knocking again, three months later. This time he was just about bowled over by the great winger in his eagerness to sign up!

"I just wish I'd signed the first time," says Kirwan, "because it meant I then had to undergo a crash fitness course to try and get

John Kirwan

John Kirwan . . . his haul of 35 test tries is easily the record for an All Black.

myself ready for the 1995 season."

Kirwan would play two full seasons as a winger with the Warriors, finishing 1996 as the side's leading tryscorer.

League would change his ideology on football. He confessed in his book Running on Instinct that he played rugby purely for the love of the game and for the amusement value.

If you were tempted to compare Kirwan, as New Zealand rugby's leading tryscorer, with Sir Richard Hadlee, New Zealand cricket's leading wicket taker, you would place them at opposite ends of the spectrum in terms of goalsetting.

Hadlee knew exactly how many wickets he'd taken, and how many more were needed to surpass a particular milestone. He used those targets for motivation.

Kirwan admits he never had a clue how many tries he'd scored or how many tests he'd played, even though he would overtake two of the game's greatest achievers, Bryan Williams on the one hand and Colin Meads on the other.

But all that changed when he started playing league. Not because the new code varied so dramatically from rugby, but because suddenly he was a professional.

"That was the difference," he says. "I was a full time sportsman. It altered my attitude completely. I was being paid for performing – I was no longer out there just to amuse myself and entertain."

Kirwan had been paid for playing earlier in his career – during his off-seasons in Italy. But that was different. That was pocket money which allowed him to enjoy a different lifestyle in another country.

Far more serious amounts of money were involved when in early 1997 he headed for Japan and a contract as player-coach with the NEC club, a position previously held by Joe Stanley.

It represented an exciting new challenge for the fellow who started his working life as a butcher's apprentice (in his father's shop at Onehunga) but whose footballing talents would make him a household name throughout the rugby world.

There weren't too many pointers to JK's genius as a rugby player in the early days, although he did make the Auckland Roller Mills under 8st team. But at De La Salle College he was hidden away in the first XV at halfback, undergoing a startling transformation in 1980 when he grew 12 inches in the year.

John Kirwan

Ric Salizzo, the team's No. 8, who would become Kirwan's business partner (and the All Blacks' first media liaison officer), claimed he started the season with a dwarf behind him and finished it with a giant.

"I wouldn't say I rated as one of the greatest halfbacks," admits Kirwan now. "My passing was not the most consistent. The first-five used to say that catching my passes turned him into a gymnast!"

Growing so rapidly in one year would rebound on Kirwan in later life, leading to a condition called 'Sherman's Disease' which placed stress on the sciatic nerve and that in turn manifested itself in hamstring problems.

Kirwan's greater passion in those early days was for surfing. He still loves to ride the big ones but the opportunities for surfing were seriously eroded when his rugby career exploded into life.

After college, and employed in the butcher's shop, he played his rugby with the Auckland Marist club, being lured along by his brother-in-law John Ah Kuoi.

"It was," says Kirwan, "a great social year, one that really turned me on to rugby."

It was the fifth grade coach Peter Snedden, a former Auckland representative, who can take credit for converting Kirwan into a winger. "I wanted to play centre," says Kirwan, "but Snedden said, 'No, mate, get on the wing and just go for the corner. I've been doing that ever since.'"

Kirwan instantly excelled in the winger's role, demonstrating the pace, strength and skills that would soon dazzle opponents worldwide. Not surprisingly, he came to the attention of the under-18 selectors and donned the Auckland jersey that season.

The next year he automatically went up to the third grade from where he again represented Auckland at under-18 level. By now he was taking rugby more seriously, training harder, socialising less.

Unbeknown to Kirwan, his performances were creating excitement among astute rugby observers. One of these was Paul Little, a Marist club stalwart who had played 10 tests for the All Blacks in the early 1960s. Little telephoned the new Auckland coach, John Hart, and suggested he might like to take a look at an unusually talented player in the club's third grade team.

On his way to Eden Park one Saturday, Hart dropped in at Liston Park, Marist's home ground, and inconspicuously observed what he termed "a big, raw-boned winger." He was impressed.

So impressed that early in the 1983 season, when Kirwan, having rejected an invitation to join the Marist senior squad – "because I wasn't ready for it" – was still operating for the third grade side, he went along to have another look.

This time he took the former All Black winger, and former Auckland coach, Eric Boggs, with him. Although Kirwan received scant opportunities, Boggs saw enough to be impressed. "Take him," he said to Hart.

The rest, as they say, is history . . . spectacular, record-smashing, crowd-thrilling history.

Kirwan, just 18, was given a try-out in a Barbarians team stacked with Auckland representatives, faring well enough to clinch selection for Auckland's big centennial fixture at Eden Park against the President's XV (once Hart had cleared it with Kirwan's parents Pat and Patricia).

"It was," says Kirwan, "an incredible experience. Two weeks before I'd been sticking my head in a barrel of brine in the butcher's shop and going to third grade training and now here I was about to run on to Eden Park for Auckland against such great All Blacks as Andy Dalton, Mark Shaw, Stu Wilson and Dave Loveridge."

Kirwan pays a special tribute to Andy Haden for helping him adjust so rapidly. "He was like the Godfather of New Zealand rugby," says Kirwan. "He had a hard time when he first made the All Blacks for the 1972-73 tour of the UK and he was determined that wouldn't happen in teams with which he was subsequently associated."

Kirwan went well enough in his debut to secure the wing berth for the season, going on to save a try, in heroic circumstances, against the British Lions (in a game won 13-12) and emerging as the team's leading tryscorer.

One try that wasn't awarded was a spectacular effort in the Ranfurly Shield challenge against Canterbury at Lancaster Park, the touch judge ruling he'd put a foot in touch. Auckland lost that game 31-9, probably the low point in John Hart's coaching career. Two years later Hart and Kirwan would return and make amends in stunning fashion.

Kirwan credits Hart with teaching him self-analysis which he considers fundamental to success. "He taught me not to dwell on my mistakes but to acknowledge them, think about them and set about putting them right. There is little to be gained, he asserted, by focusing only on those things you do right."

Kirwan went on to play for the New Zealand Colts and North Island in 1983, narrowly missing selection in the All Black team to tour England and Scotland. Amazingly, considering the force that Hart's team would become the next season, there wasn't a solitary Aucklander in the touring party.

The coach, Bryce Rope, didn't make any apologies for that but was moved to issue a public statement concerning Kirwan. The selectors had considered him but felt that, at eighteen, he was too young.

If 18 was considered too tender, 19 was okay for the national selectors, especially after Kirwan had stolen the thunder in the 1984 trial match in Hamilton. In scoring a hat-trick of tries against Bernie Fraser, Kirwan was, according to the Rugby Annual, "magic – combining his skills of speed, strength and anticipation." The crowd gave him a standing ovation after his third try.

Kirwan's test selection, as the third youngest All Black (after Edgar Wrigley and Pat Walsh) was celebrated at the Marist clubrooms where Andy Haden told him that being an All Black was all very well, but being a good one was more important.

Thanks to Jean-Patrick Lescarboura, Kirwan launched his All Black career, one which would run a full decade, on a winning note. The French had the New Zealanders on toast at Lancaster Park but Lescarboura missed four dropped-goal attempts in the final six minutes, allowing the All Blacks to escape with a 10-9 victory.

The All Blacks took a lot of stick for their showing in Christchurch but made amends at Eden Park, beating the Frenchmen 31-18. Although Kirwan had yet to do what wingers are selected to do, score a try, he'd come through his introduction to international rugby impressively.

The tries would come well enough on the forthcoming tour of Australia. In theory, they would. In practice, they didn't. Because Kirwan lasted only 12 minutes of the tour, until the New South Wales winger Matt Burke (not the same one currently starring at fullback for Australia) flung him to the ground, dislocating the AC joint.

Following an X-ray at the next port of call, Adelaide, Kirwan underwent an operation, during which a screw was inserted, and was flown home to recover.

Fate works in cruel ways. His replacement in Australia, Bernie Fraser, ended up as leading tryscorer, with 14 touchdowns, while Terry Wright, who took his place at representative level, finished up scoring 19 tries, a record for an Aucklander in one season!

The All Black selectors inquired if Kirwan was available for the short tour of Fiji in October. Kirwan was eager but the doctors advised against it, suggesting he should wait until 1985. What an extraordinary year that would prove to be. It should have been the year the All Blacks toured South Africa, but politics intervened and the tour was cancelled.

In June of '85 Kirwan fulfilled a promise to his father, who the day before the first test against England in Christchurch had suffered a heart attack, by scoring a try in the rematch at Athletic Park. There would be 66 more before his illustrious All Black career wound down.

He headed the tryscoring count for Auckland that year, among the most valuable being his touchdown in the epic Ranfurly Shield encounter at Lancaster Park. Auckland needed every five-pointer that

One of the most famous and spectacular test tries ever scored – John Kirwan's 90 metre effort against Italy in the World Cup opener at Eden Park in 1987.

John Selkirk

afternoon, hanging on grimly to win 28-23, to end Canterbury's glorious reign.

Kirwan was one to benefit from the All Blacks' substitute tour to Argentina at season's end, bagging four tries in the two internationals in Buenos Aires. The satisfaction of those touchdowns would have to last some time because he failed to score any tries in six internationals in 1986.

From Argentina, Kirwan went to Benetton for his first taste of rugby Italian style. While there he fielded a call from All Black captain Andy Dalton who advised him the players had organised a rebel tour to South Africa. Was he available?

"I said no, for two reasons – I wasn't prepared to jeopardise my All Black career and my father was suffering from heart problems and I wanted to return home as soon as possible."

Kirwan linked up with several of the Cavaliers-to-be at the IRB centenary matches in the UK, finding conversation difficult with them. Brian Lochore, the frustrated All Black coach who had nothing to do with the Cavaliers, asked Kirwan if he was going to South Africa. He assured him he was not.

He and halfback David Kirk would be the only two original selections not to travel to South Africa. They would be replaced by Bernie Fraser and Andrew Donald.

"The decision not to become involved with the Cavaliers was entirely my own," says Kirwan. "There weren't many people I could turn to for advice. In the end, I acted on gut feeling. Something deep down inside me said, 'Don't go'.

"I have absolutely no regrets. It was probably the best business decision I've ever made, although business considerations didn't enter into it. As soon as the news of the tour and my non-participation broke, I was the golden-haired boy and the business started to flow in. An example was a TV ad for Carter Holt that Andy Haden was supposed to do."

Despite the lingering feeling of letting his teammates down, Kirwan says he would not have missed the Baby Blacks tests – particularly the one against France – for the world.

"The success of the Baby Blacks was the nicest thing about deciding not to go. Hearing Joe Stanley's name read out after mine when the team was announced to play France was also a real buzz."

Rugby Greats

Kirwan found the public support overwhelming . . . "probably because, for once, the All Blacks were the absolute underdogs. There was no parochialism at Lancaster Park. We were fifteen New Zealanders against the odds and the public was right behind us."

Kirwan says Brian Lochore was one of the few coaches who could have "made it happen" in the extraordinary circumstances that existed. "I guess," says Kirwan, "that he had had to make the same decision as I had about South Africa. It must have broken his heart to have the original tour cancelled and then witness almost his entire team take off as rebels."

Kirwan reflects on the Baby Blacks as "an incredibly tight unit", the like of which he has not experienced again. "Normally, a team will sort of spread out on the bus, the veterans in the back seat and so on, but on this occasion we all sat together in the front half of the bus."

Displaying great resolve and commitment, and not a little skill, the Baby Blacks defeated France 18-9, Mike Brewer scoring the game's only try after Kirwan had risen high to reclaim a Frano Botica 'bomb'.

The fairytale ended there. The Baby Blacks fully extended the Wallabies in Wellington, losing by a solitary point, but the inevitable happened, with the Cavaliers, their two-match suspensions completed, reclaiming their test positions.

Kirwan was named a player of the year in the Rugby Annual. It was said of him that, "He may not have scored many tries but he created more, and broke more tackles, than any other player in the land. Eden Park came alive in 1986 every time he touched the ball."

Kirwan describes the 1987 World Cup as "the sort of dream from which you never want to wake up". The All Blacks didn't just win the tournament, they demolished every opponent, scoring 43 tries while conceding just four.

"We had the hunger, the keenness and the pure, uncomplicated, undistracted will to win the World Cup," he says. "Nothing else mattered. We didn't just want to beat the other teams, we wanted to destroy them."

Kirwan finished with six tries (equal best with Craig Green), two of which remain vividly in the memory – the astonishing 100 metre effort in the tournament opener against Italy and the clincher in the final against France.

Kirwan himself singles out his covering tackle on Ieuan Evans in the semi-final against the Welsh at Ballymore as an event equally as satisfying as any of his tries.

The field-length effort against Italy was a follow-up of two equally spectacular long-range tries at Eden Park for Auckland in the South Pacific Championship series that preceded the World Cup.

Kirwan's stunner in the final was remarkable for the fact that early in the first half he felt his hamstring pull. "In other circumstances I might have come off," he says, "but never in a World Cup final."

With the adrenalin flowing, he admits he didn't feel a thing until he had plunged over in the corner for the try that put New Zealand 20 points ahead. "When I cooled down later I remember thinking I'd done the hammie a fair bit of damage."

It is not just enough to win a world crown, it must be defended worthily. And that's something the All Blacks did majestically from the moment of their triumph in the final at Eden Park in 1987.

Commencing with the World Cup successes, they went 50 games without defeat (which included 22 test wins) over the next three years, with an average winning score in excess of 40 points.

Kirwan flourished throughout this period, scoring 17 tries in 13 tests at one point and picking up a further five in two unofficial internationals in Japan. This despite suffering a crippling leg injury at Pontypool which invalided him out of the tour of Wales and Ireland. Well, that's not entirely accurate. Following an operation in Cardiff to repair his torn Achilles tendon, he was invited to remain on tour with the All Blacks, which he did, notwithstanding the difficulty of getting on and off buses and planes while on crutches.

Nothing is forever, of course, and the wheels of the All Black wagon, after loosening in 1990, sheered off at the second World Cup in the UK in 1991. After a series of muddling performances, in the Bledisloe Cup games and in pool play at the World Cup tournament, the All Blacks bombed out against Australia at Dublin.

"We weren't as hungry for success as in 1987," says Kirwan. "We were probably as fit but we'd become a little bit lazy and reluctant to put in that extra effort at training. I also think that as individuals and as a team we'd lost a bit of that physical hardness that other countries expect, and fear, in All Black teams. We weren't disciplining ourselves, making sacrifices, doing the little things that make a hard mind and a hard body.

"Two of the All Blacks' great strengths historically have been that sense of brotherhood within the team and the individual and collective pride in the silver fern and in representing New Zealand. There were times in 1991 when I felt we showed signs of slipping from those high standards. If one word sticks out in trying to establish what went wrong, that word is unhappiness. Perhaps the show had been on the road with the same cast for a year too long."

The disappointments of the World Cup were set aside a week later when, with a large gathering of All Blacks among the guests, Kirwan married Fiorella Tomasi in Italy.

The wedding was big news back in New Zealand. So was an interview Kirwan had given to Television New Zealand's Brendan Telfer which implied that if John Hart was not now appointed coach he would have second thoughts about playing for the All Blacks in 1992.

The comments created a furore back home, Kirwan claiming he was "set up".

In the event, Hart was not appointed coach for '92. He didn't even win a place on the selection panel, Laurie Mains getting the big job, with Earle Kirton and Peter Thorburn his assistants.

Kirwan did return for the new season and retained his place in the All Black squad, which was more than could be said for a few other senior players, most notably the test captain Gary Whetton and his brother Alan.

However, after one outing, against the World XV at Christchurch, a game the All Blacks lost rather ingloriously, Kirwan, for the first time in his international career, found himself dropped to the reserves bench.

"It was the first time I'd been available for a test and not selected," he says. "I know Laurie and the guys were wanting to experiment at that stage, but, to me, a test's a test, and you always select your best fifteen."

Kirwan was reinstated for the decider at Eden Park, which the All Blacks won well, and was a first-choice selection for the remainder of season, which featured the nailbiting series in Australia and the brilliant victory over the Springboks at Ellis Park.

He scored a stunning try against the Boks after linking with Frank Bunce and running off him at an angle. It was a move they'd perfected at training. It hoisted Kirwan's aggregate of tries for New Zealand to

66, equalling Bryan Williams' record. But it would be 23 months before he claimed the record for himself.

After failing to score against the Lions, the Wallabies and the Western Samoans in 1993 he was sensationally dropped for the tour of England and Scotland.

"Ironically, my axing came a week after I'd scored eight tries for Auckland in a Ranfurly Shield game against North Otago," says Kirwan. "The selectors' decision came out of the blue. People were saying I hadn't been playing well, but I didn't think that. The dropping came as a huge shock."

Kirwan, approaching his 29th birthday, considered he still had plenty of rugby in him. So while the All Blacks were overseas he plunged into a furious training regime which had him fighting fit for the new season.

He demonstrated his readiness by scoring two tries, and starring, in a trial at Napier. Another star that night was 19-year-old Jonah Lomu. They would team together in the two tests against France, both of which would be lost.

Lomu was sacrificed but Kirwan survived for the series against the touring Springboks, getting the try in the first test at Carisbrook that would finally see him eclipse Beegee Williams' record.

He admits that the significance of the try means more now than it did at the time. "I didn't focus on milestones like Sir Richard Hadlee, I just played for enjoyment. Maybe I should have set goals, but at the time that try meant everything to the team, not to me. After the losses to France, we were under enormous pressure. It's horrible to play under that pressure, so I saw that try at Carisbrook as 'saving arse' not establishing a record."

He was promptly dropped for the Bledisloe Cup test in Sydney, declining Mains' offer to accompany the team as a reserve.

"It was obvious I didn't feature in Laurie's World Cup plans so, after undergoing a knee operation to remove bone chips, at the end of the season, I retired.

"I felt at the age of thirty I'd achieved everything there was to achieve in rugby and that I should now devote myself to my job (with Targetti Lighting) and to my family."

That philosophy survived until Ian Robson invited him, a second time, to become a Warrior, which he did.

Rugby Greats

He thoroughly enjoyed his two seasons in league. There was a fair league pedigree to start with, of course, for his grandfather Jack had played for the Kiwis in the 1920s and later coached at Auckland Marist.

In rugby, Kirwan knew the touchline was always the winger's friend. In league, he quickly learned the touchline was his enemy, yielding possession to the opposition. "Run into touch and you are quickly subbed off in league," says Kirwan. "It was a painful lesson I absorbed pretty quickly!"

The other situation he took a while to adjust to was running the ball back hard after fielding a kick. "In rugby, you naturally looked for teammates to link with, if you weren't going to slam the ball into touch. In league, it was all about running hard and straight and retaining possession."

Kirwan became a favourite of the fans at Ericsson Stadium, as he had at Eden Park, but after two years, and with his contract not renewable, he refocused on rugby, which had gone professional in his absence, after receiving an offer "too good to refuse" from NEC in Japan.

He, his wife Fiorella and children Francesca and Niko were off to Abiko, near Tokyo, in February 1997, his sporting career still very much alive.

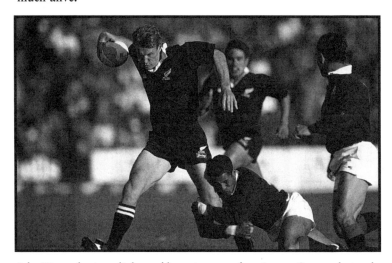

John Kirwan having a little trouble getting away from Jeremy Guscott during the series against the British Lions in 1993.   Neil McKenzie (Photosport)

Jonah Lomu

The scene was the National Stadium in Hong Kong during the 1994 international sevens tournament. The youngest member of the New Zealand team, 18-year-old Jonah Lomu, was sitting next to his hero Eric Rush watching the action.

Who should plant himself down beside Lomu but the celebrated Wallaby winger David Campese, captain of the Australian sevens team.

"Hello, Jonah," he said, "how are you?"

"Er, good thanks," replied Lomu rather bashfully.

Lomu turned to Rush. "Hey, Eric, David Campese knows me."

"Good," replied Rush, unphased by Campo's arrival.

Lomu, however, was awestruck. "Wow, a legend knows my name. What a buzz!"

About an hour later Lomu found himself opposing Campese in the final of the tournament. More than that, he'd been put in the clear by Rush, and who was the only person barring his passage to the goalline? David Campese.

"I remember thinking, 'Here comes the great Campo, the greatest winger in rugby. What am I going to do? The moment will stay vividly with me for the rest of my life. It was the first time I had confronted a great opponent, someone I'd marvelled at on television.

"All I could think of was that I had the greater body weight. I would use it."

Campese tried valiantly to stop Lomu but the odds against him were almost insurmountable. He was conceding 30kg (not to mention a dozen years) to the stampeding Tongan.

Lomu scored his try, dragging the helpless Campese across the line with him, and the New Zealanders went on to claim the title.

Lomu was operating on the wing at Hong Kong because the coach Gordon Tietjens had had a request from the New Zealand selectors to use him there.

"Gee, I was green at the time," admits Lomu, then five months out of school. "I was really scared to have a go because I was lacking in confidence. It was Rushy, as much as anyone, who got me thinking positively. He told me I had to be a leader, that I had to lead myself into battle."

The fact Lomu had played all his rugby to that point at lock or No. 8 didn't matter hugely at Hong Kong because sevens is played at such a frenetic pace with everyone backing up everyone else.

But within three months, after just two outings for Counties and a successful trial, Lomu would make his test debut – as a winger against France, the youngest All Black test player in history.

Little surprise he was bewildered and exploited by the foxy French, then dropped by the selectors, a test reject at the age of 19.

The Lomu story could have fizzled out there, if he'd been a quitter or taken any of the easier options offering. But Jonah Tali Lomu was determined to come back, fired by a burning desire to be not just an All Black but a good All Black.

There would be a share of dramas before Lomu returned to the All Blacks 11 months on. When he did, he would assert himself as much more than the good All Black he wanted to me. He would emerge as a sporting colossus, a phenomenal achiever who would have the world's media grasping for superlatives to describe his exploits.

Five appearances at the World Cup would catapult him to stardom. He would become contracted to two of the world's corporate giants, Reebok and McDonalds (even having a hamburger named after him), and find himself an international celebrity.

Not bad for a kid who grew up on the wrong side of the tracks and was put on detention within two hours of starting college.

The Jonah Lomu story is a remarkable one.

It began in a place about as remote as you can possibly get from the great international rugby stadiums of the world, in Ha'apai, one of Tonga's small outer islands.

Jonah Lomu

Jonah Lomu . . . a test reject at 19 who would come back to dazzle the sporting world in 1995.   John Selkirk

Rugby Greats

That's where little (if that adjective ever applied, because he was almost 6kg born) Jonah first began to sample life, in a beautifully uncomplicated Pacific Islands way.

Having been taken to Ha'apai by his parents Semisi and Hepi when he was one, he spent most of his time as an infant on the beach, becoming known as The Water Rat by his friends. He was brought up "the Polynesian way" by his mother's sister.

"Until the age of seven when the family returned to Auckland, I virtually lived on the beach," says Lomu. "If I was thirsty, I would climb a palm tree and bring a coconut down and drink the milk. If I was hungry, there were chickens running wild which we would catch, pluck and roast on a fire.

"It was a basic lifestyle on Ha'apai because there was no electricity, no sealed roads, not much at all really. Cooking was done underground. But it was a wonderful place to grow up – I lived on the beach."

The Lomu family departed Ha'apai the day before a hurricane devastated the island. It was probably just as well, for Jonah's uncle's house was blown across to the other side of the island.

Jonah's schooling back in Auckland thus didn't begin until he was seven by which time he had the build of a 10-year-old.

"My size instantly became an embarrassment," he says. "At every sports event, I was challenged about my age. So from the age of seven or eight I took to carrying my passport to save arguments!"

When he was eight, Lomu was invited by his friends to try his hand at league, fitting in effectively with the Manukau Magpies. He made sufficient impact to be invited along to an Auckland trial.

Problem. It was on a Sunday and Jonah's parents' strong Methodist affiliations militated against sport on Sunday. He said he was unavailable.

But when he was selected for another trial a month or so later, he decided to get shrewd, inviting himself across to his cousins on the Saturday evening so he could play. The inevitable happened – he was selected as an Auckland age grade representative.

"But guess what?" says Jonah. "Yep, the rep game was on a Sunday. So that was that."

Fortunately for rugby, Sunday scheduling consistently frustrated Lomu's attempts to play representative league. And he was stymied, once and for all, when, at 13, his mother packed him off to Wesley College, a Methodist boarding school near Pukekohe.

Mrs Lomu had recognised that her son was developing undesirably aggressive tendencies. He was the quickest tempered of her children and it was a trait she felt needed straightening out.

Lomu explains that his aggressive nature had much to do with the environment in which he grew up, the 'jungle' attitude that existed in south Auckland.

Both his uncle Dave Fukoa and one of his best friends Danny Sekona were knifed to death in what amounted to revenge attacks by ethnic groups.

"There was a lot of violence in the neighbourhood where I lived which impacted on me" says Lomu. "When I was attending intermediate school, if you didn't know how to fight, you got beaten up.

"You had to stand up against the bigger guys. Fortunately, I had size on my side. Instead of becoming hardnosed and fair, I would hit guys and ask questions later. It reached a point where if anyone looked threateningly at me, I would whack them!"

When Lomu started behaving aggressively towards the family, his mother became concerned. She could see her son finishing up like his uncle. That's when she decided decisive action was called for, and she enrolled her emerging giant at Wesley College.

Within two hours of starting school he was on detention!

A seventh former made the mistake of calling him a "turd" when he pushed into the wrong line. Now that might have been an entirely appropriate thing to say to 99 per cent of the green-as-grass third formers at Wesley College that morning. But it had entirely the wrong effect on Jonah Lomu, who at 1.83m and 96kg was undoubtedly the largest boy among the new intake.

"I began beating the crap out of him," says Jonah, "until my cousin pulled me off him. It was a record for a detention at Wesley, less than two hours."

From that moment, Lomu confesses he began to mellow, for which Wesley's principal Chris Grinter can take a huge amount of the credit.

"He recognised that I had trouble controlling my temper," says Lomu, "so he set up a punching bag in the gymnasium and gave me a key.

Rugby Greats

"'Whenever you feel angry,' he told me, 'you let yourself into the gym and take it out on the punching bag, instead of on your schoolmates'.

"I used it many times. On one occasion, I was so wild, I ripped the punching bag clean off its chain! When Chris Grinter saw the damage the next day, he commented that 'at least it's serving its purpose!'"

Thanks to Wesley's principal and the people who would guide his destiny in rugby, Lomu has entirely eliminated anger from his personality. "I came to realise that displays of temper achieved nothing, that they only reflected badly on me. Now, if someone tries to provoke me, I laugh at them. Instead of retaliating, I make them the fool."

Grinter, who had coached the great 1987 New Zealand secondary schools team to Japan (the one that featured John Timu, Craig Innes, Walter Little, Va'aiga Tuigamala, Jasin Goldsmith, Jason Hewett, Pat Lam and Jamie Joseph – All Blacks all) soon appreciated that in Lomu he had an extraordinarily gifted sportsman.

When he saw Lomu, as a fourth former, nonchalantly slam dunking while playing basketball, he asked him if he wanted to play rugby (which, it should be stressed, was the only football game played at Wesley). Lomu said yes, but emphasised that he had, until that point, only ever played league.

Grinter was unconcerned, putting him on the reserves bench for the first XV's next game. After three weeks observing, Grinter got him involved in the second half of a game, at lock.

"I played out of my skin," says Lomu, "because I wanted to impress the coach. Obviously I did, because the next week I was in the starting line-up."

He would not be displaced until he completed his schooling in the seventh form. But it wasn't all plain sailing because Lomu's league instincts stayed with him for a while. "I wouldn't let go of the ball, even when there were guys standing all over me. I've got some pretty good scars to show how long it was before I got league out of my system!"

Lomu took to rugby with a passion. "I quickly grew to love it and became dedicated to it." Mind you, he started his rugby career as part of an uncommonly good schoolboy team, Wesley in 1990 winning what was to become known as the Top Four competition, beating

Jonah Lomu

Gisborne Boys' High in the final in Invercargill, fielding a forward eight heavier than the current All Black pack. Lomu, who scored a try in the final, was one of four forwards weighing more than 100kg!

Lomu's dedication startled his schoolmates, particularly when he started running up and down the rugby field alternately pushing and pulling the heavy roller which usually remained idle until needed to flatten out pitches in the cricket season.

"I think the guys thought I was a bit loopy when I began working out with the roller," says Lomu, "but when I started to excel, a few of them began turning up in the mornings, asking if they could have a turn!"

Lomu channelled the aggression which had become such a concern for those who knew him into his sport. But now it was a controlled aggression. "If I said I didn't undergo a personality change, I'd be lying," he says. "And rugby had a lot to do with that. Through rugby I learnt about discipline, on and off the field."

Lomu began making waves as a rugby player and one who was hugely impressed, in 1991 when Lomu was a fifth former, was Eric Rush. "After I'd stepped him in a touch tournament and he couldn't catch me, he invited me to Singapore to play sevens. What an invitation for a schoolboy. Of course, I said yes!"

Rush's team, playing as the Mongrels, won the tournament. This was the event, vividly described in Frank Bunce and Walter Little's biography Midfield Liaison, at which the incorrigible Lindsay Raki, asked by a local official to identify the New Zealand team's outstanding individual to become the recipient of the prestigious player of the tournament trophy, nominated himself (and he'd only been a reserve). He had the audacity to go on stage and receive it, feigning humility as he began his acceptance speech with . . . "I don't deserve this!"

Lomu is enormously grateful to Rush for giving him first big break. "Rushy's a master of sevens. He's a great teacher of the game, making it sound so simple and uncomplicated. He knows all the tricks of the trade. Rushy taught me heaps about becoming bigger and stronger, about running faster, about beating opponents.

"Mind you, he also jerks all the young guys. He gave me two minutes' notice before I had to make the thank you speech on behalf of the New Zealand guys at the High Commission in Suva after a

Rugby Greats

Jonah Lomu runs in one of his four tries during the All Blacks' incredible blitzing of England at Cape Town during the 1995 World Cup.   John Selkirk

sevens tournament there."

Lomu's awesome mix of pace, power and athleticism began impressing more than just Eric Rush. Word that he was something special began spreading and in 1991 he locked the scrum (with Andrew Blowers) in the New Zealand under-17 team that blew Australia away, 25-nil, in Hamilton.

He felt immense pride at wearing the black jersey. "I remember thinking, if this is what playing for the under-17s feels like, imagine what it would be like playing for New Zealand schools and the All Blacks."

He wouldn't have to wait long to find out. The next year, having turned 17, he represented New Zealand schools against Ireland at New Plymouth and on a three-match tour of Australia.

All matches were won, the Irish game in nailbiting manner, 27-25, after Jeff Wilson slotted a difficult 45-metre penalty goal as the final act of the game. "I'll never forget it," says Lomu. "The Irish guys slumped to the turf, many of them in tears. Our guys meanwhile were screaming with joy. I remember lifting Jeff up in my excitement. He was definitely 'Goldie' from that moment. The incredible thing is that his kick went in a huge arc. The only time it looked like going over was when it got to the posts!"

The wins in Australia were far more clearcut. With Wilson electrifying the team from fullback, Carlos Spencer running things from first-five, the 2.00 metre Chresten Davis dominating the lineouts and Lomu leading raids from No. 8, the New Zealanders ran up scores of 112 and 65 before hammering Australia 31-8 under lights in Sydney.

Lomu chuckles about the century scoreline in Melbourne. "We felt sorry for the opposition and one guy in particular who tried his heart out. We decided he deserved a reward, so we deliberately fell off our tackles when he next got the ball, presenting him with a clear run to the goalline, which made the final score 112-5.

"The problem was next day our coach Clive Williams expressed concern that our tackling had been sub-standard and ordered a rugged session with car tyres!"

Lomu's performance in the test against Australian schools brought him to the attention of league scouts for the first time. The Canterbury Bulldogs were prepared to pay $100,000 for him. "It seemed an outrageous amount at the time," the club's president has since remarked. "If only we'd realised his true potential, we could have gone to one million dollars."

The schools team of '93, with Lomu still at No. 8, was even more potent than before and demolished England 51-5 at Carisbrook and Australia 32-7 at Rotorua, Lomu scoring three tries in the two games and terrorising the English, in particular, with his powerhouse running.

He remembers the English behaving condescendingly at a mayoral reception in Dunedin. "We were there to mix and mingle," says Lomu, "but they were playing mind games with a bunch of Polynesian kids. Not smart. They gave us all the motivation we needed, and we went out and wasted them."

Lomu labels an incident in the England international as one of the funniest of his rugby career.

"We possessed a huge set of loose forwards in Isitolo 'The Hitman' Maka, Duncan Blaikie, Andrew Blowers (who was used as a reserve) and myself," recalls Lomu. "We were all well over six feet tall and weighing in at more than 100kg.

"Well, England's number eight came around the openside, saw Duncan and me, went oops! and decided the blindside might be the better option. But there he ran into Isitolo, and there followed this bloodcurdling groan as Isi picked him up and dumped him! I felt sorry for him and started pumping air into him, as play moved on."

Lomu at that stage of his development regarded No. 8 as his favourite position. "I always thought I would specialise in that position or as a blindside flanker. But that all went out the window when I got to the sevens in Hong Kong the next season."

Lomu relished the Hong Kong experience. "I was overwhelmed by it all, having never played in front of such a vast crowd. It was an incredible experience, and we all responded well to Rushy's leadership and inspiration.

"It was during the Hong Kong tournament that Lomu first sensed that All Black honours could lay ahead for him, when coach Tietjens told him the selectors were looking at him as a winger.

"When you hear something like that," he says, "you take notice. I was thrilled to be involved with the national sevens team and regarded the All Black jersey as the next target. I'd have to say I didn't think it would come quite so soon."

The All Black coach of the time, Laurie Mains, says the selectors realised the potential of Lomu as a winger after watching him in action at the national provincial sevens tournament in Palmerston North that year. "He was an extraordinarily talented young footballer. Looking ahead to the World Cup, he was exactly the kind of player we wanted to develop – as a winger, not a lock or a number eight."

Va'aiga Tuigamala had gone to league, Jeff Wilson, the find of the All Black tour of Scotland and England in 1993, was carrying an injury and John Timu was concentrating on the fullback berth, leaving an opening on the wing for the series against France.

Mains approached the then Counties coach Ross Cooper and asked him if he would mind playing Lomu on the wing, a position, to that point, totally foreign to him.

"Who would be capable of stopping him, if he was given room to move?" asked Mains. He would later reflect that the All Black midfield at the time – missing Walter Little who was injured – was not good enough to create the necessary opportunities to get Lomu firing.

Cooper was happy to meet the selectors' wishes and played Lomu on the wing against Horowhenua and Hawkes Bay. "While he was lethal with the ball in hand," recalls Cooper, "he was, understandably, struggling with the defensive requirements of the new position. He didn't know when to move forward, when to drop back. There was a lot of publicity given to the fact he scored three tries at Levin in his representative debut, but in the same game he let Horowhenua in for two tries."

Cooper didn't play Lomu next up against Manawatu – despite extreme pressure from local officials who saw him as drawcard – but instead arranged for Hugh Blair, a champion tryscorer for Manawatu in the 1970s, to sit with him and explain the finer points of wing play.

After a bold showing in the trial match in Napier, Lomu was selected for the series against France, taking the field at Lancaster Park aged 19 years and 45 days, making him the youngest test All Black (by 32 days).

What should have been an experience to treasure became a nightmare for the teenager. His attacking opportunities were minimal, his defensive shortcomings were crudely exposed by the French, the All Blacks lost both tests (a miserable first against France) and he was dropped for the series against the Springboks.

"While it was a huge thrill to be wearing the black jersey," says Lomu, "I really didn't know what to do. I had this primal fear and the French found me out."

While Lomu admits it was a perplexing experience, he wasn't too disenchanted. "I realised I wasn't ready for test match play as a winger. But having tasted international rugby, I wanted more. I was determined to apply apply myself and to get back."

After the French tests, Lomu asked Phil Kingsley-Jones, the Counties coaching co-ordinator with whom he'd become extremely close, if he would become his manager. Kingsley-Jones agreed and Lomu said he would prepare a contract. "How much do you want – ten per cent?" asked Lomu.

"I want something more than that," said Kingsley-Jones.

"Twenty per cent?"

"I want more than that."

"How about forty per cent?"

Rugby Greats

"I want more than that."

"I couldn't do better than fifty per cent."

"Jonah, I don't want your money. I'll be your manager if you give me your next All Black test jersey."

Lomu offered one of the jerseys he'd played in against France.

"No, Jonah, listen carefully. I want your next All Black test jersey. That'll make me the happiest man on earth."

It can be recorded here that following the opening encounter against Ireland at the World Cup in 1995, Lomu presented Kingsley-Jones with his jersey.

The Jonah Lomu comeback saga has been well documented and doesn't need to be repeated here. Sufficient to say, he began to learn the winger's trade with Counties, making nine appearances in '94 and finishing up as the team's leading tryscorer. He also featured when the New Zealand Colts defeated their Australian counterparts at the Sydney Football Stadium.

Although there was a brief suggestion he might revert to the forwards, after scoring a hat-trick of tries for New Zealand Barbarians in a much publicised end-of-season charity match at Ericsson Stadium, Laurie Mains and his fellow selectors had firm plans for him as a winger at the World Cup . . . if he could survive the summer training camps!

Taupo was the most brutal of the camps. Some individuals, like Mark Cooksley and Waisake Sotutu, failed to measure up and were released from the squad. There were many who thought Lomu would suffer the same fate as he laboured through the 150-metre sprints.

The breakthrough came on the World Cup road show, when the players travelled by double decker bus from Invercargill in the south to Whangarei in the north.

Most players were expected to give five days to the road show. Laurie Mains told Lomu he was on tour for 10 days.

"All I did was train," says Lomu. "Martin Toomey (the All Blacks' trainer) was with us, overseeing all the sessions. The most 150s I'd managed before then was nineteen. By the end of the road show, I was up to thirty-four, and almost enjoying them!"

A crisis point in Lomu's career came when a Television Three journalist mischievously ran a 'story' in their main news bulletin claiming that Lomu was no longer in contention for the World Cup.

Jonah Lomu

*Another try coming up for Jonah Lomu at the 1995 World Cup – this one against
Scotland in the quarter-final at Pretoria.*   *John Selkirk*

It had a devastating effect on Lomu who, by chance, was watching the
TV3 news that evening.

"It just hit me – splat!" he says. "Appearing as a major news item
like that, you had to presume there was a strong basis of truth. I
wanted to go to the World Cup more than anything, but here I was
being told I was being written off."

Lomu went walkabout, and at about 4am telephoned Kingsley-
Jones. "He was crying," says Kingsley-Jones. "and in a terrible state.
He said he was ready to go to league. I assured him Laurie Mains
would never make a statement like that, that I'd been in constant
touch with him. I told Jonah to put it out of his mind and get down
to Dunedin for the North-South game. Fortunately, he went."

After the road show and the Hong Kong sevens – where he was
named player of the tournament – Lomu was, in a word, "fizzing",
particularly when he arrived in Hamilton for the Harlequins (the All
Blacks in disguise) game against Waikato. "I'd never been so fit, it was
incredible how I was suddenly getting around the field. By then, I
wanted to be in the All Blacks so badly. I wanted to show I had the
heart and determination of everyone else. I was prepared to give my
right arm to get my All Black jersey back."

Rugby Greats

Lomu says he was "almost a nervous wreck" by the time the 26-man party was named in Whangarei for the World Cup. "When my name was read out, I wanted to jump up and down. I was an All Black again! Then I realised there were guys around me who hadn't made it. It's one of the things you learn when you become an All Black – remaining humble whether you're winning or losing. But I still wanted to jump up and down!"

Lomu departed New Zealand ostensibly as the second choice left winger to Marc Ellis who'd played the test against Canada. But it was Lomu in the No. 11 jersey against Ireland for the All Blacks' World Cup opener.

He sat in the dressing room for fully 20 minutes cradling his jersey in his arms, gazing at the silver fern. "I almost cried, I'd been waiting so long to pull the All Black jersey back on," he says.

"As kick-off time approached, and I donned the jersey, I tensed up. Would I be able to produce the goods on the field? I remember Earle Kirton coming across and commenting that I'd got my chance. 'Was I ready?' 'Yep.' 'Sure?' 'Yep.' Fortunately, he turned away and didn't see me throw up in the bin in the corner!"

Lomu was ready, all right. He was a sensation against Ireland, also against Wales and performed heroics again, in the quarter-final, against Scotland.

But his most incredible performance came in the semi-final against England at Newlands when he scored four tries and made Tony Underwood's life pure hell.

He admits he didn't sleep a wink the night before. "I stayed awake the whole night, I was so nervous. I played the whole game the next day on adrenalin."

Of his own performance, he remembers only the first try, the ugly pass from Glen Osborne, turning and going outside Underwood, having his ankles clipped by Will Carling and trying to keep his balance as he went at, and over, Mike Catt.

"That's honestly all I remember of my play. Everything else was a haze, apart from a bit of verbal sparring with Tony Underwood. He said he was going to run around me. I said, 'Come on, let's see you go.' When he did get a chance, I flung him across the touchline and said, 'Is that the best you can do?'

"I remember Zinny's dropped goal, Robin's up and under and

Jonah Lomu

Fitzy's words of encouragement, but little else. When we got to the dressing room, I remember Laurie Mains saying, 'What the hell have you been on, boy?'"

Lomu prefers not to recall the World Cup grand final which he describes as "one immense disappointment". "We had the worst possible preparation, being all ill. In the circumstances, I'm surprised we got as close to the Springboks as we did.

"One memory that stays with me, though, is Walter Little's pass which the referee (Ed Morrison) ruled forward. To me, it was not forward. But that's part of the game – it happened.

"Losing the final has given me another goal. As Zinny said when he returned to South Africa the next year . . . the All Blacks had unfinished business."

For his achievements in 1995, Lomu would become the first recipient of the Kel Tremain Memorial Trophy as the New Zealand player of the year. He also received the award as the best sevens player.

If Lomu's rugby was awesome, ponder for a moment his appetite. When he first entered the All Blacks it was not uncommon for him to have 14 eggs (boiled) for breakfast.

Lunch was often taken at McDonalds: Six Big Macs, two hamburgers, a 20 piece box of chicken nuggets, two large milk shakes and a Coke!

Dinner: "Well," says Jonah, "I'd eat for hours. In restaurants, people would be going up for their first helping, and I would have finished my third."

His favourite food, he confesses, is chop suey, corned beef and taro. "Mum used to make chop suey in a huge pot which she'd ladle out into salad bowls for us."

His diet is a little more under control these days. "I still eat large portions but spread the meals out more evenly. And I'm big into salads now."

Lomu, sadly, wouldn't recapture the lofty heights of his World Cup displays in 1996, but there were extenuating circumstances. Having never had a major injury in his life, he tore the medial ligament of the left knee in the first international against Scotland.

Rested at Eden Park, he did further damage in the cold and mud against Australia in Wellington, this time tearing cartilage and the lateral ligaments, which caused his knee to swell up "like a melon".

Pumping himself up for more onfield heroics – John Lomu working out at the gymnasium during the 1995 World Cup in South Africa.   John Selkirk

The knee would plague him throughout the remainder of the season and cause him to miss all four internationals in South Africa in August.

But it didn't stop he and Eric Rush leading a stirring haka from the reserves bench at the conclusion of the Pretoria test after Fitzpatrick's men, with their victory, had become the first All Black team to win a series on South African soil.

Back home, Lomu declined surgery on the knee, preferring to let nature take its course. "I've seen a lot of players undergo knee surgery," he says, "and not many heal one hundred per cent. I preferred to rest the leg and strengthen the muscles around the knee with exercises."

The knee recovered in time for Lomu to play for the Barbarians at Twickenham in December, while the warm-up game at Huddersfield provided the first occasion on which he has seen snow falling. "Boy, it was cold there," he says. "Alama Ieremia stood with his hands under his arms and kept calling miss-passes that went straight to me!"

His journey to the UK was via Kimberley in South Africa where he went through a second wedding ceremony with Tanya Rutter, whom

Jonah Lomu

he had met at Bloemfontein during the World Cup in 1995. Their first marriage, a more secretive affair, had taken place in New Zealand at the beginning of the year.

Hopes of a spectacular Lomu comeback in 1997 were dashed when he was found to be suffering from nephrotic syndrome, a rare disease of the kidneys, the obvious symptoms of which are swollen ankles, puffy face and general lethargy.

In January he was prescribed a six month course of drugs, designed at having him back in action mid-year.

Andrew Mehrtens

In the spare room of the house where Andrew Mehrtens lived at the rural Maori community of Tuahiwi in north Canterbury as a young schoolboy was a large chest.

In the chest were two black jerseys that he would come to treasure. Both bore the silver fern.

The one was a 1928 All Black jersey belonging to his grandfather George, the other a New Zealand Juniors jersey which his father had worn against the Springboks in 1965.

"There was something mystical about them," says Mehrtens, who would go on to achieve the test status that had eluded his father and his grandfather. "I would often take them out, look at them with fascination and finger the silver ferns.

"It's funny, I never put them on, because they just seemed so special. There was an aura about them. I remember being intrigued by the number one on the back of the All Black jersey, which was the number the fullback wore in those days."

Young Mehrtens, who would come to be known as 'the skinny little white kid', never knew his grandfather who died at the age of 47. But George Mehrtens, a builder, had played three times for the All Blacks in 1928. Although they were a second string selection, with the best 30 players away in South Africa, the side he represented included two of the nation's most famous players, Bert Cooke and Cliff Porter. Grandfather Mehrtens, a fullback, wore the black jersey twice against New South Wales and once against West Coast-Buller.

Terry Mehrtens, Andrew's dad, didn't get to play for his country

Andrew Mehrtens

Andrew Mehrtens with his father Terry. The one is a celebrated All Black, the other represented New Zealand Juniors 30 years ago.   Joanna Caird (Photosport)

but was obviously in the selectors' minds, for twice they selected him for New Zealand Juniors sides, as a first-five against the Springboks in 1965 and against Taranaki two years later when he came on as a replacement for Grahame Thorne.

He was in celebrated company on the second occasion at New Plymouth. From that particular Juniors team came several All Blacks, Ian Kirkpatrick, Peter Whiting, Graham Williams, Gerald Kember (whom he would oppose at international level in 1970), John Dougan, Bill Currey and Thorne.

Operating mostly at first-five, but occasionally at fullback, Terry Mehrtens never achieved regular selection in the Canterbury team, being kept out by All Black Bruce Watt.

Although the national selectors obviously identified the potential in him, the Canterbury selectors never did. He was given only six outings in the A team over six seasons, all at first-five. There would be a dozen appearances for the B team.

So early in 1970, married and having long abandoned hopes of representing his country, Mehrtens headed for South Africa. Rugby wasn't the purpose of this great adventure, although within a few weeks of his arrival in Durban he would be playing for Natal.

Rugby Greats

Terry Mehrtens and his wife Sandra (no, she's not South African, as many rugby writers have claimed since Andrew became an All Black – she was born in Kaiapoi) set off for South Africa to see the game reserves.

"That was the battle plan," he says. "We were a couple of schoolteachers intending to spend a year away to check out as many game reserves as we could. Well, we finished up living there for five years and returned home only after Andrew was born. We both taught and enjoyed a great lifestyle."

The Mehrtens' were met as they stepped off the ship at Durban by another Kiwi, who'd also played rugby in the 1960s for Canterbury, Peter Hatchwell. And also in town was Mehrtens' best man Ken Sampson.

"Before I knew what was happening, Peter had me down training with the Berea-Rovers club," says Mehrtens senior, "and next thing we were both turning out for Natal which in those days was a second division union."

The highlight for Mehrtens was to appear at fullback against the 1970 All Blacks. Mehrtens' opposite was Gerald Kember, his teammate from the Juniors trial match three years earlier. "Thank God it wasn't Fergie McCormick at the other end," says Mehrtens, "he'd have been a handful!"

Andrew Phillip Mehrtens was born at Durban on April 28, 1973, and when only a few months old made the long trek to New Zealand with his parents who settled at Tuahiwi, a tiny rural community.

It would be 22 years before their son would pull on the All Black jersey but there were many signs, even in his infancy, that he was unusually talented.

His father recalls his obsession with kicking. "He had this brown plastic ball we gave him and as a two-year-old he could kick it over the schoolhouse fence.

"To be honest, he was a blessed nuisance. I'd come home from school after a hard day, looking forward to a quiet cup of tea and Andrew would insist on dragging me outside to kick the ball to him.

"He was the despair of his mother when he was at intermediate school after we moved to Kaiapoi – I hate to think how many shrubs he ruined kicking the ball. The rugby ground was only about eighty metres away, but he insisted on practising his footy on the back lawn!"

Andrew Mehrtens

Mehrtens senior says the one virtue he stressed to his young prodigy was the need to kick with both feet. "He was never that strong kicking with his left foot, although he's got better, but he can get prodigious distance with his right foot."

Mehrtens senior exits this chapter on a forlorn note. Still playing rugby at 38, his career was terminated for him by guess who? He who would become an All Black, and an impish prankster, whipped the chair away from under his father one evening.

In yielding heavily to gravity, Terry Mehrtens so damaged his shoulder it required an operation. "Get him out of here!" he remembers saying as he lay groaning on the floor, his rugby career in tatters.

"I've never forgiven him for that," he says, with a twinkle in his eye. "It didn't cure him. He still tries to crash tackle me into the corner when he calls in at home."

Andrew Mehrtens remembers barbecues at Tuahiwi when his father's South African friends called in during the rumbustious events of 1981 when the Springboks toured.

"I was always proud of the fact that I was born in South Africa," he says. "It made me feel slightly different, as a consequence of which I was a full-on supporter of the tour in '81. I hated Hart and Minto and anyone who tried to interfere with the tour."

The young Mehrtens wanted to be a halfback and a goalkicker. "I was able to satisfy half of my ambition because there weren't usually many kids who wanted to kick. I'd always make it known I was a kicker before volunteers were called for!"

Although lightweight, his natural skills, and his goalkicking, ensured that he made representative teams regularly in North Canterbury from the age of eight through until he moved into the city to attend Christchurch Boys' High School. A cracked collarbone kept him out of the Canterbury under-16 team for the South Island tournament.

Mehrtens was to play only one season in the Christchurch Boys' High first XV, 1990, and from all accounts it was the worst year in the history of the school's rugby team! "We managed to lose every one of our traditional matches," he says. "I don't know that we were that bad, all the other teams just seemed to be fired up."

In August of '90, Mehrtens undertook his first overseas trip in the cause of rugby – to Argentina with the college team. "We had a great time, visiting places like Cordoba, Rosario and Buenos Aires. The rugby was sometimes bizarre, with the Argentinian backs seeming to run in arcs most of the time, but it was a mighty experience."

Chosen as a reserve for Canterbury schools, Mehrtens didn't rate himself as an accomplished first-five when he was 17. "I had a bit of speed but because I was so light I always felt vulnerable," he says. "I wasn't prepared to have a go. It took a while before I had the confidence to run. It was something I had to work at."

Mehrtens describes himself at that stage as being better as "an organiser and a kicker" than a runner.

The next year, when he attended University, his rugby career began to take off, predictably at the expense of his studies. Finding it hard to apply himself, he fell a couple of papers short of a degree. After initially studying Law, he switched to a BA, taking history to stage three.

Mehrtens played his club rugby with the High School Old Boys under-19 team, finding the experience stimulating. "I wince when I hear of schoolboys stepping straight into senior ranks," he says. "It's important to do it in steps, allowing young players to find their feet. I made a lot of good mates that year. We lost the final but had a great time."

A couple of Justin Marshalls came into Mehrtens' life in 1991.

The first one was a flanker for the club under-19 team, an outstandingly good flanker who became a reserve for Canterbury and now plays for Bedford along with such celebrities as Martin Offiah and Junior Paramore.

The other Justin Marshall, a famous All Black now, was the halfback for Southland at the South Island under-18 tournament in Christchurch. Also starring for his team was Jeff Wilson while the Canterbury backline featured Mehrtens at first-five and Tabai Matson at centre. They were all selected (by Vance Stewart) for the South Island tournament team.

Mehrtens finished up with Jeff Wilson's badge. "Anyone want to swap?"

Wilson was impressive but he remembers Marshall as being awesome. "He was an aggressive and strong runner, just like he is now," recalls Mehrtens. "There was a confrontational approach about him."

Andrew Mehrtens

Vance Stewart had progressed to being coach of the New Zealand under-19 team by 1992 which probably helped the advancement of Mehrtens' career.

"When I turned up at the trials in Wellington," recalls Mehrtens, "I was the odd one out, the skinny little white kid no one had ever heard of. All the graduates from the New Zealand schools team knew each other, but I didn't know anyone apart from Tabai Matson, although I remembered Justin Marshall from the previous year. He had slipped through the schools net too.

"Somehow, I made the team, which I'm sure was as big a surprise to all the other trialists as it was to me. I was hardly a commanding figure, weighing in at 70kg!"

The under-19s developed into an extremely good team, amassing 87 and 74 points in their warm-up games (in the second of which, at Timaru, Mehrtens played the entire second half at halfback) before dealing to their Australian counterparts 23-3 in the test at Dunedin.

Marshall and Mehrtens teamed up together for the first time, an exciting prelude of things to come. The team exuded talent, with Norman Berryman thundering in for eight tries in three outings and Adrian Cashmore, Matson and Milton Going excelling. The pack included Nick Broughton, who went on to represent Scotland, and Taine Randell.

Mehrtens rates 1992 and his time in the under-19s as an important part of his "learning cycle".

"I wasn't as experienced as a lot of the kids around me," he says, "so I was happy to let others make the backline decisions. At school, Daryl Hansen, the second-five, called the shots and in the under-19 team it was Kenny Pourewa, also at second-five, who did the job. I was happy to be the link man – and kick the goals. Not having to make decisions took the pressure off me. It allowed me to observe others and learn. It was an important time in my career. Every game I learnt more and more."

The prodigious punting that would become a hallmark of Mehrtens' play was beginning to manifest itself by this stage.

He's living proof that size doesn't relate to the distance you can kick a ball. Grant Fox was another player of smallish stature who could achieve vast distance with his punting. Mehrtens describes it as "a whole body thing". "Because you're smaller, you snap your body into

Rugby Greats

the kick, and with good timing you get great distance," he says. "It compares to golf – it's all about weight transfer."

During the second half of the 1992 season, Mehrtens was promoted to the High School Old Boys senior team, an event which provided colourful material for the local rugby correspondents who were aware that he represented the third generation of Mehrtens to play senior for the club. He didn't let the family name down, scoring all 15 points as HSOB defeated Sydenham. Pinpoint goalkicking combined with an electrifying break down the blindside won him rave reviews. He describes it as one of the few totally mistake-free performances of his career. His fellow teammate, flanker Stephen Dods might have helped. "He warned me about one of the Sydenham loosies who had a reputation for damaging opponents off the ball," says Mehrtens. "Stephen told me to never let my guard down. That had the adrenalin pumping and I was on my toes waiting for him the whole game. But he never came near me!"

During the summer of 1992-93, Mehrtens put a lot of effort into conditioning. He worked with New Zealand athletics coach Geoff

"And make sure you miss the last drop-kick!" South Africa president, Nelson Mandela, is introduced to Andrew Mehrtens before the World Cup final at Ellis Park in 1995.   John Selkirk

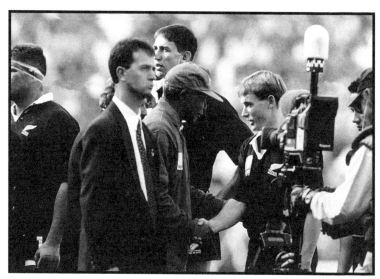

218

Baker to sharpen his sprinting, there was a lot of beach work and he even managed a few weights. He would be well rewarded for the effort, for he made exciting advancement in his rugby in 1993.

Stewart was now coach of Canterbury and although he continued to use the experienced and talented Greg Coffey as his first-five and goalkicker, Mehrtens was soon drafted into the squad and given his first outing (like so many notable Canterbury footballers down the years) against Mid-Canterbury at Ashburton. It was a bonanza for Mehrtens. The team won 90-6, he converted 10 of the team's tries and the first three times he handled the ball he ripped through the Mid-Canterbury defence. In his next full outing, a non-championship game against Otago at Lancaster Park, he accumulated 25 points, from two conversions, six penalty goals and a dropped goal. Two outings as a goalkicker, 45 points. The Mehrtens representative career was under way in impressive fashion.

In between these two games he represented New Zealand Colts against the Australians at Eden Park. At the Colts' first team meeting, coach Peter Thorburn told Mehrtens he'd seen him play at first-five, second-five and fullback. "I'm not sure what position you prefer," he said. "Prop!" was the answer Mehrtens fired back. It was at first-five Thorburn used him in the international against the Aussies. Although Mehrtens sparkled, his team was over-run in the forwards, going down 31-8. He didn't get to team with Justin Marshall, the preferred halfback being Elton Moncrieff.

Stewart gave Mehrtens a run at first-five ahead of Coffey in the NPC game against North Harbour at Takapuna. At one stage he was on the end of a crunching tackle from Frank Bunce, being sandwiched between Bunce and Ron Williams. "Suddenly Rob Penney arrived," says Mehrtens, "dived in, got the ball and moved it on. He then picked me up and said, 'Come on, young fella, let's get to the next one'. I felt proud I hadn't lost the ball in the tackle."

Preferring to retain Coffey as the pivot but eager to take advantage of Mehrtens' exciting attacking skills, Stewart placed Mehrtens at fullback for the season's final three encounters, against Otago, Taranaki and Wellington. "It was a gamble by Vance," says Mehrtens, "but I was eager to play anywhere and we won two of those matches, including beating Wellington at Athletic Park."

The Rugby Annual recorded that "the development of Mehrtens

was a blessing for Canterbury, especially since the incumbent, Coffey, a skilful player and superb goalkicker, announced his retirement at the season's end."

It was time for something completely different. Through the summer of 1993-94, Mehrtens played with the second division club Calvisano in Italy, an excursion organised for him by his good friend Dean McKinnel. He loved the experience, finding the rugby "fiery and undisciplined". He achieved mixed results with his goalkicking but was on target with his dropped goals.

Stewart, who had been retained as Canterbury coach (a notable achievement, the two before him, John Phillips and Alistair Hopkinson getting just one season each) faxed Mehrtens in Italy, encouraging his return. He wasn't to be the only M featuring in the backline in 1994. Mark Mayerhofler had come south from North Harbour and Tabai Matson had been promoted. Collectively, they would electrify the Canterbury team, in 1994 and the seasons ahead (when Justin Marshall would make it four Ms).

Mehrtens found the long bus trip through the Southern Alps didn't do anything for his muscles when Canterbury took on West Coast at Hokitika. Early in the game his hamstring tore, the first significant muscle injury he had ever suffered. It would ground him for five weeks.

He then became involved in a tug-of-war in July '94. He'd been selected for New Zealand Colts but didn't depart with the team because Canterbury wanted him for the match against the Springboks, a game in which he didn't play well, missing a sitter of a kick at an important stage. Next morning he was on a flight to Sydney, hurrying through to Port Macquarrie to link up with the Colts. "It was a rather unsatisfactory stage of my career," recalls Mehrtens. "I had another poor game midweek for the Colts, and lost my position to Carlos Spencer for the test in Sydney."

However, reunited with the Ms in the Canterbury, he soon began to fire, a promising season becoming a vintage one for the red and blacks when they lifted the Ranfurly Shield from Waikato in Hamilton. "We took it to them," says Mehrtens. "We had the confidence to run the ball and scored some classic tries."

After the buzz of taking the shield, Canterbury struggled next up against Taranaki in New Plymouth. At one stage, Taranaki's veteran lock Kevin Barrett trod on Mehrtens' hand. "Welcome to the big time," he told the fresh-faced fellow he had pinned to the turf. "I didn't react to that too well," says Mehrtens. "I performed like a smart arse for the rest of the game."

Ranfurly Shield fever engulfed Canterbury. When Mehrtens turned up for the Counties challenge – disappointed that injury was keeping Jonah Lomu at home – he expected about 15,000 to watch the game. "Instead, there were about thirty-five thousand there, screaming their heads off," he says. "It was incredible, a reminder of the extraordinary powers of the shield. Within forty-eight hours of us defeating Counties, the Otago challenge was sold out."

Otago came north optimistic it could outgun the team it had whipped 56-25 earlier in the season. The game would produce one of those heart-stopping finishes that have decorated shield rugby down the years. "It was a frantic time for the fans, I know," says Mehrtens, "but I was always confident we would win. Every time we went down their end, we scored points. I was always confident of landing the winning goal because I'd been striking the ball sweetly all afternoon." Mehrtens' four penalty goals allowed Canterbury to sneak home 22-20.

There was more to Mehrtens' omission from the All Black World Cup squad announced in October than met the eye. Coach Laurie Mains deliberately didn't name him because he knew Mehrtens was touring the UK with Canterbury. "We didn't want him under the microscope over there," says Mains. "If the Brits had thought he was going to be a vital player at the World Cup they would have monitored him closely indeed, because that's their way."

Mehrtens was introduced to the squad at the second of the summer camps, in Auckland. "We had followed his progress with interest during 1994," says Mains, "and when through injury Marc Ellis was no longer an option at first-five, we focused on Mehrtens. We rated him highly but his tendency for loose, inaccurate punting and occasional defensive lapses meant we wondered if we could get him ready for test rugby by May 1995."

To cut a not particularly long story short, the mix of Mehrtens' prodigious natural talent and Mains' technical instruction had the Canterbury ace primed and ready to explode on to the international scene a month before that. Mains would write in his biography (published in 1996), that, "If we'd set down on paper, after the frustrations of 1994, all the qualities we sought in the ideal first-five, we could not have improved on Andrew."

After missing the inter-island game at Carisbrook with a haematoma, Mehrtens was named for the World Cup after a 96-point romp by the Harlequins (the All Blacks in disguise) against Waikato. "I always thought if I made the All Blacks, it would be a rousing occasion at the clubrooms or at home," says Mehrtens. "When Laurie announced the team the players were together in a motel in Hamilton. All very low key."

Mehrtens was rooming with Zinzan Brooke whose World Cup prospects were in serious jeopardy after he suffered serious damage to his Achilles tendon. "I came to appreciate the dedication of those top players," he says. "He was up every two hours throughout the night icing his leg."

Mehrtens would create a world record in his first outing in the All Black jersey, his 28 points as New Zealand sank the Canadians 73-7 at Eden Park representing a record for a player on test debut. Another All Black, Matthew Cooper, held the record at 23 (set against Ireland in 1992). Scoring points was fun, but his greatest buzz came from his rapport with Walter Little and Frank Bunce. "I didn't have to run the backline," he says, "because there was so much feedback. "I never questioned anything. They'd say, 'Let's do such-and-such' and I'd say, 'Yep, beauty, let's do it!'" Mehrtens had no concept that he was approaching a world record. "If people think I concern myself with things like that, they're seriously off the mark."

Mehrtens would emerge as one of the superstars of a super team at the World Cup, a team that would take the concept of attacking rugby to new heights. Achieving incredible distances with his punting at high altitude, deadly accurate with his goalkicking and able to blitz the best defences with his startling pace, Mehrtens had a dream tournament . . . until the last few minutes of the final against the Springboks at Ellis Park.

That's when an opportunity to assure himself of immortality presented itself. Notwithstanding the poisoning which had thrown the All Blacks' test preparation into chaos (with Mehrtens the first to drop and one of the worst sufferers) and the clever strategy applied by the Springboks, the game was still there for the taking with five minutes to play, the scores locked at 9-all. Following another brilliant Ian Jones lineout take, Mehrtens set himself for a dropped goal, about

Andrew Mehrtens

Andrew Mehrtens in full cry during the Bledisloe Cup game against Australia in Sydney in 1995.   Andrew Cornaga (Photosport)

33 metres out, directly in front of the posts. It sliced outside the right hand upright. "It was," he reflects, "a kick I would expect to land nine times out of ten. I was terribly disappointed, because that was what I was supposedly there to do. But do I feel I lost the game? No. That was just one moment in the one hundred minutes that made up the final. I felt bad about it, but there were dropped passes and a host of other mistakes that lessened our effectiveness that afternoon."

There would be further disappointments for Mehrtens in 1995. Canterbury would lose the Ranfurly Shield to Auckland, being clinically dissected by Graham Henry's team and losing by an unbelievable score, 35-nil. Mehrtens was presented with a huge dilemma soon after the start, after damaging the AC joint of his shoulder – to go off or stay? "Obviously, I should have gone off," he says now, "but at the time, the adrenalin took over and I elected to tough it out. I did no one any favours."

That injury was insignificant compared to what would happen in the opening encounter of the All Blacks' tour of Italy and France at Catania. In endeavouring to run the ball out from his own 22, he contorted his knee, seriously damaging the anterior cruciate ligament. "I tried to change direction in mid-air," he says, "but years of inflexibility and muscle imbalance suddenly caught up with me. There was a horrible graunching sound and my knee gave way." He was flown straight back to New Zealand.

It required intricate surgery to repair the considerable damage. The tendon that runs over the kneecap was taken out and threaded through the thigh and shin bones and a replacement ligament was secured in place with titanium screws. After a couple of months, those screws were healed over and the new ligament was a permanent item.

About seven months after the injury, Mehrtens was back in action, ever so tenderly at first . But he steadily recaptured fitness and confidence and was back in the No 10 jersey when the All Blacks, under new coach John Hart, launched into their 1996 test programme against Western Samoa at Napier.

Mehrtens, who'd aggregated 149 points in his first eight test outings, was immediately into prolific scoring mode again, picking up a further 118 points in seven tests in 1996, before putting a huge fright into the All Black camp when he went down clutching his knee at training at Port Elizabeth in August.

Andrew Mehrtens

It turned out to be nothing more serious than cartilage damage. Mehrtens was flown immediately to Johannesburg where corrective surgery had him back in action in a matter of days. It cost him two test appearances, Simon Culhane deputising at Durban and Pretoria where the All Blacks completed a stunningly successful season by winning a series on South African soil for the first time.

Mehrtens had been a major contributor throughout '96, not least in the Bledisloe Cup encounter at Ballymore when, with the scores locked at 25-all, he daringly called a move which he'd participated in a few times with Canterbury. "After the World Cup final, I wasn't that eager to risk everything on a dropped goal," he says. "We practise these moves all the time at training, and hardly ever use them. I don't think the Wallabies expected us to attack from there. Frank (Bunce) put me beautifully into the gap and it was the sweetest feeling to realise I had two of the fastest players in the world, Christian Cullen and Jeff Wilson, in support. It's moments like that you live for as a rugby player."

Murray Mexted

ndy Haden branded him one of rugby's most adventurous socialisers. Murray Mexted himself wrote in his autobiography that if something was worth fantasising over, it was worth doing . . . an individual who, until the incomparable Zinzan Brooke came along, was New Zealand's most capped player in the demanding No. 8 position, taking advantage of the opportunties rugby had to offer like no other.

One week before the All Black trial at Hamilton in 1984, he was paddling a dugout canoe in the Okavango Swamps in Botswana. The day before the inter-island match in Rotorua that same season he was surfing at Mt Maunganui.

He sold scrum machines in France, he surfed the biggest and best waves in South Africa, he travelled the world to participate in spoofing contests. And in 1986 he married Miss Universe, Lorraine Downes.

The son of an All Black, Mexted possessed a great zest for life and a passion for rugby at which he was fiercely competitive. Good enough to restrict Buck Shelford to the reserves bench until he retired after the 1985 season, he made 34 consecutive test appearances.

After finally stepping aside from the international scene, he didn't just fade into the background. He wanted to give something back to Wellington rugby. For three years he served on the union's management committee, he assisted coach David Kirk as a selector and in 1997 he is coaching the Wellington sevens team.

New Zealand's armchair fans, certainly those with Sky installed,

Murray Mexted

Murray Mexted . . . possessed a great zest for life and a fierce passion for rugby.
Mike Brett

know him as a knowledgeable and authoritative television comments person. He's taken to his TV role with great enthusiasm. "I've always been a person who's concerned himself with *why* something was happening on a rugby field, not *what* was happening," says Mexted. "In my television role I'm striving to explain to listeners *why* things are going on, and I hope they appreciate that."

Because of a High Court injunction served on the NZRFU in 1985, Mexted was denied the opportunity of touring South Africa with the All Blacks. While it wasn't quite the same as participating, he derived enormous satisfaction in describing, from the commentary box, the achievment of John Hart's 1996 team in winning a series on South African soil for the first time.

When Mexted hands you his business card, as the general manager of Mexted Motors at Tawa, you are drawn to the line which reads: Three generations of integrity, service and commitment. Still diligently putting in a 50-hour week is Murray's 70-year-old father Graham who back in 1950 was sensationally plucked from the Tawa senior second division team and placed at No. 8 in the All Blacks for the fourth test of the series against the British Lions at Eden Park, going on to tour Australia the next year.

At the time he was selected, he'd played one game for Wellington B and two for Wellington A. It was, his son observes, fairytale stuff. But there would not be the same fairytale trimmings associated with Murray's advancement to the All Blacks. He would get there at the age of 25 in 1979 for the unofficial tests against Hugo Porta's Pumas. Personally, he thought he should have been selected to tour the UK the previous year.

And the reason he reckoned he should have gone was because he was tall. "They took Ash McGregor from Southland instead," he says. "I'd beaten him in the lineouts in the inter-island game without even jumping. He was too short. As a result, the poor guy got only three outings on the whole tour. Gary Seear was the only giant among the loosies. To compensate, they converted John Fleming from lock to number eight. In the circumstances, they were lucky to get away with a Grand Slam."

Once the New Zealand selectors acknowledged Mexted's height and athleticism, they found they couldn't do without him. The test No. 8 jersey was his for six years.

Murray Mexted

But for the sage advice of a London soccer club's physiotherapist in 1973, when Mexted was enjoying the first of many Overseas Experiences, those selectors would never have had to concern themselves with the rangy kid from Tawa. Having ruptured the cruciate ligaments of his right knee while playing fullback in a match of no consequence, his sporting future looked bleak. The soccer physio encouraged optimism. If Mexted strengthened the quadricep muscle sufficiently, there was no reason why he shouldn't play again. Starting that day, he built the muscle with sandbag exercises which seemed to last an eternity.

That first OE took him well beyond London, to exotic destinations such as Spain, France, Greece, North Africa, Yugoslavia and even Russia. He enjoyed the role of traveller so much he missed the entire 1974 rugby season back home, which was probably a good thing for his knee. OE became a way of life for him, too exhilarating to be a one-off event. He would travel overseas many times, mostly to his favourite rugby destinations, France and South Africa.

Back with Tawa in 1975, coming up 22, he helped take the club through to senior second division status and was chosen for Wellington B. Not everyone appreciated the involvement of a Tawa player in the B side. Paul Quinn, later to captain Wellington, told him his selection was an insult to all the first division number eights. Which only served to strengthen Mexted's resolve.

With Wellington B, he was required to be nothing more than a No. 8. In a Tawa jersey, he also captained the side, kicked the goals and usually handled the touchfinders as well. The coach, Jack Oldershaw, was firm. "With Tawa, you might do everything," he said. "Here, you concentrate on being a number eight, which means jumping at seven in the lineout."

His debut was against Marlborough at Blenheim where his opponent just happened to be the All Black Alan Sutherland. A huge shove in the back as he was readying for a classical take at the first lineout let him know who the senior partner was down the back of the lineout. "He had the edge that day," says Mexted, "but I took on board some important lessons." Sutherland, then 31, had been impressed with his young rival, commenting to a teammate that he possessed the vital attribute of height.

The most important development in his career that year was not that he played three times for Wellington B, or even that the Wellington A coach Ray Dellabarca, mindful that his captain and No. 8 Andy Leslie would be touring South Africa the next year, had involved him in a few training sessions and put him on the reserves bench a couple of times. No, the biggest step he took in 1975, after heeding the advice of Oldershaw and former All Black Graham Williams, was to switch from second division Tawa to first division Wellington.

Although it was like severing a family connection, once with Wellington his career took off with a roar, albeit involving a degree of controversy he could have done without. Dellabarca, obviously attracted to Mexted's height, used him in preference to Leslie before the All Blacks headed for South Africa in '76, then sensationally stayed with Mexted once the tour was over.

"The newspapers interpreted it as a direct snub of the All Black captain and inexcusable," says Mexted. "It wasn't something I needed as I was trying to establish myself at representative level." Anyway,

The long arms of Murray Mexted make passing difficult for British Lions prop Graham Price during the fourth test of the 1983 series at Eden Park. John Selkirk

Murray Mexted

Mexted appeared 17 times for Wellington that season and Leslie, who'd led his country with distinction in South Africa, once.

The Petone connection meant Mexted took a step backwards in 1977. Once Ian Upston replaced Dellabarca as coach, it was inevitable that he would reinstate Leslie at No. 8. After playing in only three of Wellington's first dozen matches, Mexted approached Upston and asked when he could expect to become involved. "I had to wait for my turn," replied Upston, none too impressed. "You will have to wait for yours – your time will come." His frustration was compounded by the fact he had been rated good enough by the national selectors to appear in the All Black trials at Wanganui in May.

At the end of 1977, Mexted first visited California and the UK with the Wellington club and then skipped across to Agen in France where, having written offering his services, he had been invited to play the season. He was "announced" in the local newspapers as a great All Black. The first major French club to import a player of his stature – even if he wasn't a real All Black – Agen reaped substantial rewards. The average attendance for home games was up 2500 which Mexted calculated, too late to benefit personally, was worth about $150,000 to the club.

His reward that first visit was a basic wage for working as a cheese truck driver, accommodation, car, petrol and several meals a week. When he returned in 1980, as a genuine 18 carat All Black, he worked a lot less and was paid a lot more.

The Leslie challenge had disappeared by 1978 and Mexted enjoyed a full season's action with Wellington. Although he missed selection for the All Black trial in July (Seear and McGregor opposing each other at No. 8), in September he was up against McGregor in the North-South clash at New Plymouth.

At halftime, South led 10-4, and it seemed South's coach Eric Watson was heading for a fourth straight victory. But at halftime North's think-tank, coach Peter Burke and captain Graham Mourie, decided on a complete change of emphasis in the lineouts. Everything would be thrown down the back to Mexted who towered over his opposite McGregor. The tactics worked like magic. South had no one to combat Mexted and the whole course of the game changed, North going on to win 29-13.

"While I was personally disappointed at losing out to McGregor when the team to tour the UK was then named," says Mexted, "I could not believe that such a basic blunder would be perpetrated. He was 6ft 1in. He was given two games at number eight and one on the side of the scrum in a tour of eighteen matches."

Mexted would have loved to have broken into the All Blacks for the home series against the French in 1979 to have competed against his Agen teammates Daniel Dubroca and Christian Beguerie, but Seear, the test incumbent, was retained. However, his stocks slumped when the All Blacks were outrun by the French at Eden Park and then lost to Australia in Sydney.

At this point All Black coach Jack Gleeson (who would die of cancer a few months later) decided to start from scratch and build a new team for the tour of England and Scotland. "It was obvious many of the existing All Blacks had lost form," he said. "A fresh approach was necessary." No players who featured in the series against France were used against Argentina.

Mexted was part of that 'fresh approach'. He and Ken Stewart combined brilliantly to shut down the maestro Hugo Porta. As Porta *was* the Argentinian team, it allowed the New Zealanders to fashion two impressive test victories. The selectors were suitably impressed – they named the entire fifteen who won at Athletic Park (with the exception of John Ashworth who was unavailable) for the UK tour.

Although he'd worn the silver fern against the Pumas, Mexted didn't regard those matches as the real thing. *Now* he was an All Black, selected as the best No. 8 in the land. In fact, he was the only No. 8 taken away, as a consequence of which he played in nine of the eleven matches.

After he'd scored several tries and was starting to enjoy himself, coach Eric Watson brought him sharply back to earth. "Would you like me to get you your own ball?" Watson asked him. "Then the others can have a game too."

Even Watson had to concede that Mexted's solo four-pointer in his test debut against Scotland at Murrayfield was a classic. Mexted brands it 'an Andy Dalton original'. On Graham Mourie's initiative the All Blacks had switched to two-man lineouts (involving Mexted and Andy Haden) to neutralise the efficiency of Scotland's tall forwards.

"Early in the second spell Andy said to me, 'You should have a go from one of these lineouts'. "The thought hadn't occurred to me. When we were thirty-five metres from Scotland's line, I told Dalton I'd balk backward then run forward for his throw. My marker took the bait. Andy's throw was perfect. I had it in my hands, went through the gap and past a surprised halfback, beat a couple of flatfooted props and bolted to the goalline."

Considering that six All Blacks were making their test debuts, the 20-9 victory was most encouraging, and there were smiles all round when Mourie's men held on for a one-point victory over England a fortnight later, after being crushed by Northern Division at Otley along the way.

Mexted found he responded superbly to the inspiring and calculating leadership of Mourie. Two years previously, Mourie had defined the No. 8's role as he understood it, which varied substantially from how Mexted at the time was playing it. Mexted believed that from a scrum or lineout, he should take off *behind* his backline. "Not so," said Mourie, "the number eight should be the second person to the ball, going forward, right behind the openside flanker. I have to get to the stage where I know you are behind me. Whatever I do, you must be there to support me."

Mourie had wielded a significant influence on how Scotland operated against the All Blacks. He had told Mexted that because of his respect for the flyhalf John Rutherford he would run wide and cut their backs off. "That will force Rutherford to kick, have a go himself or come back into the forwards," he said. "But be careful because he is very elusive."

Mexted believes that Mourie's absence when the All Blacks toured Australia in Fiji exposed shortcomings in Watson's ability as a coach. "I enjoyed Eric and he had a lot of fine qualities," says Mexted, "but he operated best in harness with Mourie. He was rather stereotyped left to his own devices, too constricted in style and pattern.

"In Australia, where we played on hard grounds against quality opposition, Eric persisted with setting up rucks when there should have been acceptance that in these conditions we spread the ball to our wings. Mind you, the selectors had left behind one of our best attackers, Bruce Robertson. His omission ranks as the greatest selection blunder of my time."

For reasons which are hard to fathom now, the All Blacks took only 25 players along for the 16-match tour of Australia and Fiji in 1980, and only four of them were loose forwards. Mexted and Leicester Rutledge both made 12 appearances and Mark Shaw 13. The most lightly used loosie was Geoff Hines who had nine outings.

The series should have reached a perfect climax at the Sydney Cricket Ground in mid-July after the All Blacks and the Wallabies had claimed a test apiece. But a severe bout of food poisoning that flattened the tourists seriously diminished their prospects. Mexted and Shaw vomited so incessantly they were taken to hospital for injections only four hours before kick-off. A debilitated Mexted failed to see out the game which the Australians won 26-10.

That result brought down the wrath of the New Zealand fans and Watson was lucky to survive as coach. But survive he did, and his team made amends with a triumphant sweep through Wales a few months later. He was reunited with Mourie and the tactics that had failed on the hard surfaces in Australia were most effectively employed on the softer fields of Wales.

The All Blacks had required a controversial late penalty goal to nose out Wales in 1978 but this time – in Wales' centennial test – Mourie's team gave a commanding performance. And no one played better than Mourie himself. The great former Welsh flyhalf Cliff Morgan paid him the ultimate tribute when he said, "I can go happily to my maker because today I saw, from Graham Mourie, the greatest loose forward display the world could ever wish to see." Mexted lavishes praise on *both* his fellow loosies that day. "It was vintage Mourie," he says, "but 'Cowboy' Shaw's performance was as memorable in a different way. He stunned them with the velocity of his game."

The series that survives most vividly in Mexted's memory is that against the Springboks in 1981 with its backdrop of howling protests and controversy. Mexted says that much has been made of the stresses under which the Springboks played. "But less has been made of the anxiety and stress under which the All Blacks operated," he says. "Our proximity to home and families placed pressures of an emotional sort none of us had had to handle before. Our homes and families were under threat, whether mental or physical, from our own countrymen. We were subjected to personal abuse and obscene phone calls, threats to destroy our properties. We were spat upon by fellow New Zealanders, taunted, reviled."

Murray Mexted

Wedding time in 1986 for Murray Mexted and former Miss Universe, Lorraine Downes. Sharing the happy event with them is Leeanne Hoskin who represented South Africa at the 1983 Miss Universe contest.   *Peter Bush*

The All Blacks' response could only be on the field and it became a matter of compulsion to win the third test at Eden Park once the Springboks had squared the series in Wellington. "There could be no other result," says Mexted. "To lose at Eden Park would have been a shattering emotional experience for every player."

It was vital to lock out all the extraneous events surrounding the game, which was not easy, given the All Blacks were being transported from their north shore hotel to Eden Park at 8.30am, to protect against protestors blocking the Harbour Bridge.

Mexted had been developing in Wales a combination with Mourie and Shaw that would make them the most celebrated loose forward combination in the world. But at Eden Park he had neither Mourie nor Shaw with him. Cowboy was injured and Mourie was back on the farm making his personal protest against the tour. Mexted's partners that day were Frank Shelford and Geoff Old. "In the most important match of my life, I was partnered with two flankers I had never played with," says Mexted. "We were playing a team of awesome size and power, with a dangerous kicker at flyhalf (Naas Botha) and speedy wingers. If ever we needed a competent loose forward unit, this was it."

Mexted was sometimes accused of being a 'frivolous' player but that incredible afternoon at Eden Park his concentration was so intense he confesses to being almost unaware of the endless buzzing of the ground by the pilot of a Cessna. "Afterwards, when someone said the plane had made fifty-seven passes, some of them crazily low, I didn't believe it. Obviously, there were occasions when it was there, but what I was later to see on film I found unbelievable."

If the dramas off the field weren't enough, the teams conspired to draw level at 22-all going into injury (and flour bomb) time. It seemed that Botha's wide angle conversion attempt of Ray Mordt's third try would decide the game. "If this goes over," Mexted remembers saying to Haden, "there's absolutely no justice in the world."

"When it missed, I felt no elation," he says. "The scores were level and that was neither good enough nor fair enough. When Allan Hewson took his final kick, I knew it would go over. It seemed right that it should. But after he'd kicked it, the danger man became referee Clive Norling. His self appointed star status had us over the edge."

Mexted considers 25-22 a fair reflection of the game. The Boks, in his opinion, didn't deserve a draw. And his final word on an unbelievable game is for Hewson. "I doubt anyone else would have kicked that pressure goal. Hewie had his faults, but he was a rare artist, possessed of freakish skills. He was so very calm, one of the most in-control footballers I have played with."

Hewson and Mexted continued to combine forces as Wellington not only took out the NPC title in 1981 but brought untold joy to the capital's rugby followers by lifting the Ranfurly Shield from Waikato. They were together again, with Mourie and Shaw back in the pack, as the All Blacks completed a hat-trick of test victories in Romania and France to bring a satisfactory conclusion to an extraordinary rugby year. Mexted actually came off against Romania with rib damage, a notable happening, being the only occasion in 34 test appearances he left the field.

Through 1982 and 1983 the All Blacks continued on their winning way, proving themselves decisively superior to the Wallabies and the Lions. A major factor in the whitewash of the Lions was the closing

Murray Mexted

down (by Mourie, Mexted and Shaw) of the tourists' danger man Ollie Campbell.

Then came the low point in Mexted's international career, the tour of England and Scotland, minus half a dozen of the team's most senior forwards and a few backs. It was a jacked-up tour, a replacement destination for Argentina which was off limits following the Falklands conflict. With no Graham Mourie, no Andy Haden, no Andy Dalton and no Dave Loveridge, the All Blacks needed a fresh captain. Coach Bryce Rope ignored the more obvious qualities of Mexted and Shaw and instead, indulged a whim by appointing Stu Wilson to lead the side from the wing.

"Stu wrote in his biography that he found the role frustrating to the point where he himself was in turmoil," says Mexted, "and that he received little understanding from the manager Paul Mitchell. There were only two serious candidates for the captaincy, Cowboy and myself, but Rope rejected both of us. Then after Peter Wheeler's Midlands team had devised tactics at Leicester to disrupt our drives, Rope decided that in the test at Twickenham, we wouldn't drive at all. Can you believe it – an All Black team abandoning the drive? Suddenly we were a team not to be feared. At the end (with England winning 15-9), I felt as low as I ever have. We had failed to switch tactics when the state of the game screamed for it."

The big men returned to the All Black pack in 1984 and the team, normal tactics restored, went back to winning, taking out the home series against France before gaining revenge for the '80 series loss in Australia. Displaying remarkable resilience, Mexted, as the only No. 8, appeared in 10 of the 14 matches in Australia. The *Rugby Annual* observed that he "thrived on his demanding schedule, producing No. 8 play of the highest level. Many first-fives throughout Australia must be experiencing nightmares of Mexted stampeding towards them. He captained the side with distinction on five occasions."

Mexted didn't need to go to South Africa in 1985 to experience the country. He'd done that in 1982 when he mixed surfing at Jeffreys Bay with representing Natal, completing a formidable loose forward trio in Currie Cup matches with Springbok captain Wynand Claassen and another Kiwi, Craig Ross. He'd returned to New Zealand in time for the test series against the touring Australians. In '85, he was going purely to play against the Springboks, the ultimate challenge for any

New Zealander. But, of course, lawyers and High Courts intervened, and the tour was abandoned. While the replacement tour to Argentina was enjoyable, Mexted finding that country refreshingly different as a rugby destination, nothing could compensate for the disappointment of being denied the opportunity to tackle the South Africans on 'their own soil.

"We'd all made huge sacrifices to be at peak fitness for the tour in 1985," says Mexted. "Touring there is unique, something which comes to players only once in their careers. It's the ultimate challenge for New Zealand rugby players, which is why we went as the Cavaliers the next year."

Although Buck Shelford had emerged as a serious challenger to his position, Mexted was at No. 8 for all four tests. Because of his height, and with wind never a factor, the All Blacks consistently threw to Mexted at the back of the lineout. But although they won enough possession, they didn't possess the backline pace of the Springboks. "We seriously missed John Kirwan," says Mexted. "It didn't matter so much that David Kirk wasn't there, but JK's pace would have been a great asset."

Mexted considers the tour was valuable for New Zealand rugby in that it groomed several players for test play, notably Grant Fox, Alan Whetton and Murray Pierce. "Foxy went there as understudy to Wayne Smith but returned as number one. It was on that tour he learnt as a first-five how to control a game. South Africa had a lot of high profile first-fives and Fox learnt from them."

It disappointed Mexted when the NZRFU subsequently dealt the Cavaliers a two test suspension. "We had been encouraged unofficially by New Zealand councillors to go ahead," he says. "We felt we had a consensus, but once we were out of the country we were condemned. We felt we were sold out by many, including the NZRFU."

Following the Cavaliers tour, Mexted retired. He was coming up 33, with 114 matches for Wellington and 72 for the All Blacks behind him. "I knew the fitness standards required to play at that level and decided I'd had enough. Buck asked me what my intentions were and I told him I was quitting."

Mexted had met Lorraine Downes, Miss Universe, in South Africa in 1984. They became engaged the next year, the day after the All

Murray Mexted

Black tour was cancelled, and married in 1986, honeymooning in the wine regions of France.

Mexted did play some more rugby, for his old club Tawa, helping it win promotion in 1988 to first division where it has survived since. When he finally tossed his boots away, he turned to administration, serving three terms on the Wellington union, pulling out after 1995 because he felt he had more to offer through coaching.

He and Lorraine have a son, Hilton, aged four. Having taken time out to concentrate on being a mother, Lorraine, having sold her model agency, is running a corporate grooming consultancy from their home.

Formerly a force on the rugby field, Murray Mexted now makes an impression as a television comments person.   Photosport

Mark Shaw

It was at Cardiff Arms Park in 1980 that Mark Shaw realised his destiny. Bruce Robertson, who had lead the All Blacks on to the field for the international against Wales in the one hundredth game for his country, had tears streaming down his cheeks as the New Zealand national anthem was being played.

"I looked at Bruce," says Shaw, "and I saw what the black jersey and the silver fern meant to him. I realised it meant the same to me and I determined then that no one was going to get my job – I was going to play as many games as I could for my country.

"I might have got there with no pedigree but I realised that this was what I'd been put on earth for. I was staying, and anyone who wanted my position was going to have to fight me for it!"

Shaw, then 23, would miss only three internationals out of the next 33 played, making the All Black No 6 jersey his own for virtually seven seasons, until A. J Whetton finally displaced him.

Popularly known as 'Cowboy', he would win international recognition . . . make that notoriety . . . as one of the game's toughest, most respected, competitors. He would become the All Blacks' Enforcer, achieving legendary status for the potency of his left hook.

It's not a title that sits easily with him; indeed, it touches a raw nerve.

"I got angry with journalists who branded me a dirty player," says Shaw. "John Reason called me the Wild Man from Borneo and T. P McLean labelled me a thug.

"Well, I might have broken a few jaws and I might have sat a

Mark Shaw

Mark Shaw . . . proved you can make it to the top without a pedigree. Here he does his thing for Manawatu in a representative match against Wellington.

Peter Bush

couple of opponents on their backsides, but I tell you what, I never started any trouble, I never kicked anyone and nor did I ever take on anyone smaller than myself. I never hit a back in my whole career.

"The guys I tangled with were always bigger, heavier, meaner, and usually uglier, than me, forwards who deserved what they got because they were trying to give their side an advantage by unsettling my team.

"Sometimes I'd be asked by a teammate, Andy Haden or someone, to sort out a player who was deliberately obstructing at the lineout. Other times I'd identify troublemakers and deal with it myself.

"If I saw an opponent putting the slipper into one of my teammates, I couldn't help myself. It was the law of the jungle.

"I became pretty hard-nosed. It was apparent some teams realised they couldn't outplay the All Blacks so they sought to outmuscle us. When they started causing havoc, well . . . someone had to front."

Shaw was disappointed when the impression was sometimes given that he was selected only to fill the role of the Enforcer.

"I played sixty-nine matches for the All Blacks and the number of times I was involved in incidents wouldn't have reached double figures. But, of course, the incidents always made the headlines."

They say that Mark, the younger of two children, was a chip off old man Bill's block. Bill Shaw, who'd played senior club rugby for Kia Toa in Manawatu, was a popular personality as a publican, initially of the Railway Hotel in Palmerston North and later, when his son's rugby career was beginning to unfold, at the Waikanae Hotel on the Kapiti coast.

The move to Waikanae didn't help Shaw achieve a rugby pedigree. He attended Kapiti College at Raumati, an unfashionable rugby school; indeed, because the college fielded only one rugby team, Shaw concentrated on golf in his third and fourth form years, sharpening his game on the well manicured links of the Paraparaumu Beach club where the New Zealand Open is regularly staged.

Not until his fifth form year was he considered worthy of Kapiti College's first (and only) rugby fifteen. He made an immediate impact, winning selection for Horowhenua at under-16 and under-18 level, although he concedes that the standard of those representative teams was "pretty average".

By his standards, a far greater achievement was his attaining – "on an absolute minimum of study" – School Certificate, passing in all five subjects. He scored 63 for geography and 50 in each of his four other subjects. "My mates and teachers could never work out how I could achieve the minimum pass mark of fifty in so many subjects!"

In his first year out of college, he secured a job working as a chippie and hammer hand on the Wellington overbridge but the travel from the capital to Levin became a burden when the Horowhenua selector-coach, Leo Fitzgibbon, who'd been impressed with his displays as a blindside flanker for the Paraparaumu senior team, introduced him to his representative squad.

"It was all rather fortuitous," recalls Shaw. "To eliminate the travel, my old man gave me a job in the pub at Waikanae, working in the public bar and running the wholesale."

One of Shaw's regular customers was Cliff Porter, a local personality whose greatest claim to fame was captaining the 1924-25 All Blacks on their 'invincible' tour of the UK and France. "We'd often yarn about rugby," says Shaw. "He brought his scrapbooks in a couple of times. He was a great man, an inspiration for a young footballer like myself."

Another Waikanae identity was Gary Knight who would achieve fame as an All Black front rower but whose focus in 1974 was the Commonwealth Games as a wrestler. "There weren't too many heavyweight wrestlers in the district for him to practise against, so I used to help out," says Shaw. "I could wrestle a bit, although I'd have to say I was more proficient at boxing.

"Anyway, one night Axle (Knight) lost concentration, was a bit slow and I pinned him. He was cheesed off in a big way. Next thing, he picked me up and threw me, head first, through the wall!"

Shaw's debut for Horowhenua was in a nondescript game against Wanganui but in his third outing he found himself up against a Manawatu side chock full of players who were either in, or on the fringe of, the All Blacks.

He was given the thankless task of jumping against John Callesen, a 6ft 5in test player. "It was obvious who was going to win that contest, so I resorted to a few dubious practises to try and level things out a bit and finished up with a black eye, courtesy of Kent Lambert!"

When Shaw lined up against Manawatu the next season it was a Ranfurly Shield challenge, the green and whites having wrested the 'log' from Auckland. This time Shaw was delegated to jump at No. 8 against Sam Strahan, another towering international.

"I won the first two lineouts," recalls Shaw, "and he won the rest."

Although Horowhenua did tolerably well to hold Manawatu to 36-18 it was obvious to Shaw he was operating in a team with an extremely modest skill level, so at season's end, rating OE ahead of rugby and not yet 21, he headed for London.

Shaw and his Kiwi cobbers assessed the major rugby fixtures coming up. "We picked out a home international in each country, cranked up our campervan and took off.

"We drove to Edinburgh first, had two weeks in Scotland, saw a test at Murrayfield, then headed for Cardiff, and did the same. That way, we checked out all the great stadiums – Cardiff Arms Park, Lansdowne Road and Twickenham, as well as Murrayfield.

"I loved Cardiff Arms Park. That was a great experience just being there for a rugby international. Who would have thought that less than three years later I would be out there representing the All Blacks!"

After experiencing the summer delights of such exotic destinations as Portugal and Spain, Shaw and his mates headed for France, timing their arrival to coincide with the 1977 All Black tour.

Shaw's old wrestling partner, Gary Knight, arranged tickets. Sleeping throughout in their campervan, they missed only the opening encounter at Brive, getting to see the other seven matches, including the international at Toulouse where Knight had his eyes gouged by the nefarious French prop Gerard Cholley.

Shaw noted with interest the relentless obstruction the French forwards indulged in, which contributed massively to their first test victory. The All Blacks circumvented it brilliantly in the rematch at Paris by using two man lineouts and playing the game at breakneck speed.

There were other, more direct, ways of dissuading opponents from wreaking such havoc, Shaw mused. It wouldn't be long before he would, most effectively, demonstrate his methods!

The kitty empty, but fortified by his travel experiences, Shaw returned to New Zealand at Easter, 1978, settling in Palmerston North where he turned up at his father's old club, Kia Toa.

"I was told politely I would have to start in the lower grades," says Shaw, "but through a sequence of injuries I finished up playing for the seniors that first week."

He soon came to the attention of Manawatu coach Graham Hamer who used him as a No. 8 while Geoff Old was touring Australia with the New Zealand Juniors. His five outings for the green and whites that year were at Pukekohe, Auckland, Timaru, Dunedin and Invercargill.

Mark Shaw

It wasn't to be instant stardom for Shaw. Manawatu, rejoicing in the presence of the Ranfurly Shield, used Old, Kevin Eveleigh and Terry Clare as a loose forward trio for the important, domestic, encounters, until North Auckland came to town and unexpectedly muscled away the prized trophy.

Shaw never advanced beyond the reserves bench for the major fixtures, not once getting to sample shield rugby before the trophy left town.

His career began to take off in 1979, from the moment he switched from No. 8 (where he'd played all his rugby) to the blindside flanker role.

First, he was accommodated in the Manawatu side by Hamer and then the All Black selectors chose him for the New Zealand Juniors' internal tour.

"It was," says Shaw, "my first sniff of the big time. I'd received some good press after Manawatu defeated Auckland in Palmerston North. Apparently, the selectors were looking that day.

"I'd come that far with no pedigree, no involvement with national age grade or schoolboy teams. Teams in those days were picked largely on pedigree, so to suddenly win recognition was a source of great encouragement. I started to back myself.

"The national selectors had identified me as being all right. I reasoned that if I was a New Zealand Junior, I was probably only three or four places from being an All Black. I concluded that I must have been better than I thought I was!

"It was time to get serious. No one knew what my potential was because I had no background. I think Hamer only introduced me to the Manawatu squad as a back-up but suddenly here I was, a New Zealand Junior. The future was beginning to look exciting."

Shaw played all six matches on the Juniors' tour and appeared in 13 of Manawatu's 15 games, variously as a lock, a flanker and a No. 8. The *New Zealand Rugby Annual* singled him out as the union's most promising player of '79.

If 1979 had stimulated Shaw, the next year would, in his words, blow his socks off!

His performances with the Juniors had obviously impressed the selectors because he was summoned to Hamilton in early May for the All Black trial, before Manawatu had even played a game.

Mark Shaw . . . anyone who wanted his All Black jersey was going to have to fight him for it!   John Selkirk

The trial preceded the selection of the All Black team for the full-scale tour of Australia and Fiji. With established internationals Graham Mourie and Ken Stewart unavailable, there were positions up for grabs.

That was the good news. The bad news was that a week before the trial, playing a club fixture at the Showgrounds in Palmerston North, Shaw took a heavy knock on the hip.

He was in two minds whether to travel to Hamilton. "It was one of those difficult situations a player can find himself in," says Shaw. "A golden opportunity beckons but you know you should really rest the injury.

"I decided to bite the bullet and go. I shouldn't have. There was extensive bruising on the hip and I lasted only sixty minutes before giving way to Stu Conn. The zambuck looked at the bruising with some horror and said I was wasting my time trying to get back on.

"Instead, I was taken to hospital for an X-ray. I felt my performance probably wasn't good enough to clinch selection, but on the way back to the ground, in the liaison officer's car, the touring team was announced – and I was in it!

"I was an All Black. I.didn't know what to think – it was unbelievable. It took a while to sink in as everyone came up and shook my hand. I felt elation for myself and sadness for the guys who'd missed out."

Shaw says he was dispensed advice that evening by his father, who'd journeyed to Hamilton to watch the trial, for which he has been forever grateful.

"I was probably blowing my trumpet a bit, once my new status had sunk in. My old man called me aside.

"'Mark,' he said, 'you've cracked it – you're an All Black. Don't ever forget your mates and your family. They're they ones who knew you before and they're the ones who'll be around when your rugby career ends. That could be tomorrow if you break your leg. You'll make a lot of mates on your way through who won't remember you when you're no longer an All Black. Don't become a hot shot and forget your friends.'

"It was," says Shaw, "great advice, something I've never forgotten. And the old man was right, the friends I had at the start are the best friends I've got now."

It was in the early stages of the Australian tour that Shaw acquired the nickname of Cowboy, given to him by Stu Wilson.

"A lot of people seem to think I was called Cowboy because I might have whacked a few people. That wasn't it at all. I was working as a freezing worker when I was selected for the All Blacks and I had plenty of rough edges, no track suit and the arse out of my trousers. Stu compared me with John Wayne and then started calling me Cowboy. It stuck!"

Remarkably, for a tour comprising 16 matches including four tests (three against Australia and one in Fiji), the All Blacks went away with only 25 players. And only four of those were loose forwards – Murray Mexted, Leicester Rutledge, Geoff Hines and Shaw.

Mexted, the solitary specialist No. 8, would appear in 12 of the games, Shaw in 13 (including eight in succession) and Rutledge in 12.

Hines, an openside flanker, went away as the rising star but after a disastrous first outing against Sydney dropped back to fourth in the pecking order.

"Coach Eric Watson went cold on him and promoted me to the top line-up, switching Leicester across to the openside. Whacko, that suited me, I was like a pig in shit. I'd have played every game, if Eric had wanted me to."

The *Rugby Annual* noted that Shaw "took a while to establish himself but then came on rapidly, and excitingly, ranking as probably the forward find of the tour. Hard and rugged to the point of being uncompromising, he slotted in well to the driving All Black forward pattern."

Shaw won notoriety for the short, sharp left handed punch that broke Wallaby lock Steve Williams' jaw in the second test at Ballymore, a game the All Blacks won through a magnificent late try by Hika Reid. Shaw's lethal jab came at a tense stage in the match as both sets of forwards traded punches.

Williams made the mistake of targeting Shaw but missed with the haymaker he threw. Cowboy didn't miss with his short arm jab and Williams retired injured a few minutes later, his jaw shattered.

Although Shaw revelled in being an All Black and enjoyed the competitiveness of the series in Australia, he was annoyed that the Bledisloe Cup went to the Wallabies, two tests to one. It would be the only losing series he would experience as an All Black until 1986 when his career was winding down.

"I've heard it described as a disappointing tour," says Shaw. "I'll tell you what, there were no disappointing All Black tours. I never went on a bad one. I'd have gone to Stewart Island, if they'd teed one up there, and enjoyed that too!"

There would be no further reversals in 1980 for Shaw. He would not play in another losing game.

Manawatu, featuring such stars as Frank Oliver, Gary Knight, Geoff Old, Mark Donaldson, Doug Rollerson and Shaw, went through to take out the NPC stylishly, winning their last seven matches in succession, dropping only one of their 10 matches, that to Wellington.

And then the All Blacks, their tactics better suited to the softer fields of the UK than the rock-hard surfaces in Australia, swept triumphantly through USA, Canada and Wales, taking the gloss of the Welsh centenary celebrations by hammering them 23-3 in the international in Cardiff.

Graham Mourie had returned to international action and, he

Mark Shaw

Mexted and Shaw would form a devastatingly effective loose forward trio that would serve New Zealand handsomely through until the end of the 1982 season (excluding the '81 series against the Springboks when Mourie stepped aside on moral grounds).

It was on the Welsh tour that Shaw had his role as a blindside flanker clearly defined for the first time.

"Until that tour, loose forwards were basically loose forwards, everyone doing a bit of everything. But in Wales, Mourie, who was a great strategist, defined the roles of the openside flanker, the blindside flanker and the number eight.

"What we put into operation on that tour became the model for New Zealand rugby throughout the 1980s.

"Mourie was the continuity player, the guy who ranged wide, shadowing opposition players, tackling threequarters, anyone who threatened. He was great on his feet, the perfect link.

"Mexted, who didn't like putting his head into rucks and mauls, had great athletic skills – he was mighty down the back of the lineout and with the ball in hand, haring all over the place.

"I didn't have the speed and skills of the other two, so I was happy crashing and bashing and driving ahead, tackling anything that moved, playing what became known as the tight-loose role.

"Collectively, we were bloody effective. It wasn't an exaggeration to say that, in those days, the team with the best set of loosies usually won. We were a team within a team and we enabled the All Blacks to put into effect the continuity game that eventually overwhelmed virtually every opponent."

Shaw thrived on touring with the All Blacks, the intensive training sessions, the physical commitment, the camaraderie. "It took over my life," he says. "By the time I'd got through the Welsh tour I'd become pretty hard-nosed about it. 'This is me,' I'd decided. It was what I'd been put on earth to do. Any guy who wanted my spot in the All Blacks was going to have to fight me for it!

"Seeing the tears in Bruce Robertson's eyes before the test in Cardiff was the epitome for me of what being an All Black is all about. Put the binoculars on Zinzan Brooke, Michael Jones and Sean Fitzpatrick now and you'll see it in their eyes, that total commitment to being an All Black."

Shaw says he was always motivated when he took the field in the black jersey and always strove to give 100 per cent. "There was never an occasion when playing for the All Blacks was just another game."

He laments that since his exit from the international scene "too many players have got the All Black jersey and not respected it" and he cites the decision to take 36 players to South Africa in 1996 as an example of this. "It helped us achieve an historic series win there, I acknowledge that, but should those guys who were taken along simply to play midweek matches have been full All Blacks?"

From 1980 through until the Cavaliers' tour made such a shambles of things in 1986, Shaw would miss only three test matches.

He watched the infamous 'flour bomb' test against the Springboks at Eden Park in 1981 from his lounge after injuring his hip playing for Manawatu against Southland the previous Saturday.

"I was given twenty-four hours to come right after assembly, didn't, so was flown back home to Palmerston North, thus missing all the drama that surrounded the Auckland test.

"I wouldn't say I was instrumental in getting my Manawatu teammate Geoff Old into the team but when the selectors asked for my opinion, I told them Oldie was the obvious choice to replace me. He'd been a reserve for three years, knew all the calls and was bloody talented. He went out a played a boomer."

The only other tests Shaw missed were the second and third on the tour of Australia in 1984 after teammate John Ashworth had trodden on him in the first international in Sydney. "I've still got the bloody scar!" Frank Shelford replaced him on those two occasions.

Shaw considers he produced his best rugby in 1982 and 1983. "That was when I was really humming," he says.

In 1982, he thought he was going to win a Subaru car which was to be presented to the player of the series. "Bob Dwyer (the Australian coach) voted for me, but not enough others did and it went to Allan Hewson.

"They were the days of strict amateurism and Hewie's club, Petone, relieved him of it and sold it. I think all Hewie got out of it was a weekend for two at Taupo and a bottle of wine. My club was prepared to sell the car and share the profits with me. Such is life!"

Having been replaced by Shelford in the test line-up in Australia in '84, Shaw was grimly determined to re-establish himself the next year.

"The All Blacks were going off to tackle the biggest, meanest, toughest opponents in the world, the Springboks, on their fields. To have missed selection would have been the end of the world. I would have been suicidal!

"So I trained like a demon through the summer. Ken Maharey set me a personal programme which was pretty revolutionary at the time. He even had me doing track work – now that was something special! There was no way I was going to be left behind."

But, of course, every All Black was left behind when a High Court injunction forced the abandonment of the tour, an event which Shaw brands the biggest disappointment of his rugby career.

Shaw was among a group of All Blacks invited to participate in the IRB centenary matches at Cardiff and Twickenham in early 1986 before flying down to Johannesburg to link up with the Cavaliers.

"It wasn't the way we wanted things to happen," says Shaw, "but at least I can say I played a test series against the Springboks in South Africa, and that is the ultimate for any New Zealand rugby player."

The rugged itinerary – four tests on successive Saturdays with midweekers against powerful sides such as Western Province, Natal and the South African Barbarians – combined with the strength and pace of the Springboks took its toll, the Cavaliers managing just a solitary test victory.

Shaw played the first three tests before giving way to Alan Whetton.

His final official test outing, back home, was against Alan Jones' Wallabies at Eden Park, a game the All Blacks dropped 22-9.

Shaw doesn't reflect too kindly on his captain, David Kirk, for what happened. "We won enough ball to win three test matches that day, but Kirk just kept shovelling it on and the Aussies kept knocking us over. I went to him at one stage and said, 'Give us the ball, we'll turn this around,' but he wouldn't. With a Dave Loveridge there, we'd have rescued that game."

Although he toured France at the end of '86, it was as a midweeker, the test No 6 jersey having been claimed by Mike Brewer who had established himself as a Baby Black while the Cavaliers were away.

Shaw made a strong bid for inclusion in the World Cup squad the next season. "I came out fighting, having trained hard through the summer, but I'd passed my use-by date. Brian Lochore pre-warned me that I wouldn't be in the squad, which I appreciated."

Rugby Greats

Although 1986 was a confused year for New Zealand rugby, Shaw gives it a special rating, because he played under and was controlled by three individuals who meant so much to him – Brian Lochore, the All Black coach, and Ian Kirkpatrick and Colin Meads, who were manager and coach of the Cavaliers.

"Whenever you shuffle the cards, those three guys come to the top. They are three mighty men, three of the giants of rugby."

Having played 87 games for Manawatu, Shaw rounded out his representative career with Hawkes Bay, making 20 appearances for the Hawkeye guys from 1986 to 1988.

It wasn't long before he was making his mark as a coach and in 1991 he guided Hutt Old Boys to Jubilee Cup glory – for the first time since 1934 – in the Wellington senior club championship.

The NZRFU has recognised his talents. They sent him as assistant coach to Lane Penn on the New Zealand Divisional team's tour of the Pacific Islands in 1988 and he was appointed a New Zealand under-19 selector in 1995, becoming assistant coach of that team to Wayne Smith in 1997.

The manager of the steel structural division of Dimond Industries, Shaw lives on the waterfront at Paekakariki with his wife Mandy and their four daughters, Lisa, Sarah, Jackie and Karen.

Mark Shaw demonstrating his skills against the British Lions in 1983. Coming at him is fellow flanker Peter Winterbottom. Fotopacific

Wayne Shelford

He was unrivalled as a winning captain. As an All Black leader on 31 occasions, he never had to make a losing speech. The New Zealand Maori teams he led dropped just one game in 13 – to mighty Auckland – and his teams never lost in the All Black trials.

It was an awesome record that Wayne 'Buck' Shelford built up, which made the telephone call on 11 July, 1990, from Alex Wyllie, the national coach, to Peter Thorburn, coach of North Harbour, so extraordinary.

Shelford was outside his Whangarei motel practising lineouts in preparation for that afternoon's NPC game against Northland when the call came through.

Thorburn called Shelford into his room.

"He had tears in his eyes," says Shelford. "He had just fielded a call from Grizz (Wyllie) advising that I had to play really well that day because they were considering dropping me. John Hart (a national selector) would be at the game."

Thorburn took the news worse than Shelford. He couldn't believe what he'd just heard.

"Buck probably hadn't produced his best form in the series just concluded against Scotland," says Thorburn, "but he had been absolutely dynamic on the tour of Ireland and Wales at the end of 1989, and you only had to look at his record. Teams under Buck performed."

North Harbour's laboured 9-6 victory didn't provide Shelford with the sort of opportunities he needed to convince Hart that, at the age of 32, he was recapturing his finest form.

The next day the fateful call came from Wyllie. He told Shelford the selectors weren't considering him for the first test against the Wallabies. "We think you're carrying a knee injury," he told him.

Shelford replied that he didn't have a knee injury.

"What's that bandage on your leg?" asked Wyllie.

"I've been having sciatica," replied Shelford. "I'm wearing the bandage to keep the hamstring warm."

"That's your decision," said Wyllie, "but we're not choosing you."

Shelford sat down trying to comprehend the significance of what the All Black coach had just told him.

Before he'd made any sense of it, the phone rang again.

"It was Grizz back. He wanted to know what leg it was that was injured. I felt angry at that stage and said, 'Print what you want' and hung up."

Shelford, a veteran of 48 All Black appearances over five years and a hero of the triumphant first World Cup campaign, would never play for his country again.

He would make a bid to regain his position but Zinzan Brooke would wear the No. 8 test jersey throughout 1990 and on to the second World Cup after which Shelford would cut his ties with New Zealand and play out his rugby career in England and Italy.

He still wonders about the events of 1990.

"I was disappointed that no one gave me a decent reason why I was dropped," he says. "The injury story was nonsense. I played right through the season with North Harbour.

"I don't believe I performed that badly against Scotland. There were others who played worse and survived.

"At the end of the day, it was a set-up. They'd taken me out of the equation. I'd been an All Black since 1985 so they knew my play. Don't tell me they would drop someone on the strength of one NPC game."

Shelford's sacking shocked the country and would engender amazing "Bring Back Buck" fervour, the campaign surviving till long after Buck had passed his Use By date.

In the wake of his departure from the All Blacks, innuendo flourished. The most popular story was that he and Grant Fox had

Wayne Shelford

No one led the haka with greater passion than Wayne 'Buck' Shelford. With their tongues in the right place for this performance at Eden Park are Bruce Deans and Richard Loe.   John Selkirk

come to blows in the dressing room. Another had him trading blows with Alex Wyllie.

"None of that happened," says Shelford. "It's all nonsense."

What he believes is closest to the truth is that Fox, reacting to comments Shelford made after the narrow victory over Scotland at Eden Park, told Wyllie that if Shelford played for the All Blacks again, to count him out.

"That's the most likely scenario," he says, "one player putting pressure on the coach, but nothing's ever come out, so who knows."

Being dropped was something Shelford hadn't experienced since he was at intermediate school in Rotorua. On that occasion his father had had an earnest discussion with the coach, and he was reinstated for the next game!

Shelford's father didn't intervene on this occasion but undoubtedly there were dozens, probably hundreds, of his supporters up and down the country who passionately expressed their disappointment to the selectors at the dropping of a footballer who in his lifetime had achieved legendary status.

Shelford had the bloodlines to excel in sport. His father had played rugby and league to senior level, his father's cousin Bill Shelford had won the world 14-inch standing block woodchopping event while on his mother's side, one brother (Bill McLennan) had played league for New Zealand while two others, Gordon and Jack, had represented Otago at rugby.

At Western Heights High School, Shelford, who was playing rugby from the age of five, made a deep impression on the coach, Dick Gordon. "During his two seasons in the first fifteen, he played every match, thirty-four in total," says Gordon. "He was as hard then as he was when he became an All Black. Hika Reid was in our team, too, another player destined to go to the top.

"Wayne's rugby was not unlike that of Colin Meads. My memories of him are of his storming runs down the park, ball in one hand. His intensity was apparent. He never gave less than one hundred per cent."

When he left school at the end of 1974 – better qualified in sport than academically – Shelford moved to Auckland to join the Navy. He signed up for eight years, being based initially at HMNZS *Tamaki* where he underwent BCT (basic common training). Shelford, who came to be recognised as one of the fittest, and hardest, men in rugby, concedes that in those opening months in the Navy he wondered what had hit him. "It became easier after about three years, but for a start the training was brutal," he says. The early training involved lifesaving, swimming, working with ropes, learning naval history and fitness training.

Shelford wanted to become a physical training instructor and was disappointed when told he couldn't until he had completed four years training. So he started as a junior communications officer, quickly switching to the gunnery section when confronted with the complexities of morse code.

Super fit, Shelford excelled on the rugby field, being granted extra leave to play for the Navy under-18 team from where he was selected as a No. 8 to represent Auckland under-18, a team that also featured Joe Stanley and Nicky Allen.

He acknowledges that he was a hothead in those days. "I was too quick with my fists and too ready to use head high tackles. I was seriously lacking in discipline. At that stage I equated roughness with good play. I had a lot to learn!"

Shelford's career over the next few years became a stimulating mix of shipboard life, overseas exercises and rugby. Assigned to HMNZS *Otago*, he visited such exotic destinations as Darwin, Singapore, Manila, Pago Pago, San Diego, Portland and ports on the west coast of Canada almost as far north as Alaska.

His rugby career developed promisingly. The Navy team of which he was a member won the national Services tournament in 1977 and the next year he was selected as a New Zealand Colt, the team undertaking a four match internal tour.

When he missed selection for New Zealand Juniors in 1979, he concentrated his attentions on life in the navy, undertaking a number of overseas trips aboard *Otago*, resuming his rugby career in earnest in 1981, at the age of 23.

First, he transferred from the Navy club, which was languishing in second division, to North Shore to achieve better quality rugby. It was, he considers, the first time in his life he had demonstrated any ambition regarding his rugby.

Bryan Craies, the Auckland coach, disregarded him that first year but John Hart snapped him up in 1982 and used him at No. 8 throughout the successful NPC campaign.

As a newcomer, Shelford found it hard to be accepted. At training one night he suggested the locks weren't tight enough. "For the next several scrums Andy Haden and Gary Whetton bound together so snugly, I couldn't get my head in!"

Maori rugby began to assume a special significance. Shelford had been a reserve for the national team's game against the Springboks in Napier in 1981. When he then featured prominently in Northern

Maori's Prince of Wales Cup victory the next season, he rated himself a contender for the New Zealand Maori team's big end-of-year tour to Wales and Spain.

There was a Shelford in the touring party. But not Wayne. It was his second cousin Frank, a dynamic flanker who'd broken into the All Blacks in '81.

Buck Shelford, based at Wigram, Christchurch, at the time, was hugely disappointed when the selectors preferred Carlos Baker and Colin Cooper as their No. 8s. At the time the Maoris were heading for Wales, Shelford was being transferred to Blenheim on a training course.

He had been out walking the snowlines for three days and when he returned to camp there was a telegram informing him that he was to replace Cooper who had damaged his medial ligaments.

"It was the opportunity I was looking for," he says, "although I had to take some reference books along to study as I had an exam to sit upon my return."

Shelford was undervalued by the Maori selectors, being used only twice, against Llanelli and the Spanish President's XV at Barcelona. Jim Love, taken as a lock, was the No. 8 against Wales while Carlos Baker was preferred against Spain.

Shelford found fault with the team's management. "It was in many ways an undisciplined tour," he says. "Many areas needed improving – the coaching, the management and even the calibre of the players chosen. The training was disorganised and the social commitments excessive. The match strategy seemed to be to throw the ball about without being constructive, as a result of which there were as many losses as wins in Wales."

Shelford still couldn't secure a place in the Maori team in 1983, Dale Atkins having come through to claim the No. 8 jersey. However, he did become involved in the two tests against Tonga as a replacement, enough for him to score three tries.

It wasn't a vintage year for Shelford. Hart used him eight times as a blindside flanker, a position with which he was never comfortable. "I was blamed for missing a couple of vital tackles in the Ranfurly Shield challenge against Canterbury (which Auckland lost 31-9)," he says, "and didn't fare much better when we drew nil-all with *Otago* in the mud at Carisbrook. After that, Harty dropped me for the final match of the season. That was a fair kick in the teeth."

Wayne Shelford

Shelford's career began its upward spiral in 1984, largely thanks to the misfortune of Glenn Rich who snapped his Achilles tendon. That created an opening at No. 8 which Shelford filled, Alan Whetton becoming the blindside specialist.

"It was the opportunity I was waiting for," he recalls. "Auckland played magnificent rugby all season to win the NPC which boosted us all as individuals. It led to me getting an All Black trial early in the 1985 season."

The *Rugby Annual* identified loose forwards Shelford, Whetton and Grant Dickson as a "potent striking force" whose well organised defensive patterns meant only 15 tries were scored against Auckland in 21 matches. At the not inconsiderable age of 26, Shelford was named Auckland's most promising player of the year.

If Shelford feared that the move across the harbour bridge to the North Harbour union in 1985 might hamper his rugby career, he couldn't have been further wrong. It took off in the most spectacular fashion.

In rapid succession in '85, Shelford progressed from participation in the New Zealand sevens team at Hong Kong, to North Island selection, to an All Black trial, to captaincy of New Zealand Maori against Waikato, to captaincy of the New Zealand Emerging Players team on an internal tour, to selection for the All Blacks (who should have gone to South Africa but who toured Argentina instead) to captaincy of the New Zealand Combined Services team on its tour of the UK.

Shelford was back in New Zealand from the Argentinian experience – where he toured in the shadow of Murray Mexted after making his All Black debut against San Isidro at Buenos Aires – only 48 hours before flying out with the Services team which was to enjoy enormous success. They won all eight matches including the 'tests' against the British Police and British Combined Services, scoring 47 tries and conceding just one.

He found the servicemens' approach contrasted dramatically with the All Blacks who were utterly dedicated to representing their country. "The servicemen wanted to socialise a lot more," he says. "You couldn't discourage that or they would revolt. Often on the night before matches they would drink and get out the guitars. They were playing rugby for different reasons to the All Blacks! It wasn't

Trouble looming for French fullback Serge Blanco as Wayne Shelford moves in on his prey during the World Cup final at Eden Park in 1987. Following the action is Eric Champ.

John Selkirk

my way but I could appreciate where they were coming from."

North Harbour prospered in its first season. Shelford became the union's first All Black while the team advanced to the second division by crushing Nelson Bays in the NPC play-off, a match in which Shelford scored two tries.

It seemed North Harbour would progress unhindered to the first division the next year, but Waikato proved a stumbling block. A last-minute runaway try allowed the Mooloo men to gain promotion while the new boys stayed put in division two. "That probably was a good thing," says Shelford. "Instant promotion might have given some of the players an over-inflated idea of their ability. It gave the union time to reflect and assess where it was going. That extra year in second division made us stronger."

When Shelford shared in New Zealand's thrilling sevens victory at Hong Kong in March of 1986 he little suspected that a month later he would be back there, en route to South Africa, as a member of the unsanctioned Cavaliers team.

Wayne Shelford

The team that should have toured in '85, with two exceptions (John Kirwan and David Kirk), were off to do battle with the Springboks, regardless of what the High Court and the Government, not to mention the NZRFU, thought.

From a playing viewpoint, nothing much had changed since 1985, with Shelford still understudy to Mexted, although he was accorded the honour of captaincy for the matches against the Barbarians at Ellis Park and Western Transvaal at Potchefstroom.

After the tour captain Andy Dalton had his jaw shattered, by a punch, in the second match Jock Hobbs took over the leadership.

Shelford feels that despite the (3-1) series loss, and the subsequent two test suspension imposed on all the players by the NZRFU, the Cavaliers were justified in touring. "Our democratic rights had been usurped in 1985," he says, "and we were determined to get there. A test series against the Springboks is the ultimate for any New Zealand rugby player and for many of our guys this was their only opportunity to fulfil that desire."

Shelford resigned from the Navy to tour with the Cavaliers. He didn't want to, but they refused to grant him leave (with or without pay). So he applied for immediate dismissal which, notwithstanding his 11 years' involvement, was granted.

Upon his return to New Zealand, Shelford applied for readmission to the Navy. After three weeks, he was advised there were no jobs available. The Navy would advise him if there was a job coming up. Shelford says he knows that at the time they were six short in his rank.

"The Navy bosses didn't want me back after the ruckus my departure had caused," he says. "I wrote again and this time was informed I would not be considered for any position in the Navy.

"Because I felt I had been unfairly treated, I took my case to the Ombudsman. Unfortunately, the gentleman handling my case died. His successor eventually informed me that he supported the Navy's stance. And that was that."

So Shelford turned his attentions to the Army but upon a directive from Wellington, he was blocked there too.

Concerned about his lack of income, he linked up with Murray Deaker (now a radio and TV personality) at FADE, the Foundation for Alcohol and Drug Education, presenting school lectures and promotions. That kept him going until 1988 when he joined the Apple

Rugby Greats

and Pear Board before joining the IMG marketing group

A broken hand kept Shelford out of the last two tests of the 1986 series against the Wallabies but he returned to international duty in France at season's end, making his test debut at Toulouse. He marked it sweetly by scoring New Zealand's only try in a hard-taken 19-7 victory.

The rematch at Nantes a week later survives as one of the most painful memories of his rugby career. Not only were the All Blacks destroyed – being flattered by the 16-3 scoreline – but Shelford was forced from the field with horrendous injuries. He lost three teeth, was concussed and had the right testicle ripped out of his scrotum, 18 stitches being required to repair the damage.

If that was a low point in Shelford's celebrated career, it was followed by the highest of highs only seven months later – victory at the first World Cup, with Big Buck a commanding performer throughout.

Indeed, after the All Blacks had demolished all six of their opponents, including France in the final, the French unhesitatingly singled him out as the All Black who made the greatest impact on the tournament. Pierre Berbizier, their coach, said Shelford was so impressive because he always kept his team going forward. "Even if only by fifty centimetres, he always makes progress."

Shelford was used at No. 8 in all matches except the pool game against Argentina when Andy Earl was given an outing. He received glowing reviews except when he punched Welshman Huw Richards in the semi-final at Ballymore. Fortunately for Shelford, referee Kerry Fitzgerald didn't see his punch which left Richards dazed. When Richards came to, it was to discover that the referee had ordered him off!

The 29-9 defeat of France in the final was adequate compensation for the agonies of Nantes, although there was a tinge of sadness associated with the triumph because the true captain, Andy Dalton, had not been able to participate after pulling a hamstring.

"Our personal reward," says Shelford, "was a gold medal and I recall clutching it in the manner I'm sure medal winners do at the Olympic Games. The changing room was abuzz for more than an hour and we even did a victory haka."

David Kirk, who'd inherited the captaincy after Dalton's

262

Wayne Shelford

misfortune, led the team to another outstanding victory, against the Wallabies in Sydney, then headed for Oxford University to take up his Rhodes Scholarship.

With Dalton and Hobbs easing out of top-level rugby and Brian Lochore stepping down, the positions of captain and coach of the All Blacks were up for grabs. Shelford was the natural choice as leader but there was a fair old dog-fight over the coaching post. John Hart was in charge in the All Blacks to Japan but Alex Wyllie, his deputy there, came through to win the appointment at the beginning of 1988 that technically would run through to the second World Cup.

The Wyllie-Shelford partnership would guide New Zealand with spectacular success through until Shelford's unexpected axing in 1990.

With Shelford leading from the front, and unnerving opponents with his aggressive haka, the All Blacks swept aside such proud opponents as Wales, Australia, Argentina, France and Ireland, their average winning total in 11 internationals during 1988 and 1989 being an astonishing 36 points. They twice hit the half-century against Wales and put 60 points on the Pumas.

They came through a 13-match tour of Australia and a 14-match tour of Wales and Ireland unscathed, consistently producing high-quality, 15-man rugby that delighted the fans.

Shelford admits that he revelled in the captaincy. "I know that David Kirk found the job a burden and frustrating at times and that Jock Hobbs used to hibernate, but I always tried to be available. I called the shots on the field but I was a captain who liked to mingle with his team."

By 1989, Zinzan Brooke was challenging Shelford for his position. Before the team departed for Wales and Ireland, Zinzan approached Shelford and said that John Hart had told him he would be playing in the test matches.

Shelford was relaxed about the situation. "Well, Zinny, if you are playing better than me, I'll step down. We're good friends, let's see how it goes. John Hart is not the coach – Grizz is."

As it turned out, Shelford produced some of the finest rugby of his career and his test position was never under threat, although he did give way to Brooke during the Barbarians match.

That was because Shelford had seriously damaged neck vertebrae in the test against Ireland. "A welcoming committee of three Irishmen crunched into me early in the game," recalls Shelford. "I've never known such pain. It was like a burning rod. Our physio repaired me well enough to see out the game."

Against the Barbarians a week later, Shelford took another blow on the neck, after which he had trouble lifting his arm. "It was affecting my tackling, so in the interests of the team, I came off."

The downfall of Shelford as a captain was being plotted in 1989, he was to discover several years later. "Meetings were going on behind closed doors," he says, "meetings I didn't know about. Gary Whetton was directly involved. Essentially, they wanted me out and Zinzan in."

It came to pass after the All Blacks struggled to defeat Scotland at Eden Park in June, 1990, that Brooke did replace Shelford, thereby ending what had been a comparatively brief, but certainly illustrious, 22-test career.

There was an element of controversy associated with Shelford's final test appearance. It directly involved Fox but it was something that went much deeper than that, something Shelford considers eventually undermined the All Blacks' 1991 World Cup campaign.

"By 1990 the players had started doing their own thing," he says. "The big forwards were no longer doing the hard, grinding work. They were looking for the plums instead. I personally felt that only Alan Whetton, Michael Jones and myself were getting stuck in.

"At halftime in the second test against Scotland the guys said they wanted to spin the ball. I said, 'No, put it in the air and let's get stuck into them.' It was only Foxy's boot that allowed us to escape."

At the press conference, Shelford, defending the team's tactics, said that because he had his head in the scrum, Fox was his eyes. "He's the general I rely on." This was interpreted by some as a criticism of Fox, although it was never intended as such.

Unwanted by the selectors, Shelford headed for the UK, joining Northampton as a player. The first game he watched, the side lost 60-nil to Orrell. He wondered what he was getting into.

But taking their inspiration from him, Northampton developed into a powerful unit, progressing to the final of the Pilkington Cup against Harlequins, by which stage the whole town was in behind the team. "We'd gone from attendances of about thirty to six thousand," says Shelford proudly.

He missed the final when he returned to New Zealand for the trials,

Wayne Shelford

Wayne Shelford, wearing his Northampton jersey. Taking inspiration from him, the club developed into a powerful unit, reaching the Pilkington Cup final.

Fotopacific

hoping to win a place in the World Cup squad. Although he performed well enough opposite Brooke, the selectors didn't want him. Brooke, Mike Brewer and Arran Pene were all rated higher, although Shelford observes wryly that the day the World Cup team was announced, he was the only one fit.

Shelford did attend the World Cup, as an accredited journalist, watching with dismay as the All Blacks went down the gurgler. "They were the worst organised All Black team ever," he says. "The danger signs were there in the Bledisloe Cup games but no one did anything about them."

Shelford would have nothing more to do with New Zealand rugby until 1995 when he returned home to assist Chas Ferris with the coaching of North Harbour.

He had three enjoyable seasons with Northampton, reaching the semi-finals of the Pilkington Cup on two more occasions, before moving on to Italy where he linked with the Roma Olympique club as a player-coach, occasionally nipping across to England to conduct coaching seminars.

He found the commitment of the Italian players "fantastic" but their skill level "pathetic".

"Once they travelled beyond the hills of Rome, they didn't care. They were dynamic at home but in away matches they had no heart. It's hard to get a grip on their mentality."

He got Roma through to the semi-finals both years, but they were no match for the 'big boys, Milano and Benetton, although in his farewell appearance the Roma players, giving the performance of their lives, downed Benetton in front of 15,000 Benetton fans. "Benetton had put sixty points on us in the first semi in Rome, so they advanced to the final."

Shelford involved himself with a none-too-successful North Harbour side upon his return in mid 1995 but stepped aside from all serious rugby the following year while he settled into the role of owner/manager of the Wade Hotel at Silverdale, 20 kilometres north of Auckland, where he lives with his wife Joanne and children Lia, 15, and Eruera, 12.

For 1997, he was appointed coach of the North Harbour Development squad, in which position he was to be working closely with Harbour's representative coach Peter Thorburn.

Wayne Smith

Wayne Smith made more than 100 appearances for Canterbury and the All Blacks and many of them survive vividly in his memory.

Oddly, right up there with them is a game he didn't play for Waikato in 1978. It was a game that could have had a profound influence on his career.

As a promising young first-five from Putaruru, he'd been included in the Waikato representative squad and named by coach George Simpkin to make his debut in the annual Queen's Birthday clash against Auckland.

At least, he remembers being named in the starting fifteen. But when he assembled with the team on match day, it was to be told that Alan Hopson had been preferred.

"To this day, I have never established why I was replaced," says Smith. "I sat on the reserves' bench and watched Waikato win, as they always did in that holiday weekend fixture.

"I never did get to take the field for Waikato. I wasn't bitter about the Auckland game, just mystified."

The encouragement of a representative appearance could well have influenced Smith, then 21, to stay in the Waikato. Instead, at the beginning of 1979 he headed south to the enrol at Teachers College in Christchurch.

"I chose to go to Christchurch because I'd noted that Doug Bruce had retired and felt there might be an opening for a free-spirited first-five." It was an optimistic attitude from someone who hadn't

Wayne Smith takes his exit from Carisbrook, Dunedin, after being injured during the third test against the British Lions in 1983. Many of the New Zealand players wore thermal vests to protect against the cold.   John Selkirk

advanced beyond the Waikato B.

Yet before the year was out, Smith would not only secure a position in the Canterbury team but would be placed on standby for the All Blacks' tour of Scotland and England. The man who might have decorated the Mooloo backline went on instead to become one of the favourite sons of Lancaster Park.

After making the journey south in 1979 in his trusty Valiant, Smith turned up at an early season training session of the Christchurch club but, discouraged at finding 90 players there trying out for the senior squad, went away.

His cousin, who worked at the Belfast freezing works, suggested he consider Belfast, an unfashionable senior team possessing powerful forwards (headed by All Black prop Billy Bush) but no backs of any consequence.

"There were only thirty people trying out at Belfast, very few of them backs," says Smith. "I said, 'This'll do me'. I began training with them, trialed there, and I've been a member of the club ever since!"

Coming from Putaruru – where his earliest rugby memories were of playing barefoot on frosty winter mornings – Belfast, based 10 kilometres north of Christchurch, appealed to Smith because it was essentially a country club in the city.

"They were in the bottom eight when I joined," recalls Smith, "but we soon worked our way up to the top four. Our forwards were always powerful and the backline really sparked when Kieran Keane (an All Black to Britain in 1979) came across from University."

The Belfast executive were pretty excited about their new first-five, to the extent they telephoned Canterbury selector Gerald Wilson and suggested he make the journey out to Belfast to check out the Smith boy first hand.

As a consequence, Smith was added to the representative squad. When Canterbury then stumbled in successive matches against Queensland and, believe it or not, Mid-Canterbury, Wilson and his fellow selector-coach Tiny Hill decided to give the boot to their first-five, 19-year-old Robbie Deans. They replaced him with Smith.

"It was probably the best thing that could have happened to Robbie," says Smith, "because he concentrated on fullback after that and went on to become one of Canterbury's greatest achievers."

Promoted to the representative team for the 'friendly' against South Canterbury in Timaru, Smith wasn't sure what he found the more terrifying – debuting for Canterbury or coming under the influence of the team's legendary captain Alex 'Grizz' Wyllie, who was in his 16th and last year of representative play.

"Alex had a frightening reputation, especially with the young players," says Smith. "I remember Gary Barkle telling me about his first bus trip when he was summoned by Grizz and ordered to drink a fearsome amount of beer, or have his ears whacked. He called him Mr Wyllie!"

Smith managed to gain Wyllie's approval both on the field and in the bus.

Against South Canterbury, Wyllie ordered a kick "into the box" from a set piece on the right hand side of the field. "I think it was a test to see if I could kick with my left foot," says Smith. "Well, luckily, it was a dream kick, right where he wanted it. As we advanced downfield, he patted me on the shoulder. He maintained a dignified silence, but it was an enormous boost to my confidence."

On the bus trip home from Timaru, John Collinson, who'd been a reserve that afternoon, did the unthinkable, and pilfered some of the great man's beer. "Well, you can imagine the uproar that caused," says Smith. 'Who's taken my beer?' he thundered. We all cringed because it was probable that the beers Collinson had given us belonged to Grizz. Luckily for me, Billy Bush was his henchman and, being a fellow Belfast player, he gave me a wink and declared me 'clean'. It was a close shave!"

Smith describes Wyllie's influence on the team as remarkable. "He was a total autocrat, which in other circumstances might have been a problem. But Grizz had amazing vision and understood the game totally. He controlled the whole show, calling every move. You didn't argue, you just did what he called."

A classic example of Wyllie's absolute authority came in one of Smith's early games at Lancaster Park. "We'd only been playing about five minutes, in cold, wet conditions, when Grizz called a 'Lefto' move which involved the blindside winger running into the backline outside me.

"As Grizz was sticking his head into the scrum, I informed the winger of the Lefto move. He shook his head, claiming he wasn't warmed up. 'Over-rule it,' he said. So I booted for touch. 'What the hell's going on?' asked Grizz as the scrum broke up. 'I ordered the Lefto move.' I told him the winger had over-ruled it because he wasn't ready.

"'Is that so?' said Grizz, switching his attentions to the winger. The winger confirmed that he wasn't ready for such a move. 'In that case,' said Grizz, 'you can f— off!' Whereupon he signalled to the grandstand for a replacement. The referee stopped the game until Wyllie had finished making the substitution."

Smith valued his association with the Canterbury team because it presented the opportunity to stay in quality hotels and eat nourishing meals. Which certainly wasn't the situation back at his student flat in Christchurch.

"The pad we lived at in Kenilworth Ave was an absolute dive," he recalls. "We boarded up the holes to keep the cats, and the cold, out. In the depths of winter, because we couldn't afford fuel, we used to burn strainer posts from a farm nearby. It's fair to say I wasn't satisfying my nutritional requirements while I lived there either!"

Canterbury had to settle for fourth in the NPC that season, losing their chance for glory with a mid-season slump. The *Rugby Annual* recorded that while Canterbury's forward strength was evident "the backs were disappointing".

The exception was Wayne Smith who was described as the backline's "only real star".

The All Black selectors were impressed with Smith too, placing him on standby for the tour of England and Scotland. "That provided a huge buzz," says Smith, "and made me train my heart out. I went on a Teachers College trip to Mt Aspiring and walked the Routeburn track. To sharpen my fitness, I would run from hut to hut while the others were walking. I watched every match on their tour with nervous excitement but the two first-fives, Murray Taylor and Eddie Dunn, came through unscathed!"

Smith wouldn't have long to wait before graduating to All Black honours. In May of 1980 he was matched up against Auckland's Lindsay Harris in the trial at Hamilton, with the selectors resting the test incumbent Murray Taylor. It was a winner take all situation for Smith and Harris.

Smith had the better game and was duly selected. Adding to the pleasure of achieving All Black honours was the fact that the trial (and the announcement of the team) happened in the Waikato, his home territory. "I reckon half of Putaruru turned up at Rugby Park to cheer for me," says Smith.

A combination of extreme fitness and inadequate diet meant that at the time of his selection for the All Blacks, Smith weighed only 70kg, almost jockey weight.

Smith would survive only six matches, including the first test, before tearing his hamstring and returning home. His international debut was against Sydney where his opponent was the great Mark Ella. Ten minutes into the game Murray Taylor, the second-five, injured his leg and was replaced, bringing Gary Cunningham and Tim Twigden together in midfield.

"I called a Wipers move," says Smith, "but Gary said he couldn't kick and Tim said he couldn't kick either. So in my All Black debut I was saddled with all those extra responsibilities."

Smith came through well, drop-kicking a goal which allowed the

All Blacks to escape with a draw. He was duly named the New Zealand *Sunday News'* player of the match and arrived home to find a new toaster waiting for him.

He wouldn't remember his test debut so fondly, the genius of Ella creating a spectacular late try for the Wallabies to win 13-9. Smith acknowledges that he kicked poorly, allowing the Australians' big-booting fullback Roger Gould to emerge as the player of the game. "It was pretty devastating to go one down in a three test series."

The team moved north to tropical Townsville where Smith made his sixth appearance in eight matches, coming to grief with his hamstring severely torn. He was flown home and replaced by Nicky Allen.

His frustrations continued back home, with the injury slow to respond to treatment. He returned to duty with Canterbury but never recaptured his best form. Nor, for that matter, did Canterbury which finished a disappointing seventh in the NPC.

Ironically, the only success in Canterbury's last six outings was against Auckland at Eden Park, continuing an astonishing run of success Canterbury enjoyed during Smith's days in the red and black jersey. Canterbury defeated Auckland seven years in a row from 1977, the trend not being arrested until John Hart's team picked up the pace in 1984.

The season of 1981, when the visit by the Springboks threw New Zealand into turmoil, was a forgettable one for Smith. On the comeback trail, he broke his jaw which put him out of contention for the tests against Scotland. Doug Rollerson, who'd established himself on the tour of Wales the previous year, was used at first-five for the entire series against the Boks.

Smith, his jaw out of alignment until a second operation straightened it, managed only six games for Canterbury in what was a catastrophic season for such a proud union. They finished ninth in the NPC (with only Hawke's Bay and Southland below them).

Canterbury rugby would be dramatically rejuvenated in 1982 with the return, this time in the role of coach, of the one and only Alex Wyllie.

Not just because Grizz was taking over, Smith embarked on a weight-training programme through the summer, ran a lot and worked diligently on his skills, particularly his kicking.

Wayne Smith

"I was concerned about the up-and-down nature of my rugby," he says. "I wanted to achieve a routine that would build greater consistency, one that would load the odds my way."

By the time 1982 rolled around, Smith was working as a sales representative at the Canterbury Sports Depot where he came across a book called Peak Performances which fascinated him.

"It was about establishing pre-game routines and how to react in situations which demanded decision making," he says. "It helped me shape my rugby strategy."

The improvement in Canterbury rugby under Wyllie was instant. For a start, he reintroduced trials and selected his squad on merit. He demanded fitness and discipline. Smith found he complemented his own rugby philosophy perfectly.

"A lot of people think because Grizz was a forward, he was dour and unimaginative" says Smith, "but as a coach, he was tactically brilliant. Few people appreciated his skill. He was a revelation for me." Smith found him something of a bush psychologist. "He quickly came to appreciate which players needed massaging and which ones needed a boot in the bum. He allowed players the space in which to prepare."

There was never any question that Grizz *was* The Boss. Before a warm-up match against Marlborough at Blenheim, he ordered Smith to "run only twice" in the game.

"I'd used up my two runs in three minutes and thought 'What now!'" says Smith. "My game was an attacking one, taking on the defence, but Grizz obviously wanted to assess the talents of other players that day."

Wyllie introduced Bruce Deans at halfback ahead of Steve Scott. Initially, Smith was concerned that Deans' passes weren't as long. "But I quickly came to appreciate that it's not the length of pass that is important, but the speed with which it is delivered.

"Bruce's passes suited my game perfectly. They allowed me to get a flying start and develop my running game."

Things started to happen in '82. Warwick Taylor arrived from Otago, Craig Green from Mid-Canterbury and Vic Simpson materialised from the University club.

"They were three wonderfully talented players," says Smith, "but there were only two midfield places available to them. One of them was going to have to play on the wing. Vic, one of the few individuals brave enough to challenge Grizz, insisted it wouldn't be him. Craig, however, was happy to play anywhere to get a game. It prompted one of Grizz's more prophetic statements. 'Craig Green,' he snapped at Vic, 'will be an All Black before you'."

Smith was concerned that he might be remembered as an All Black who never made it, so he was delighted to be selected for the '82 Bledisloe Cup series against the Wallabies when for the first time he came under the influence of Graham Mourie whom he describes as "a great thinker on the game".

Smith, anxious to be a good All Black, was happy with his form throughout the series. "I didn't set the world on fire, but my kicking had improved out of sight. I felt I could dictate a game with either foot if I had to. My self esteem had risen and I knew that would count when I returned to Canterbury."

What sensations were to follow at representative level. Smith would be lauded as a hero before season's end after Canterbury, in a fairytale turnaround in fortunes, lifted the Ranfurly Shield from Wellington and retained it, albeit luckily, against two challengers.

Smith was never certain he would play in the shield challenge. "It was a toss-up," he says, "between Steve Scott and Kieran Keane or Bruce Deans and me. Grizz, acting on his intuition, went for Bruce and me.

"Grizz was at his motivational best before the game. He'd procured a tape of a radio interview given by Allan Hewson in which he said that Canterbury was wasting its time. 'They might as well hop on the plane and head home now,' he said. Grizz played it over and over and you could see guys like John Ashworth and Murray Davie seething. I'm not certain Hewie's comments were actually broadcast, but never mind, they had the desired effect on our team!"

It was a desperately tense, close-fought encounter with Wellington clinging to a 12-10 advantage for much of the second spell. Smith was feeling sick because early in the second half he had bombed a try by throwing a forward pass to an unmarked Craig Green.

"You don't always get a second chance, but that afternoon I did," says Smith. "Because Stu Wilson stayed out looking after Craig, I didn't have to throw a pass this time. The gap opened and I took it."

Smith's try behind the posts, converted by Robbie Deans, secured

Wayne Smith

Wayne Smith has support from his captain Andy Dalton as he gets taken in a double tackle against England at Athletic Park in 1985.   Photosport

the famous 'log' for Canterbury for the first time in nine years. The faithful fans who'd followed the team were ecstatic, as were the thousands who clogged Christchurch Airport for the team's return that evening. Smith had to drive over a garden to get out of the car park.

"No one," says Smith, "anticipated the fever that would grip the Canterbury province with the arrival of the shield. Even Grizz was caught by surprise. We'd been playing to crowds of about five thousand maximum and we didn't think things would change much.

"We were told to assemble at the ground at two o'clock, as usual, for the Counties challenge the next Saturday. When I drove to the ground, I couldn't find a car park. None of us had car passes and we had to take pot luck. As a result, half of us were late for the team meeting.

"There were almost forty thousand packed into Lancaster Park. We'd all underestimated the power of the Ranfurly Shield, as a result of which we nearly blew it. It needed a last minute penalty goal by Robbie Deans to salvage a draw. Our shield tenure was nearly over before it started."

The Counties experience shaped the rest of Canterbury's shield era.

Never again would the team assemble on the match afternoon. "Systems were put in place," says Smith. "Thereafter, we stayed together in a hotel the night before shield challenges."

Smith would undergo some bizarre treatment in 1983 to correct painful injuries.

After straining his back lifting weights before the All Black trials in Wellington, he was in agony. Christchurch physiotherapist Brian McKenzie identified a muscle imbalance stemming from a congenital back problem. To correct it, he prescribed inversion treatment which entailed Smith hanging upside down from a rail. "Not only did it fix the problem," says Smith, "I think I grew a few inches!"

That injury caused him to miss the first test against the British Lions but he returned for the second and third internationals, only to tear his groin muscle in the icy cold conditions that prevailed at Carisbrook. This time he was out for two and a half months, Smith finally, in despair, turning to a healer after trying all the orthodox remedies.

"This fellow smashed his hands together until they turned blue," says Smith, "at which point I wondered about his mental state. But he said they were the lengths I had to go to if I wanted to play sport again. I had to breach the pain barrier.

"The treatment involved lifting a sand-filled bucket – sidewards, backwards and frontwards. I had to do until I couldn't stand the pain any longer, and then do two more!

"Incredibly, it worked. Within a week I was playing for Canterbury B. And I came back for Canterbury's last three, important shield defences, against Wellington, Auckland and Manawatu. And to this day, my groin has never given me any more trouble!"

Smith would be a vital cog in the Canterbury team throughout its glorious shield era, until Auckland came calling one day in September, 1985. And that's when a soaring up-and-under from Smith in the final minute almost completed one of the greatest comebacks of all time in what became known as the Provincial Game of the Century.

Smith singles out two individuals for their valuable inputs during the shield era – the trainer Jim Blair (who eventually defected to Auckland) and the captain Don Hayes.

"Don Hayes was an inspiration to all of us, humility personified. Right to the end, he never let anyone get carried away. He helped shape my philosophy on hard work and on remaining humble.

"The year we smashed Otago 44-3 we scored from a spectacular triple scissors move with five minutes to play. Vic Simpson and I permitted ourselves a high five. 'Settle down,' said Don, 'the game's not over yet!'

"Jim Blair revolutionised our training methods when he joined us before the 1983 season. He was the first person to ask me what my particular role entailed. 'Do you run five metres or fifty?' he asked me. I said five, and he designed my individual training schedule accordingly. We also had personal programmes prepared based on speed and strength."

Smith visited England and Scotland with the All Blacks at the end of 1983 under the "hard case" captaincy of Stu Wilson, concluding that wing is not a good position from which to captain a team. Wilson's men drew with Scotland and lost to England.

Andy Dalton, one of a host of tight forwards unavailable for the UK excursion, was back in charge against France at home and on the tour of Australia in 1984, when the All Blacks came back sensationally from one test down to take out the Bledisloe Cup.

The French should have won the first test at Lancaster Park but their flyhalf Jean-Patrick Lescarboura missed four dropped goal attempts in the last six minutes.

"He was inconsolable afterwards," says Smith. "Every time I went to talk to him he burst into tears. They possessed huge talent, the French, but never met their potential. In the second test they self-destructed, running the ball from crazy situations."

Smith felt he produced his best rugby as an All Black in 1984. The *New Zealand Almanack* agreed, making him a player of the year.

When the All Blacks toured Fiji at season's end, Smith noted the entrance of a footballer of uncommon talent, Grant Fox.

"It was great to have another training partner," he says. "Warwick Taylor and I put a lot of work into our kicking, and ball skills. It was great to welcome a player with the same philosophy. I could see it was only a matter of time before he took over as the All Black first-five because he possessed a special rugby brain."

Fox wouldn't loom as a rival until late 1985, when the All Blacks toured Argentina (the consolation trip when the trek to South Africa was abandoned).

Rugby Greats

In the meantime, Smith appeared twice against England, giving arguably his worst test performance at Christchurch followed by one of his finest, seven days later, in Wellington and in the one-off Bledisloe Cup game against the Aussies in Auckland.

In Argentina, he picked up a bad viral infection which affected his kidneys and caused his weight to increase by almost half a stone. "For the first time in my life," he says, "I was able to bump opponents off!"

Because Smith was hospitalised for a time, Fox played the first test against the Pumas, but Smith was reinstated for the rematch, a game which was drawn with the maestro Hugo Porta scoring all 21 of Argentina's points. It was to be Smith's last appearance in the All Black jersey.

He would tour South Africa in 1986 as a rebel (after participating in the IRB centenary matches at Cardiff and Twickenham), displacing Fox for the fourth test when the Cavaliers decided they would run everything at the Boks in a bid – an unsuccessful one – to salvage a drawn series.

With the Ranfurly Shield gone, Fox poised to become the All Black first-five (he wouldn't actually make it until 1987) and feeling drained, Smith took a decision at the end of 1985 to step down from representative and All Black rugby (not appreciating at that stage that the Cavaliers tour would prolong his international career).

But there was one unfulfilled goal – to win the Hong Kong sevens title. He would achieve that in 1986 in glorious fashion. As captain, he led New Zealand to stunning victories in both the New South Wales and Hong Kong tournaments, scoring three tries in the final at Hong Kong.

Smith's career took a complete change of direction in late 1986 when he took up the joint roles of coach, captain and goalkicker with the Casale Sule Sile club near Venice in Italy, a huge challenge in a foreign speaking country, which became greater when the side lost its first 10 matches. But after they'd won seven games in the second round his reputation was restored!

After two seasons in Italy, Smith returned to Canterbury where from 1988 until 1992 he coached the Canterbury sevens team, the New Zealand sevens team and the Canterbury B team (and played three more games for the union in 1989). Being an employee of the union meant he wasn't eligible to coach the main representative team.

Wayne Smith

The punting style of Wayne Smith who played 17 tests for New Zealand in the 1980s. Photosport

So in 1992 he returned to Italy, joining their premier club Benetton as coaching director, responsible for the A, B and under-19 teams, having the satisfaction of getting all three teams into the national finals.

But two years was again enough, especially as his wife Trish and twin sons Nick and Josh were having to commute there in the holidays. "It was Italy or New Zealand, and I chose New Zealand," he says.

Back home, Smith took up an appointment as chief executive of the Hawke's Bay Rugby Union and although he thoroughly enjoyed the challenge, and worked fearfully hard to put a board structure in place, he realised his heart was really in coaching.

He was able to satisfy that ambition when appointed coach of the Canterbury Crusaders for the 1997 Rugby Super 12 campaign, with former All Black hooker Peter Sloane as his assistant. The NZRFU also named him coach of the New Zealand under-19 team.

Joe Stanley

"Choose a proven provincial player and put an All Black jersey on him and he'll never let you down." The quote belonged to Brian Lochore who, as the coach, had just engineered one of rugby's most astonishing achievements, the victory by the Baby Blacks against a full-strength French team at Lancaster Park in 1986.

Lochore and his fellow selectors had been obliged to turn to the provincial players of New Zealand after 30 of the nation's leading footballers, internationals all, had defied authority and taken themselves off to South Africa to do battle with the Springboks.

Back home, the show had to go on. Jacques Fouroux's Frenchmen were coming to town, and 15 All Black jerseys had to be filled.

A couple of positions looked after themselves, notably halfback and wing because David Kirk and John Kirwan had declined the invitation to become Cavaliers. But for the perplexed national coach the prospect of fielding up to a dozen rookie All Blacks in a test against a team as talented as France was daunting.

One position that was open till the last was centre. Iain Wood and Scott Pierce had been assessed in the trial in Blenheim after Frank Bunce had opposed Murray McLeod in the inter-island fixture in Oamaru. When Bunce limped off with a leg injury, he was replaced was Marty Berry.

Five options there with no indication that the selectors were interested in Joe Stanley who'd been Auckland's centre since 1982. John Hart had been pushing his case. But Joe was 29, awfully old to be breaking into the international scene.

Joe Stanley . . . didn't make the All Blacks until he was 29 but then appeared in 27 consecutive tests. Photosport

Joe Stanley

Chances are that if any of the other five had produced a blinder at that time – and Bunce was the most likely to, but he'd gone to Oamaru with badly strained ankle ligaments – Stanley may never have got his big break.

Lochore admitted later the selectors had had Stanley in mind all along for test selection, but wanted to assess various other options."We'd seen Joe many times, and he was very much in our minds," Lochore said. "None of the others impressed, so we thought Joe would do the job we wanted. It's fair to say we regarded him as nothing more than a good, solid, reliable centre. We certainly didn't anticipate the career that unfolded. Joe was one of those players who got better, the higher the level of play."

Good, solid and reliable – that was how he was perceived in 1986. No Smokin' Joe tag then. No expectations that he was a footballer capable of influencing the outcome of a test match. Probably no thought that he would even survive the return of the Cavaliers from South Africa.

But Joseph Tito Stanley, the centre who back in '82 had been dropped by Hart after one game for Auckland, would not only survive the return of the Cavaliers, no one would wrench the test No 13 jersey from him for more than four years, not till he had racked up 27 consecutive test appearances.

He would become the strong man of the All Black backline. Like Ian MacRae two decades earlier, he would be regularly used as a battering ram, a champion setter-up of second-phase play, not a role he relished but one which he uncomplainingly fulfilled because it was expected of him.

It was surprising that Stanley's talent took so long to manifest itself at top level because as a youngster he exuded class. A teacher at the Bayfield School in Auckland in the late 1960s, Tim Haslett, would identify skinny little Joe as a star in the making. "He was the only boy I ever suggested could be an All Black," says Haslett, these days a university lecturer in Australia. "And he was only eleven. When he got the ball and ran with it, it was immediately obvious he was a class above all the others."

Joe was the third eldest, and decidedly the skinniest, of nine children born to Joseph and Nancy Stanley who, after quitting Kinleith because of the cold winters, settled in Ponsonby. Being skinny meant becoming quick. "There was no point in a skinny little bloke like me standing and trying to fight," says Stanley. "With eight boys in the family, we were always going to end up scrapping, and if I didn't take off, I copped the worst of it!"

It wasn't long before young Joe developed an affinity with the Ponsonby Rugby Club which was walking distance from where he lived. "We'd often go there on Saturday mornings and roll around in the sawdust training area."

Haslett remembers Stanley as "a super kid" at Bayfield School, an inner city school with a mix of immigrant families, mostly Polynesian, and children from affluent European families. "Joe was always quiet and co-operative as a pupil," says Haslett. "No sign of the killer instinct that would come out the moment he stepped foot on the rugby field."

Mt Albert Grammar School, whose most famous rugby pupil had been Bryan Williams, would next benefit from Stanley's talents. Indeed, in his final two years, 1973 and 1974, Mt Albert would be the dominating force in Auckland secondary school rugby. The stars of the team were Fred Ah Kuoi, who would go on to captain New Zealand at league, Lindsay Harris, who would play more than 100 games for Auckland, and a dashing winger with a giant Afro hairstyle, Joe Stanley.

Stanley remembers Ah Kuoi as the player who set the Mt Albert team alight. "He had four years in the first fifteen, a player who developed young," he says. "He was inspirational. Most of our team were league players. Probably only two of us finished up playing rugby."

The man who would become the All Blacks' champion setter up of play, in those days avoided confrontation. "I was slightly built and not keen to tangle with opponents who all seemed to be bigger than me," he says. "I couldn't kick – that never changed – but I had a decent step, pace and could swerve, so whenever I got the ball, I just went for it. It was smarter to beat your opponent than engage him in physical contact."

The tackling that would become a Stanley forte didn't feature in those days. "I knew how to tackle," says Stanley. "But because most of my opponents were bigger than me, I didn't get too involved. It wasn't until I went north and played rugby league in Whangarei that tackling became a strength."

Stanley's talents had been obvious right through. He had been selected for the Auckland Roller Mills primary school team but unfortunately had to withdraw when he fell ill but he did get to pull on the Auckland representative jersey at under-16 and under-18 level.

By the time he'd been selected for the Auckland under-21 side in 1976 as a Ponsonby third grader, Stanley appeared to be on the brink of an exciting rugby career. But he would slip through the rugby net for a couple of years, trying his luck at league in Whangarei where he made sufficient impact to be invited to a national training school at Hunua. Rugby's good fortune is that he was so hopelessly out of condition he failed the fitness tests and pulled out without ever being given the chance to demonstrate his league skills.

Stanley went to Whangarei at the beginning of '77 to stay with his brother Robin because domestically things weren't working out for him in Auckland. He picked up a job at the Marsden Point oil refinery and ended up playing premier league with the West End Jumbos. "They were a fascinating mix of guys in their late thirties and teenagers," recalls Stanley.

The Jumbos were coached, and run from standoff, by former boxing champion Charlie Dunn. He acknowledges that Stanley transformed an average team into a dominating one. With Joe achieving wonders at centre, the Jumbos won the championship for the first time in 35 years, beating the Portland Parrots in the final. Stanley was the leading tryscorer in the competition with 33. *The New Zealand Rugby League Annual* recorded that Stanley's "scorching pace and beautiful fall-away passes for his wingers made him the most dangerous back in the north".

He won selection for North Auckland and from there was invited to a New Zealand Maori league trial in Huntly, interesting because both his parents were Western Samoan! Stanley basically went along for the ride, noting that he wasn't the only Polynesian passing himself off as a Maori.

Someone recognised his talent because at the beginning of 1978 he was selected to attend league's national coaching school. "I was reluctant to attend for various reasons," says Stanley. "I'd only gone to Whangarei on a working holiday and, deep down, I knew I wanted to return and play rugby for Ponsonby. Because I wasn't told about the coaching school until the new year, I was seriously out of condition."

So seriously out of condition that he walked the final stages of the 12-minute run and returned from the road run, feet seriously blistered, by car! The Kiwi coach, Ron Ackland, came and checked out the exhausted individual. "Mate, I'm stuffed," declared Stanley. "No more sessions for me." Ackland glowered back and said, "Future Kiwis are never stuffed." "Well," replied Stanley, "I'm stuffed and I'm out of here."

Abandoning the ill-fitting shoes which had tortured his feet, Stanley jumped in his car and headed back to Whangarei where he had to endure a degree of derision for wasting a great opportunity. Charlie Dunn told him he was "a bloody idiot – a stupid, useless idiot".

Stanley's life and rugby career underwent a major transformation in 1979 by which time he had returned to Auckland and reunited himself with the Ponsonby club. That same year his father died, aged just 52, of heart failure, in Apia only 24 hours after flying from Auckland. Joe was devastated. "He had been one of my greatest fans," he says, "and I felt bad that he hadn't seen me play at senior level for Ponsonby. I determined to achieve that as a tribute to him."

Not long after returning from the funeral, Stanley was drafted into an injury-depleted Ponsonby team and found himself playing against Otahuhu on the main oval at Eden Park. "Brian Megson and Gene Thomsen, two of Ponsonby's rep players, were out injured, so I was brought in at second-five. I was so nervous, I made a fool of myself by missing my first tackle from which Otahuhu almost scored. But I came right." In fact, Stanley 'came right' so effectively he was named player of the day. And he retained his place in the star-studded Ponsonby backline for the remainder of the season.

It's stating the obvious to say that until 1979 Stanley didn't place any great emphasis on training. "I never enjoyed fitness work like a lot of Polynesians," he admits. "I used to rely on my natural skills. Until I made the Auckland team, it's fair to say I had no strong ambition in rugby – I was happy to cruise along."

Promotion to the Ponsonby seniors inspired Stanley to undertake a midweek training run around the city streets. "I thought I'd die! My body didn't know what had hit it. I was a smoker until then but I gave that up, and I have never smoked since. As the season went on, I became fitter and began enjoying my rugby more. I persisted with the running but it wasn't something I ever enjoyed. It was a means to an end."

When John Hart was appointed coach of Auckland for the 1982 season he began checking out would-be contenders for his team. The Ponsonby centre Joe Stanley was a player who had impressed him with his club performances and he couldn't understand why his predecessor Bryan Craies had never risked him. Hart knew that Stanley had a reputation for playing-up away from the rugby field.

So Hart went to the Ponsonby club, arranged to be introduced to Stanley and asked him if he wanted to play for Auckland. Not surprisingly, Joe said yes. So Hart told him he would play him against the Barbarians the next month, on two conditions: He had to show Hart he could beat a man on the outside, and if there were any stories of him misbehaving off the field, he would not be selected.

"I've never done that with any other player," says Hart. "But Joe honoured our agreement, and so did I."

Stanley duly appeared against the Baabaas in May on the same day as 'Buck' Shelford and Grant Fox. Although Auckland won the game, only Fox would survive, Shelford and Stanley being dropped to the B team. "The Barbarians game was effectively a trial for a lot of us," says Stanley, "and Buck and I didn't pass the test. I was guilty of a stupid kick in a prime attacking situation. Why I did that, I'll never know. I deserved to be dropped."

Four months later, after Auckland had lost two NPC games in succession (something which never happened again during Hart's tenure), Stanley and Shelford were recalled, both slotting in against Otago at Eden Park. They performed outstandingly, each scoring a try. For both, it was the start of celebrated rugby careers at representative (and later international) level. Stanley considers he was lucky to receive a second chance with Auckland. "There obviously wasn't going to be a third chance, so I had to make the most of it. Fortunately, the Otago game was played on a heavy field which made it a good day for tackling. My targets weren't so mobile!"

Stanley made such good progress in 1983 it seemed his career was about to take off. He appeared opposite Steven Pokere in the All Black trial at Athletic Park in May, earning this rich review in *Rugby News*: "The player who, with his strong, thrustful running, had critics

branding him a likely test newcomer was Aucklander Joe Stanley."
His reputation was enhanced with another impressive performance
for North in the inter-island game in Blenheim in September. And he
had represented New Zealand at the Hong Kong sevens tournament.

It remains one of New Zealand rugby's modern mysteries that, until
the Cavaliers created opportunities three years later, Stanley was then
completely ignored by the national selectors. Throughout 1984 and
1985, when Pokere was the preferred centre, with Craig Green and
Vic Simpson the back-ups, Stanley didn't even get a trial. This
notwithstanding the fact that Auckland was the dominating team in
the country with its wingers John Kirwan and Terry Wright scoring
bucket-loads of tries.

So it was 1986, by which time he was 29 and half contemplating
retirement, when Stanley finally progressed to the top strata of New
Zealand rugby. He says that most of the Baby Blacks, as they would
come to be known, were so eager to be involved against France, they
would have happily paid their own hotel bill in Christchurch.

Stanley describes the captain's meeting on the eve of the
international at Lancaster Park as the most electrifying he was ever
involved in. "It was spine tingling," he says. "David Kirk, our captain,
had asked each player to state what he felt and what he hoped to
achieve the next day. They say big boys don't cry, but there were a few
tears around the room that night."

Stanley's opponent was Philippe Sella, a veteran of 31 tests, and
paired with him in the centres was the sensationally fast Denis
Charvet. They would take some controlling. As he prepared to engage
in combat, Stanley remembers thinking, "We have nothing to lose –
people are expecting us to get beaten, so if we win, it's a tremendous
bonus."

The Baby Blacks scored first, built a 12-nil advantage inside half an
hour, led 12-6 at the interval and held on to score a resounding
victory, 18 points to 9. There were many heroes, Stanley among them.
He and Arthur Stone tackled mightily throughout, but one absolute
cruncher by Stanley upon winger Marc Andrieu so unnerved the
French that his fellow All Blacks later claimed the great Serge Blanco
wasn't prepared to enter the backline in midfield, only outside his
wingers.

In the dressing room afterwards, Stanley, like those around him,

Joe Stanley

Joe Stanley about to pass as he is challenged by Favio Gaaetaniello during the opening match against Italy in the 1987 World Cup tournament. In support is Warwick Taylor.   *John Selkirk*

reflected on a job well done. "It was a fantastic feeling to have won our first test. It was something no one could ever take away from us. I knew I wanted to play more tests, but I could have survived happily on the memories of that day."

Stanley did play more tests. Lots more. He shut out Pokere in 1986 and no other centre got a look-in at test level for four years. But it can be revealed now that he was extremely fortunate to get to France with the All Blacks at season's end because he'd seriously damaged his knee cartilage playing for Auckland.

He admits he doesn't know how he managed to convince the medical panel that his knee would stand the rigours of a tour. "At training it was so painful I struggled to run at times, yet three doctors checked it out and cleared me to tour. I had fluid sucked out of it regularly and needed painkilling injections to get through the tour."

With his wonky knee, Stanley was in agony by the time the All Blacks arrived in Nantes for the second test, but because more than half the test side were injured, he chose to battle on. It remains probably his least pleasant test memory. Not only were the All Blacks hammered by a ferocious French side (desperate to salvage coach Jacques Fouroux's career), some fearful injuries were inflicted upon the New Zealanders. Buck Shelford had his scrotum ripped open while Stanley was blatantly kicked in the back.

Back home, Stanley had his troublesome knee operated on by Barry Tietjens who removed an alarming amount of graunched cartilage and bone chips. While it improved the knee, if never completely corrected it, and the operation became an annual event. Stanley was to find that running only inflamed the knee, so from early 1987 he switched to working out on an exercycle.

Stanley was fortunate to be invited to undertake an early-season tour of the UK with the New Zealand Barbarians, which allowed him to regain match fitness gradually, and had him close to peak fitness by the time the World Cup kicked off.

Stanley was on the field for all but 10 minutes of New Zealand's Cup campaign. The segment he missed was the tailend of the semifinal at Ballymore after he'd accidentally collected Welsh winger Adrian Hadley's boot in the head. Missing the dying stages of the game didn't concern him but missing the team's celebrations that evening, because he was confined to bed, did.

The World Cup final was Stanley's 12th test and fourth against France. With grim memories of Nantes, he was determined to produce a top performance, especially as he was marking the player acknowledged as the best centre in the world, Philippe Sella. The French, who'd spectacularly eliminated Australia the weekend previously, were never seriously in the picture, classic tries after halftime by David Kirk and John Kirwan allowing the All Blacks to race away to victory. Not only were they world champions, they were clearly several notches ahead of the rest of the world.

And over the next three years they would demonstrate their superiority in the most emphatic manner. There was only one slight hiccup – the second test at Ballymore in 1988 when the Wallabies forced a 19-all draw – as Grizz Wyllie's men maintained a remarkable winning scoreline of almost 40 points a game.

Stanley didn't lack for motivation coming into the first test of that '88 series after Australian coach Bob Dwyer identifed him as a weakness. "We hadn't performed that well in the lead-up games," says

Joe Stanley

Stanley, "and Dwyer was going on about how the All Blacks were beatable and that I was the weak link because at thirty-one I was slowing down. His words didn't upset me, just gave me a little ammunition."

Stanley was anything but a weak link as the All Blacks blew the Aussies clean off Concord Oval, winning by 25 points. Stanley wasn't a weak link at any stage of the series, nor when Dwyer's team came to Eden Park the next year.

The battering ram role for which Stanley became renowned wasn't one he particularly enjoyed. "To be honest, I always preferred to spread the ball wide rather than take it up to create second phase possession, but I realised the benefit of the tactic to the team. If I had to do it, then I would do it well. I developed a technique of laying the ball back while my forwards protected me. I was only once booted setting the ball up, although there were countless times I was stood on. My body has its share of sprig marks. My satisfaction was in pulling myself up and seeing a John Kirwan or John Gallagher or Terry Wright racing for the line. Frustration was finding the ball knocked on. Then you knew you'd done it all for nothing!"

The Ponsonby connection was strongly represented on the 1989 tour of Wales and Ireland, with Matthew Ridge, Craig Innes and Va'aiga Tuigamala being promoted from that year's crack New Zealand Colts team. Innes, at 20, might have challenged Stanley for his test position but when John Kirwan snapped his achilles tendon in the match against Pontypool, Innes filled the vacancy thus created on the wing.

Stanley was a consistent performer throughout the tour but by a cruel stroke of fate he is probably remembered more for an ugly incident that followed the Llanelli game (played in a hurricane at Stradey Park). On his way to bed late that night, he found Andy Earl, with whom he'd been drinking, grappling with two Welshmen, who were in an area of the hotel reserved for guests. Stanley went to Earl's aid and began wrestling one of the two Welshmen, the ruckus ending a few moments later when Gary Whetton arrived on the scene.

Next morning Stanley was startled to find a complaint of assault had been laid against himself and Andy Earl. They had to accompany a Llanelli detective to the police station where they remained for several hours while all parties were questioned. While the Welshmen

Joe Stanley proudly shows off his biography Smokin' Joe, written by Phil Gifford and published in 1990. 　　　　　　　　　　　　　　　　　　　　*Vogel Photography*

were being interviewed, Stanley and Earl were held in a cell.

After they explained how they were acting in self defence, they were given the opportunity to lay a counter complaint, but Stanley told the police, "I'm happy to forget about it and get on with the tour." A final decision not to proceed with any action was not made for another two days, by which time the incident had leaked to the press, several sections of which ran exaggerated versions of the truth.

Towards the finish of the tour Stanley developed a serious neck injury which a scan back in New Zealand would reveal was a prolapsed disc. At the time it was treated as no more than a damaged muscle, Stanley being cleared to play against Ireland. "Luckily, I didn't get a heavy blow on the neck or I could have had lasting damage."

He was in so much pain during the final week, finding sleeping difficult, that there was never any prospect of him playing further rugby, so Walter Little took over for the Barbarians contest at Twickenham.

The damaged neck continued to trouble him in 1990. He got through the two Scottish internationals but with considerable discomfort. Because he was now experiencing persistent tingling down both arms, he elected to drop out of rugby, rest being prescribed as the best treatment.

Joe Stanley

He made only four appearances for Auckland that season, but turned out for Auckland B and C as he started his comeback. The All Black selectors hadn't forgotten him and took him on the end-of-year tour of France where, for the first time, he became a midweek tourist, Craig Innes, 12 years his junior, getting the tests. Stanley was given the honour of captaining the All Blacks at La Rochelle.

With an eye on the second World Cup, he reported for duty again in 1991, aged 34. He made it to Argentina, where Innes was again the test centre, but his days as an All Black were numbered. "I would have loved to have been involved in another World Cup," he says. "I know I wouldn't have played the majors but I believed I had something to contribute." As it was, he got to the tournament as the leader of a supporters group.

In early 1992, new Auckland coach Graham Henry asked Stanley what his intentions were. "I told him I was quitting," says Stanley, "that it was time to start taking life easy."

Stanley had never done any serious OE in the cause of rugby, so when an invitation to help coach the Zagara club in Catania, Sicily, arrived, he grabbed it, taking his family along and thoroughly enjoying the experience. After a short stint there, he learnt that the NEC club in Japan was keen to acquire his services as a player-coach on a long-term basis. "I wasn't that interested in playing but when I found there were basically only ten serious games involved each year, I accepted. And I've been there with my family ever since." The contract expired in March 1997, after which Stanley and his wife Evelyn were planning to return to New Zealand where they want their children – Jeremy (a threequarter with the Auckland Blues), Crystal, Brooke, Ashley, Deirdre and Joseph jun – to grow up.

Warwick Taylor

Most players if they had a brother who was an All Black would use the connection to their advantage. Not Warwick Taylor when he headed south from Matamata to Otago University in 1979 to study for a diploma in physical education. He didn't want anyone to know that he was the brother of the test five-eighth Murray Taylor. His career had been developing promisingly in Matamata but a doubt existed in his mind? Was he progressing in rugby through his own talents or was he receiving favourable treatment because his brother was an All Black?

"It was important for me to make my own way in sport, I felt," says Taylor. "No one knew me in Dunedin. I revelled in my anonymity." Taylor was proud of his brother's achievements but didn't boast them to anyone. It wasn't until after the University trials that anyone in the southern city became aware of his bloodlines.

Taylor was given an important piece of advice by his brother before he went south: Concentrate on one position. Murray, who Warwick regarded as the most talented rugby player he'd ever seen until his leg was shattered in several places, became something of a puppet in the hands of the New Zealand selectors. Of the seven test appearances he made, four were at first-five and three at second-five.

"He told me how difficult it was to adjust from one position to the other, particularly at the highest level," says Taylor. "The most valuable piece of information he ever gave me was to identify my best position, and stick to it." Second-five was the position Taylor sorted out for himself and in a distinguished career he would play 100 games

Warwick Taylor

Warwick Taylor makes a point to John Gallagher at the time of the first World Cup in 1987. They were both major contributors to New Zealand's triumph.

Andrew Cornaga (Photosport)

for Canterbury, 20 for Otago and 40 for New Zealand, virtually every one of them in the No 12 jersey.

He wouldn't command a lot of headlines and nor would he score many tries, but throughout the 1980s he would win a reputation as Mr Reliability in midfield, a sure tackler, an expert retriever of high kicks and a champion setter-up of others. Grant Fox in his autobiography would say of him: "He was the 110 per cent man. I have never seen a player so unreservedly lay himself on the line for the All Blacks."

A comment by a teammate would have a profound influence on how he played the game for the remainder of his career. At the time a first-five, he once danced through the opposition to score a brilliant solo try. His satisfaction was pricked by a colleague who, instead of congratulating him, berated him for not giving the rest of the team a chance. "You can do that all the time," this fellow said. "Why not give us a turn?"

Taylor says that it made him realise everyone in a team wanted to participate. "His comments made a lasting impression and probably influenced me to start setting up other players. I always felt I had the potential to beat opponents but I preferred to draw two of them, if I could, and put a teammate away."

Taylor grew up on a farm at Wardville, near Matamata, the second youngest in a family of five. His sisters and brothers were all achievers in sport. Elder sister Rae captained the New Zealand under-24 netball team and was a national trialist, younger sister Jan was a New Zealand under-21 netball representative, Murray was an All Black and Ross, the eldest brother, a Waikato B rugby player. When Warwick was 12, the farm was sold and the family moved to Waharoa.

Rugby was, naturally, a passion in the Taylor household, their father Torry having played for Waikato at junior level. One day the local minister called on the family, the Taylor boys having been conspicuous by their absence at church. As he was preparing to leave, he spotted a rugby ball. "Aaah," he said, "there's the thing you worship in this household!"

Taylor senior had rigged up a tackling bag in the backyard, attaching it to the frame of an old swing. "If you mistimed your tackle," recalls Warwick, "you cannoned into the side of the swing.

Warwick Taylor

Looking back, I'd say it certainly helped my tackling accuracy!"

Having two older brothers who were so accomplished at rugby – they actually played in the Matamata College first XV together, at first and second-five – naturally hastened young Warwick's development. "They had a big influence on me," he says. "They were being coached by George Simpkin at college and relaying a lot of that information to me."

At primary school, the youngest Taylor decided he wanted to be a halfback, that was until he found he had to pass the ball all the time. So he moved out to first-five, then eventually to second-five, displaying sufficient natural skill to win representative honours as a primary school player.

His entry into the first XV at Matamata College was accelerated when the two first-fives in the squad in 1975 both suffered fractures. The 15-year-old found the challenge daunting, especially when in his first outing, against Western Heights, a big Maori forward came charging straight at him. "There weren't a lot of options," he says, "but I grabbed him by the legs and fell back. It was a technique I was to employ throughout my career whenever I had to tangle with large forwards. I used their weight to bring them down."

Taylor captained the first XV in his seventh form year. In Simpkin's coaching days the team had won a reputation as one of the most accomplished in the country, but by 1978 it had lost much of its potency. "In fact," says Taylor, "I learnt to be a good loser at college. We always went out to do our best, but we were no match for schools like St Stephen's. In the four years I played against them, we never got close to them."

Taylor represented Waikato under-16 while in the fourth form and Waikato under-18 two years later and was dubbed a footballer with a bright future when he headed south early in 1979. But he'd cast aside those rugby credentials by the time he began trialling with the University senior squad in Dunedin. He was Warwick Taylor, student, with no known rugby pedigree.

"I was keen to play at senior level," he says. "If I'd missed selection at University, I would have tried another club. As it turned out, I won a place in the University B team." Running the team was Lee Smith, who would take over as coach of Otago the next season (and eventually become coaching co-ordinator for the NZRFU) while the backline included David Kirk. Taylor made one appearance for the A team, a timely one – the club final, which University A won.

Smith was also coaching the Otago B representative team in '79 and telephoned Taylor inviting him to play. But because Taylor was heading back home for a holiday break, he declined. He got a second chance later in the year, turning out against Wellington B at Athletic Park, his first major representative outing.

Otago was inches away from losing its first division status in 1979, a Steve Marfell kick which struck the crossbar costing Marlborough victory in the promotion-relegation game. Taylor listened to the commentary with fascination, little thinking he would be wearing the Otago jersey the next season. "Otago followers should be eternally grateful that Marlborough didn't displace them that year, because we've seen with teams like Manawatu, Hawke's Bay and Northland how desperately hard it is to regain your status once you're down."

When Smith stepped up to coach Otago in 1980 he installed Taylor at second-five and also nominated him for the New Zealand Colts. Taylor's version of events suggests he "got lucky" with the Colts. True, he was the last player selected, after Auckland's Mike Mills withdrew with an injury, but either Smith had considerable influence or someone had spotted him playing club rugby, because there were no trials for the team in those days. And his Otago debut didn't come until after he'd returned from the Colts' successful tour of Australia.

With Taylor in midfield and such promising individuals as Gary and Alan Whetton, Albert Anderson, Robbie Deans, Vic Simpson and Ian Dunn in the side, the young New Zealanders held on for a 10-8 win over their Australian counterparts in the 'test' at the Sydney Cricket Ground. Taylor says that the coach, Bryce Rope, discovered he was a 'one-footed' kicker and made him practise kicking with his left foot until he was totally proficient. "He also made me work on the wipers kick, which is so valuable for a second-five."

After debuting against North Otago at Oamaru (and scoring two tries), Taylor commanded a regular place with Otago throughout 1980, but the team was only marginally more successful under Smith, coming in 10th out of 11 in the NPC, beating only wooden-spooner South Canterbury and Southland. "Lee was a teacher-style coach," said Taylor, "making extensive use of the blackboard. A lot of the oldies didn't appreciate that. Personally, I felt he was ahead of his

Warwick Taylor

Warwick Taylor prepares to kick ahead as Iain Paxton comes at him at Carisbrook during his first series for the All Blacks, against the British Lions in 1983. Awaiting developments is Wayne Smith.   John Selkirk

time. Methods he used then are commonplace now."

The next year, the last before Laurie Mains took over and transformed Otago rugby, Taylor experienced a patchy season. He was replaced at second-five for the game against the Springboks by 1976 All Black Neil Purvis and missed a few NPC fixtures as well. Finally clear of the relegation zone, Otago actually won five championship games.

His diploma course at Otago University completed, Taylor had a choice of attending Teachers College in Auckland or Christchurch. He chose Christchurch, which gladdened the heart of Alex Wyllie who was taking the reigns of Canterbury rugby at the same time Mains was becoming Otago coach.

For the trial at Kaiapoi, Taylor, to his dismay, found himself placed on the wing. "Why I am there?" he inquired of Wyllie. "Because that's where you played for Otago." Taylor was mystified, then remembered that his solitary appearance (of 20) on the wing for Otago, early in the 1980 season, had been against Canterbury at Lancaster Park.

Rugby Greats

Obviously, Wyllie had been watching.

Wyllie soon enough became aware that Taylor was a midfielder, not a winger. But that compounded his problems, because he was also trying to accommodate Craig Green and Vic Simpson in the midfield. Someone would have to move to the wing. Simpson emphatically refused, although he was coerced into playing against Mid-Canterbury on the wing, after which he called Wyllie "Dad!". It was Green who resolved the dilemma by agreeing to operate on the wing. "That was a lucky break for me," says Taylor. "Alex helped mould Craig into an outstanding wing." Taylor and Green would play together the following year on the All Black tour of England and Scotland.

The Wyllie influence soon had Canterbury firing. The team which in 1981 had finished an embarrassing ninth (one spot behind Otago even!) was now among the most respected in the land. It defeated Auckland at Eden Park, something which hasn't been achieved in an NPC fixture since, and went through to finish runner-up in the championship. But, more importantly, it won the Ranfurly Shield.

The most obvious source of improvement in the team was fitness. Wyllie spared no one at training. In fact, Taylor admits that on occasions he eased off in Saturday matches so he could cope with Grizz's Sunday trainings! "There were times when I wondered if some of the squad members were going to survive those sessions," says Taylor. "I had so much respect for Grizz. He was supposedly anti-university types, but that wasn't borne out. From the start, he encouraged fifteen-man rugby, which was amazing really for someone who, as a player, had controlled games from number eight, and who, as a captain, had bawled out any back who dropped a ball."

The shield victory in Wellington was a triumph for Wyllie who'd primed his team perfectly, and that included playing a tape of the Wellington fullback Allan Hewson advising the Canterbury players to take the ferry straight back home because they had no show of winning. "That was a red rag to the Canterbury bulls," says Taylor. "Grizz insisted the interview had been broadcast on Wellington's most popular radio station. Years later I learnt it was never broadcast at all and that Grizz had dubbed the tape!"

Canterbury was lucky not to lose the shield at its first defence. "It was only a controversial penalty kicked by Robbie Deans a minute or two from time that allowed us to escape against Counties," says Taylor. "We were incredibly lucky."

Taylor was close to exhaustion at fulltime against Counties. He says it was one of only three occasions in his career when he was completely spent. The others were the Cavaliers' second test in South Africa in 1986 and the Bledisloe Cup test in Sydney following the World Cup in 1987. "Those are the times you know you've played to your limit," he says, "when there is nothing left to give."

Canterbury reigned supreme in 1983. The first division national title was taken with a perfect record of 10 wins, the British Lions edged out 22-20 and nine shield challengers turned back, including Auckland in overwhelming fashion. The team produced a rich brand of attacking rugby.

Taylor was to be on the winning side five times against the hapless 1983 Lions, for in May, following the trial in Wellington, he was named in the All Black test line-up. Taylor had proved himself defensively in the trial (against Charlie Kaka and Joe Stanley). He had to, because his attacking opportunities were nil as his team plummeted to a 32-4 defeat. He'd also proved his fitness, he and Wayne Smith being the first two home in the 12-minute run. "I didn't think of myself as an All Black," he admits. "I was mindful of the three Waikato boys who'd made it young, Lachie Cameron, Geoff Hines and my brother Murray, and who were not there now. I determined that if I made it, I wanted to be there a long time."

Taylor missed the announcement of the team, but his University clubmates hadn't and began hugging him and toasting him the moment he arrived at the clubrooms. "Five minutes earlier I didn't think I had any show," he recalls. "Then suddenly I was an All Black. It was one of the most emotional moments in my life."

When he recovered from the celebrations the next day, Taylor found doubts starting to set in. "Being selected was great," he says, "but having made it, I realised I now had to perform. I felt I had a hell of a lot to learn. An All Black was *the* best, but I didn't consider I was the best. I wasn't naturally skilled. What talents I did have, I really had to work on. I still say now, there were loads of players better in my position than me."

However, having been selected, Taylor resolved to become a good All Black. "And if it was in my powers, I wanted to be a great one."

Rugby Greats

The All Blacks achieving a clean sweep of the series at the Lions' expense, and winning the one-off Bledisloe Cup game in Sydney (when Taylor scored his first test try) certainly kicked his international career off on the right note. He was signing autographs following his debut at Lancaster Park when his brother Ross tapped him on the shoulder. "There's an old bugger in the grandstand wants to meet you," he told him. "It was dad," says Taylor. "We hugged each other and there were a lot of tears. Winning that first test meant so much to me and the other new guys in the team."

When the All Black team to tour England and Scotland (under the captaincy of Stu Wilson) was announced, it included seven Canterbury players (Robbie Deans, Craig Green, Taylor, Wayne Smith, Albert Anderson, Jock Hobbs and Murray Davie) and no one from Auckland. How things would change over the next decade!

There was the sort of hiccup teams strive desperately to avoid in the prelude to the Scottish international at Murrayfield. Robbie Deans, having forgotten his mouthguard, went back into the hotel to retrieve it, unbeknown to manager Paul Mitchell (who will not go down as one of the great All Black administrators). He told the driver to head for the ground. When Deans' absence was finally conveyed to him, the bus was turned around, with great effort. But on the way back to the hotel, they passed Deans going the other way in a taxi. Deans had to talk his way into the ground, hardly the best way to prepare for your test debut!

Fifteen minutes into the game, Taylor seriously damaged his left medial knee ligament when giant prop Scott Crichton fell on his leg. "The leg was strapped and the intention was I should stay on until Craig Green was ready to take the field," says Taylor. "In the event, I stayed on till halftime but could only run straight. If I'd taken a heavy knock, I could have been in serious trouble."

Taylor wondered gloomily about his future, but an immediate operation in England repaired the damage. "The surgeon did a brilliant job," he says. "He undoubtedly saved my career."

Taylor's mother Marjorie, who was across following the tour, brought his clothes to the hospital. "I never saw our manager once, the whole time I was in hospital," he says. Taylor discharged himself the day before the England international, on crutches, his leg in plaster. He returned home in a wheelchair, guided through customs by Hika Reid.

Warwick Taylor

Summer was spent strengthening the leg, making extensive use of weights. He also took up cycling, tying his left foot to the pedal. However, first time out he forgot this and crashed to the road when he went to steady himself with his left foot at a compulsory stop!

Taylor was concerned that Bill Osborne was attempting a comeback in 1994, especially as he was conscious of the fragility of his knee. "Alex Wyllie told me I just had to get out there and 'do it'." Do it Taylor certainly did, being reinstated at second-five for the domestic tests against France (collecting a try at both Christchurch and Auckland) and for the tour of Australia. He was his usual dependable self in every outing, but missed the third test in Sydney after breaking his cheekbone against Queensland.

Taylor was never a glamour member of the All Black backline. He was never an *Almanack* player of the year in any of the six seasons he represented New Zealand and he seldom received generous reviews in the media. He used this to his advantage. "I used to think, 'Right, you buggers, I'll show you, I'm here to stay. I'm not the flashy sort of player you're looking for – my job is to straighten the attack, draw two defenders and pass to someone in a better position than myself.'"

The 1985 season was a disappointing one for Taylor, and his Canterbury colleagues. Not only was the All Black tour of South Africa cancelled, through the High Court injunction, but Canterbury lost the Ranfurly Shield to Auckland, albeit after one of the great contests of all time. Taylor appeared in all the tests but the series against the Pumas in Argentina was a pale substitute for the long-awaited clash with the Springboks.

Determined that the show should go on, the All Blacks (minus John Kirwan and David Kirk) made it to South Africa in 1986 in the guise of the Cavaliers. With Osborne in the party, Taylor thought he might be supplanted at second-five, but he went on to play all four internationals, notwithstanding a couple of unusual physical setbacks. When he arrived in South Africa (from the UK where he had participated in the IRB centenary matches) he was suffering from haemorrhoids. A small operation corrected the problem but forced him to miss the first two tour matches. Then after posing for a photo on Table Mountain he stepped back on to a sharp bolt which cut deep into the sole of his bare foot. Twenty-four hours before the first international he was limping badly, but a painkilling injection got him

The All Blacks scored 12 tries in the first outing at the 1987 World Cup against Italy, and here's Warwick Taylor finishing off one of them.   John Selkirk

on to Newlands. "I survived the last twenty minutes on adrenalin after the painkiller wore off," he says. "I couldn't walk afterwards."

Taylor was the hero of the second test in Durban when his late try gave the Cavaliers a desperate, one-point victory. "I managed to charge down a Naas Botha kick, retrieve it and score six inches from the deadball line," he says. "I gave everything that day and afterwards collapsed from exhaustion." Taylor considers he played the best rugby of his career on the Cavaliers tour and laments the fact that no one back home saw it.

He had to fight a battle on two fronts upon his return, losing to the NZRFU and having to sit out a two-test suspension with his fellow tourists but winning (eventually, after the matter went to court) against the Board of Governors at Burnside High School who wanted to dismiss him for not formally seeking leave to visit South Africa.

Taylor was reinstated for the Dunedin test against the Wallabies but found himself dropped for the series decider at Eden Park, replaced by Arthur Stone. "I'd been playing the best rugby of my life in South Africa," he says, "now here I was dropped. Although it hurt, it was probably a good test not to be involved in. The All Blacks took a hammering."

He knew he'd slipped further down the pecking order when he missed selection for the tour of France, Stone and Marty Berry being the preferred second-fives with John Gallagher joining the side ostensibly as a fullback but appearing twice at centre.

As he contemplated a summer as an ex-international at the not advanced age of 26, Taylor took encouragement from an Andy Dalton saying: Great All Blacks come back. "I decided I wanted to be back, so I threw myself into a weight training course through the summer."

And when the World Cup squad was announced in May, Taylor was in and Stone (and Berry) out. Not only was he in, he featured in five of New Zealand's matches, being spelled only for the pool match against Argentina when Bernie McCahill was given an outing.

"We fired from the start," he says. "It was a fantastic campaign with which to be associated. John Kirwan scored some incredible tries and we played off him a lot. Joe Stanley and I stopped the opposition in close and John Gallagher came roaring into the backline at 100 miles per hour. Everyone peaked together."

In the quarter-final against Scotland, Taylor heard something crack in his ankle and feared it was broken, but it turned out to be nothing worse than bruising. It handicapped him in the semi-final against Wales when Stanley was favouring a hamstring. "We were a couple of crocks in the second spell at Ballymore, but it didn't matter because the All Blacks scored an astonishing number of points regardless."

Emotions spilled over after the All Blacks downed France in the final. "We played that final for all the All Blacks who had gone before," says Taylor. "New Zealand had been the best in the world so often, only now we had a trophy to prove it."

The one regret that Taylor has is that the All Blacks dispersed immediately after the tournament and didn't celebrate the winning of the World Cup worthily. However, there was a reunion in Sydney a month later at the time of the Bledisloe Cup contest which was billed as the unofficial World Cup play-off. Again the All Blacks won handsomely.

Taylor spent the New Zealand summer with the Venezia-Mestre

third division club in Italy. He thoroughly enjoyed the experience, apart from the five days he spent in hospital with painfully swollen testicles from a rugby injury.

Taylor's final test appearances were against Wales early in the 1988 season. They shouldn't have been, but his subsequent tour of Australia with Buck Shelford's team was a disaster. He broke his hand in three places against Australia B and in his comeback game, against New South Wales B three weeks later, tore his hamstring.

Hand and hamstring mended, he made it to the All Black trial in Hamilton in 1989, but John Schuster was now the preferred test second-five and Taylor resigned himself to playing out his career at representative level. His 100th appearance for Canterbury fell, fittingly, in the final game of the 1990 season, the bizarre 'no scrum' encounter with Auckland on Eden Park. For a player who'd prided himself on setting other people up for tries, he finished with a flourish, getting a haul of four against Bay of Plenty and one more in the finale against Auckland.

In the South Pacific Championship game against Fiji in '90 he damaged his neck which several times during the season went into spasm. Psychologically, he was concerned at doing permanent damage which forced his retirement. He made a few subsequent appearances for the Classic All Blacks until a chiropractor warned him, after another heavy blow, that he risked breaking his neck.

His association with the game continues, however, as coach of the Burnside High School first XV, a role he has filled for 12 years. No longer being a player means he has more time to dedicate to his wife Tracy, whom he met as a seventh former in Matamata, and their three children, Thomas, 8, Stephanie, 6, and Madeleine, 2.

Alan Whetton

Alan Whetton has just one regret about the celebrated playing career that involved him in 35 test matches with the All Blacks and 150 appearances for Auckland – he missed out on playing against Wales at Cardiff Arms Park.

Oh, he was there in 1989 as New Zealand's premier blindside flanker. He was there when the national anthems were being played, standing alongside manager John Sturgeon, crying with disappointment and frustration. Crying because for the only time in his 29 years he had torn a leg muscle.

It had happened at Swansea a fortnight previously, right down in front of the grandstand where his parents were sitting. In trying to stop the Swansea flyhalf, he'd slipped on the muddy service and torn his hamstring.

"It was no twinge," says Whetton, "but a great, horrible tear. I knew instantly from the pain I was in trouble." It wasn't for a lack of effort from his teammates that the muscle wasn't repaired in time for the Welsh test. It required icing every 30 minutes throughout the night. "The guys were brilliant – they came in all through the night to put fresh ice bags on the muscle."

But two weeks just wasn't enough time to repair the damage. The No 6 jersey went to Andy Earl, leaving Whetton reflecting on how cruel life could be. He'd played the previous 17 tests for his country without once being injured and it was a personal ambition to run on to Cardiff Arms Park this day with his brother Gary. But it wasn't to be.

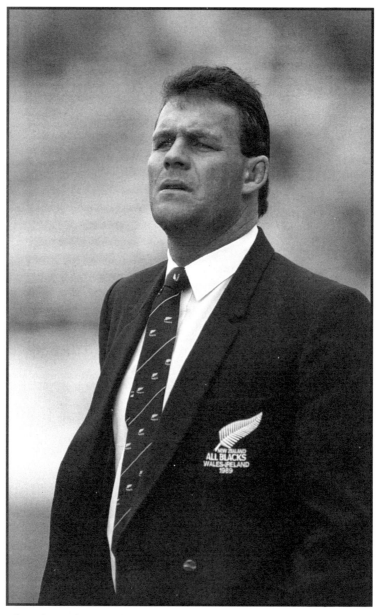

Alan Whetton frustratingly reduced to a spectator for much of the All Black tour of Wales and Ireland in 1989 after injuring his leg.   Fotopacific

Alan Whetton

"I felt gutted," he says. "Meanwhile, Sturge (John Sturgeon) was overcome by the emotion of the occasion and we both started crying. At that moment you wouldn't have known we were a couple of big, tough rugby types."

Although he felt proud as the All Blacks demolished the Welsh, continuing the stunning sequence of test successes begun at the 1987 World Cup, he didn't indulge in too much celebrating that evening. "The beer didn't taste so good," he says, "because I couldn't relive the moments with the guys. I left them to it."

Whetton hated being incapacitated. Perhaps it related to the stuttery start he'd had to his international career, but he realised on that tour of Wales and Ireland that he was a player who needed to be fully involved all the time. "I really should have flown home and allowed a fresh player to come in," he says. "I wanted to go but I was talked out of it. I finished up playing only four games, in two of which I limped off injured, in eight weeks. It was a thoroughly frustrating exercise."

Whetton's entry into test rugby had been rather frustrating, too, because his first four test outings were all as a replacement. When he did finally make the starting fifteen, against Alan Jones' Wallabies in 1986, he turned in such a shocker he was promptly dropped and subsequently left behind when the All Blacks toured France.

It was a watershed stage of his career. He either left it to his twin brother to represent the Whettons at international level or he did something about getting himself back into the All Blacks. It wasn't a hard decision to make – he wanted that black jersey badly. So with his best mate Lee Wahlstrom acting as trainer, he embarked on a furious training programme throughout the summer, emerging fitter than he had ever been. That 'everything' included a recall to the All Blacks for the first World Cup tournament. He would not only regain the No 6 jersey, he would play in all six matches, equalling the world record by scoring tries in five consecutive tests. He would be acclaimed as the world's best exponent of blindside flanker play and, notwithstanding the torn hamstring in Wales in 1989, he would go on to play 65 games for his country, including 35 tests.

In their youth, it was Alan who appealed as the brother more likely to succeed in sport. That, they both agree, was largely because Gary was "fat and lazy" and didn't apply himself seriously to any sporting projects until after he attended Outward Bound school. After they'd arrived in the Auckland Grammar School first XV together in 1977, jointly locking the scrum, Alan was an instant star, winning selection in the Northern Region schools team and the Auckland secondary schools team. The next year he captained the Auckland third grade reps. Alan trained and Gary didn't and that essentially was the difference, until Outward Bound shook Gary awake.

In 1979, Alan continued to play third grade with Grammar while Gary stepped up to senior ranks and won selection for New Zealand Colts. The following year, aged 20, they were New Zealand Colts together, starring in the narrow 'test' victory over Australia in the curtainraiser to the Bledisloe Cup international at the Sydney Cricket Ground. Alan was at No. 8 and Gary at lock against an Australian team featuring Glen Ella at fullback and his brother Gary at centre.

After Gary had represented Auckland in 1980, Alan joined him in 1981, making seven appearances in Bryan Craies' team, four at No. 8, two at lock and only one in the position in which he would achieve international recognition, blindside flanker. Of course, that was the year Gary was sensationally hoisted into the All Blacks for the infamous 'flour bomb' test at Eden Park.

At season's end, Gary was off to Romania and France with the All Blacks. Alan took off for Europe, too, cashing in on an invitation his brother had received (through Auckland) to play for the West Hartlepool club in England. "It was a great opportunity to combine OE with rugby," says Whetton, "and I got to see Gary and the All Blacks playing in France." Gary joined him after the tour and together they lifted West Hartlepool to an improved standing in the order of merit. "I loved my time there," says Alan. "I played something like forty-five games in their season. I was tempted to stay longer, but it was my ambition to play for the All Blacks, so I returned home, after some emotional farewells."

While his brother prospered at international level, Alan would have a painstaking wait before the All Black selectors determined that he was the best in his position in the land. Ah, now there's the crux of the problem. What *was* his position? New Auckland coach John Hart used him as a flanker, a No. 8 and a lock in 1982 while Bryce Rope suggested to him during the New Zealand Juniors' internal tour that his future probably lay as a blindside flanker.

Alan Whetton

Blindside flanker was the position he wanted to specialise in but when brother Gary wrecked his knee playing in Western Province's centenary games in 1983, Hart used him as Andy Haden's locking partner for the remainder of the season. By the end of that '83 season he'd represented Auckland 31 times – 13 at flanker, 12 at lock and six at No. 8. It was this versatility which would get him into the All Blacks the next year. But the 'spare parts' tag would become a source of considerable frustration.

While being a twin inevitably ensured that Alan bore a strong physical resemblance to Gary, it didn't guarantee him his brother's height. Gary grew to be 1.98m (6ft 6in) while Alan stopped at 1.93m (6ft 4in). Gary possessed the ideal stature for playing lock while Alan was obviously better suited to the blindside flanker's role. But that didn't stop coaches from using him at lock. In one of his most important outings in '93 he locked the North Island scrum with Haden.

Selection for the All Blacks should be an occasion of great moment, an experience to cherish, to celebrate with family and clubmates. That's how it was when Gary was so unexpectedly elevated to international status in 1981. The telephone rang hot and the media came searching for rugby's newest celebrity.

The celebrations are rather more muted when you're simply named a test reserve. You're an All Black, but you're not. You train with the team but if you don't get to run on as a replacement, your name will never appear in the list of *They Played for New Zealand*. So it was with Alan in 1984. John Hart made the announcement at an Auckland training session. John Kirwan, Steve Pokere, Gary Whetton and Andy Haden were All Blacks to play against France at Lancaster Park. *Congratulations, guys – good luck for the game. And Alan Whetton's in the reserves. Well done, AJ.*

"While I was delighted to be involved," says Whetton, "it wasn't the same as being named in the fifteen. I didn't feel I had quite arrived as an All Black. I was on the fringe." On the fringe he remained. Cowboy Shaw had a firm grip on the No 6 jersey and was not about to give it up. And the All Blacks completed the series against the French without needing to call on any replacements.

Whetton's All Black status was confirmed a few weeks later, however, when he was selected, as a loose forward, in the 27-strong party to tour Australia, his debut coming against Queensland B at Ballymore. He and fullback Robbie Deans would become the busiest members of the side, each appearing in 11 of the 14 games. He admits to being almost overawed by the experience. "Initially, I found it frightening to be amongst all these great players," he says. "And physically, I don't believe I was ready for the All Blacks. Although I survived okay in the midweek matches, at times I was out of my depth. I can remember thinking, 'What the hell am I doing here?' The tempo of the big matches was so much greater than anything I had experienced. No one had prepared me for it."

If Whetton felt he was struggling to establish himself at rugby's highest level, others considered he'd justified his selection as an All Black. The *Rugby Annual* said of him: "A newcomer who made considerable progress. Often looked like a losing heavyweight boxer, so regularly was his face patched up, which only served to underline his dedication to duty. Played five times as a flanker, three times at No. 8 and came on as a replacement on three occasions."

Two of those outings as a replacement were in the test matches at Sydney, first for Shaw and then for Jock Hobbs. Whetton felt he struggled in the tests. "I seemed to be two or three metres off the pace all the time – I simply wasn't used to the greater speed at which they were operating." When the All Blacks undertook a short tour of Fiji late that same season, he went along as Murray Mexted's understudy at No. 8. The position seemed to agree with him, for he scored three tries in his two outings.

Nothing changed much in 1985. Rated for his versatility, Whetton was on the reserves bench for the domestic tests against England and Australia, getting involved in the Bledisloe Cup encounter at Eden Park when Shaw came off. Then when the All Blacks toured Argentina (after the long awaited South African visit was abandoned), Whetton played all the midweek games on the side of the scrum while Shaw got the important Saturday outings. When he ran on for lock Murray Pierce at Buenos Aires, it was his fourth test appearance, all of them as a sub, which someone with a sordid sense of humour claimed was a world record. "All but one of my replacement tests gave me less than half a match," he says. "When I came on once for Cowboy, it was just before halftime, which was a bit better. At least it gave me a chance to get into the game,"

Alan Whetton

The brothers Whetton, Gary and Alan, ready for All Black duty during an overseas tour. With them is Grant Fox.   Photosport

The needle was beginning to get stuck for Whetton by the time 1986 rolled around. He was 26 and although a valued member of Hart's crack Auckland provincial side, he was nothing more than a spare parts man as far as the All Blacks were concerned. Indeed, by the end of '86 he would find himself a disposable part.

But first came the Cavaliers' tour of South Africa, and a glimmer of hope. Whetton naturally went into that series ranking behind Shaw, who hadn't been seriously challenged for his position since 1980. For the fourth and final test at Ellis Park, in front of a crowd of 70,000, with the Cavaliers trailing in the series 2-1, AJ Whetton wore the No 6 jersey. "It doesn't feature in the record books," he says, "but I regard that as my first genuine test appearance. We were overwhelmed by the Springboks at the end, but I still feel that was one of the best matches

I ever played. I was so much fitter and stronger, and better mentally prepared, than in 1984. I felt I was ready to make the step up to the All Blacks."

In the perfect world, the Baby Blacks and the Cavaliers would have merged contentedly, with the unified objective of bringing down the Wallabies in 1986. But it didn't work that way. There were serious divisions between the two camps. The Baby Blacks were saddened when 10 of their number were dropped once the rebels' suspension was over. The Cavaliers regarded themselves as the senior pros, determined to prove they were New Zealand's best players. Collectively, they were not a happy lot when they came together for the second test against the Aussies at Carisbrook.

It was not a healthy environment for Whetton to enter the (official) test arena. "It was a difficult time," he says. "Mentally, the Cavaliers weren't focused and, in hindsight, the selectors would probably have been wiser staying with their new squad. Our team was terribly disjointed and I gave a poor performance, letting Steve Tuynman through for a try which, ironically, was not awarded by the referee (Derek Bevan). It should have been Australia's matchwinner.

"I knew I'd let myself down and started drinking port after the game. I got horribly intoxicated before the test dinner because I knew I was going to be dropped. Steve McDowell kindly put me in a taxi and sent me back to the hotel where I learnt next morning that Warwick Taylor and I had been dispensed with for the final test in Auckland. Although my parents and friends wanted to blame the selectors, I accepted their decision. They'd given me a chance and I'd blown it."

The really bitter pill was when the touring team to France was announced, and Whetton wasn't in it. Mark Shaw, aged 30, was there. Andy Earl was there. Mike Brewer, the up-and-comer (who would wear the No 6 jersey in both tests), was there. But AJ Whetton wasn't. "They'd ditched me," says Whetton. "While it was hard for me that my brother Gary was touring and I wasn't, at the end of the day it was probably good that I was left behind. It jolted me into action."

As the summer approached, Whetton turned to his good friend Lee Wahlstrom (brother of referee Glen), a policeman who was a flanker with the Teachers-Eastern club and a fitness fanatic. "He told me I wasn't fit and that he was prepared to act as my trainer to get me right for the 1987 season," says Whetton. An injured ankle meant the first five weeks of training took place in a pool, but then came four months of intensive work involving running and weight training. By the end of summer, Whetton was bursting out of his skin, ready to bid for a World Cup spot.

It showed when the zonal matches were staged in April. The standout was a 22-year-old flanker from Auckland, Michael Jones, but right behind him throughout the series, and again in the main All Black trial at Whangarei, was Alan Whetton. "For the first time, at that level, I found I was not only up with, but often ahead of, the play," he says. "I was often arriving at the breakdowns *with* Michael. Fitness was manifesting itself in confidence. I was enjoying my rugby more than ever before."

He had a lucky break. Brewer, who'd made considerable progress on the French tour, was forced out of contention with a groin injury. And Cowboy Shaw, at the age of 31, would ride no more. The blindside flanker's job was all Whetton's. He, Michael Jones and Buck Shelford would make an awesome threesome at the World Cup.

"For Warwick Taylor and myself, it was specially satisfying," says Whetton. "Our circumstances were identical. We'd produced our best rugby with the Cavaliers, we'd both been dropped after the Carisbrook test and we were both to play important roles in the World Cup. I had enormous respect for Warwick. He wasn't flashy but he was one of the best second-fives in the world. He was Mr Reliability and as a flanker, I worked well off him. There were so many dynamic backs in that team for Michael and myself to support. Joe Stanley could off-load in any situation, John Kirwan, if he wasn't scoring, was holding defenders at bay till you arrived, Grant Fox achieved pinpoint accuracy with his kicks and John Gallagher timed his entries into the backline with perfection.

"Our backline was a delight to watch. That I scored five tries had everything to do with the fact that I supported them faithfully. They created the opportunities and I was lucky enough to finish several of them off."

Of the six matches that comprised New Zealand's World Cup triumph, the one that stands out for Whetton was the quarter-final against Scotland. "For us, that was *the* test of the series," he says. "The Welsh were inadequate and the French had probably played themselves out against Australia. The Scots had drawn with France in pool play and we regarded them as a team of pros. Our coach Brian Lochore handed the forwards over to Grizz Wyllie midweek for a never-to-be-forgotten scrummaging session. Someone counted more than eighty scrums. We were all bruises and scars and aching muscles afterwards. Gary and I still laugh about that session. But it paid handsome dividends. The Scots expected to pressure us through the scrums but we were the ones exerting the pressure on match day."

Scottish captain Colin Deans, a veteran of 52 tests, described the All Black scrum as one of the mightiest he had ever encountered. "They ruined so many of our scrums," he said. Despite this forward pressure, the All Blacks led only 9-3 at halftime, and it was only when Whetton scored his try in the third quarter that the New Zealand fans began to breathe a little easier.

As a blindside flanker, Whetton says that for him the World Cup was "like a jigsaw falling into place". "It's all about knowing the lines to run," he says. "You can sprint madly and not be near the ball. You need pace, certainly, but your lines are all important. You've got to know what your backs are doing and where they're going."

Three years after graduating to the 'fringe' of international rugby and almost six years after brother Gary broke into test rugby, Alan Whetton had finally established himself in the All Blacks, aged 27. His contribution to the World Cup campaign was significant. John Hart, a selector at the time, considers Whetton's contribution was vastly underrated. "He was the unobtrusive player of the tournament." Three years on, Hart said if asked to choose the best forward in the All Blacks, he would choose Alan Whetton. "He can run and pass like the others and he has a high understanding of the requirements of his position."

The tour of Japan at the end of '87 was a pleasant interlude for those involved. "It was, but it wasn't, an All Black team," says Whetton. "Not all the World Cup players went, but I was at the front of the queue with my hand up. I loved touring and Japan offered a completely different rugby perspective."

On the 1984 tour of Australia, Whetton had been a vulnerable, spare-parts player. Four years on, he was an established member of the test pack, a senior pro among the touring party (with a reputation as a great humorist, to the point of being appointed judge at the All Blacks' mock court sessions). Now he got the big games, and Mike

Alan Whetton

Brewer and Zinzan Brooke waited in the wings. The All Blacks carried on under Alex Wyllie where they'd left off under Brian Lochore, sweeping the Wallabies aside in the two Bledisloe Cup internationals in Sydney. "We struggled in the second test in Brisbane, for various reasons," says Whetton, "but in the Sydney tests we operated like clockwork. It was a marvellous team to be part of."

A hip injury suffered in the first test sidelined him for a couple of weeks, but he struggled back to full fitness, reluctant to yield his test position to any of the challengers.

The awesome All Black pack (with Whetton, Shelford and Jones as loosies, Gary Whetton and Murray Pierce locking and Steve McDowell, Sean Fitzpatrick and Richard Loe in the front row) remained intact until 1989 when injuries began to take their toll. First there was the horrendous damage to Michael Jones' knee in the test against Argentina at Wellington, sidelining him for 12 months, and then Whetton came to grief at Swansea during the tour of Wales and Ireland.

Whetton achieved a mini-ambition by playing on the Arms Park, against Cardiff, in the tour opener. But there were 20,000 empty seats that day. His personal goal was to run on to the famous field before a capacity 55,000 crowd with his brother to play Wales. But sentiment counted for nothing. After Swansea, his tour became a misery. Concentrated physiotherapy and extended periods in the pool improved the leg sufficiently for him to take the field against Leinster, but before halftime he had limped to the sideline, the hamstring torn again.

"At that stage, I should have packed my bag and headed for home," he says, "but I was pressured into staying. I wasn't enjoying being there as a passenger. What my leg most needed was rest. Anyway, the medical team finally got it right, and I managed the full eighty minutes against Ulster, not without some misgivings. At one stage I said to Mike Brewer that I thought I'd done my groin in. He said, 'Well, you're not going off – the guys have got a big game coming up (against the Barbarians) and they don't need to get involved tonight'."

Whetton came through the Ulster game so well he was given a place on the reserves' bench for the Barbarians encounter at Twickenham. When Buck Shelford retired injured at halftime, Whetton threw off his tracksuit top and looked hopefully towards coach Wyllie. "But Zinny had his tracksuit off too," says Whetton. "He wasn't going to let me get on!"

The hamstring fully repaired, Whetton resumed his test career the following season, surviving as New Zealand's first-choice blindside flanker through until the ill-fated World Cup campaign in 1991. It was not a great period for All Black rugby, and sadly it coincided with Gary's elevation to the captaincy. "Gary had a magnificent career in the All Blacks and earned the captaincy," says Alan. "The sadness was, of course, that he inherited it in such controversial circumstances, with Shelford's sacking. The Buck thing just wouldn't go away for him. And at the time he stepped into the captaincy, the mighty All Black machine was starting to creak."

On the tour of France at the end of 1990, notwithstanding two fine test victories, Whetton first detected the signs that would bring the All Blacks crashing down. "John Gallagher was missing for a start, and that was significant. But suddenly the guys were dropping passes, making mistakes . . . bread and butter things. Maybe it was a mental thing, who knows? But we were no longer the clinical machine we'd been. I was still trying my hardest, but I was a player who performed best when the team was firing. I wasn't a Buck Shelford who could pick the whole team up and carry them with me."

The calf muscle he damaged in Argentina kept Whetton out of the two Bledisloe Cup tests in 1991, when the All Blacks struggled for survival. But, to his great relief, he was named in the World Cup squad. He would play all the matches through until the loss to Australia in the semi-final, giving way to Andy Earl in the play-off for third at Cardiff (once again being denied a test appearance at the famous stadium).

Hart's appointment as co-coach with Wyllie was interpreted by Whetton as "a cry for help". "Sadly, things were beyond repair, and there was an inevitability about our fate at the World Cup. Australia played to its potential and we didn't – as simple as that. I don't believe the Australians have played that well since. David Campese and Michael Lynagh had magic games and sparked the whole team. We had periods on attack but we couldn't score tries. In fact, we never looked like it."

When the new season rolled round Whetton, now 32, had half a mind to retire. "So it didn't bother me when the new coach, Laurie

Alan Whetton

Alan Whetton on the burst against Italy during the 1987 World Cup opener at Eden Park. In support are John Kirwan and Steve McDowell.   John Selkirk

Mains, didn't call me to the trials. But I was disappointed that my brother Gary, as the incumbent captain, was never properly notified that he wasn't needed. It was just a courtesy thing."

Whetton had half a dozen games for Auckland, under its new coach, Graham Henry, before giving way to Michael Jones. After 150 appearances, which had produced 55 tries, his distinguished representative career was at an end.

He dedicated the 1993 season to his club Grammar, as he said he would, then treated himself to a season off. In 1995, responding to a call from Henry, he became Auckland's assistant coach, a position he filled for two years. "With Auckland's rare mix of legends and players of huge potential, my role was more that of a manager than a coach," he says.

He was looking forward to a third term but after selling his transport company, Philpott Carriers, he needed greater security than Auckland could offer and so accepted a coaching position with one of Japan's top four teams Kobe Steel. He and his wife Nicci and their infant children Olivia and Maddison settled in Japan in October 1996.

Gary Whetton

After an amazing career in which he played 101 games for the All Blacks, bettered Pinetree Meads' 20-year-old record for test appearances, shared in victories over every nation in the world, helped win the World Cup, captained Auckland and New Zealand and was associated with the Ranfurly Shield for six years, there didn't seem to be anything left in rugby to challenge and stimulate Gary Whetton.

That was his thinking when, in 1992 at the age of 32, he and his family headed for the small town of Castres in the south of France.

He was getting out of New Zealand because he was disillusioned, having been abandoned by the new All Black selection panel headed by Laurie Mains in the wake of the disasters at the second World Cup.

"I felt I still had a lot of rugby to play," says Whetton. "I was upset that as the incumbent All Black captain, I had been summarily dismissed, and particularly the manner in which it had happened. I played out the season with Auckland but rather than hang around holding a grudge, I decided to try something different."

Little did Whetton anticipate that that 'something different' would provide him with a rugby experience to rank right up alongside the best moments of his career.

He was a celebrity when he arrived in Castres, a delightful little town about 50 kilometres east of Toulouse. In seeking a New Zealand import, the club president Pierre-Yves Revol hoped to lure a top-class provincial player or even a former international. He didn't expect he would be welcoming the recently deposed All Black captain.

Gary Whetton

Happiness is defeating Australia in a Bledisloe Cup encounter, and doing it in style. Gary Whetton about to embrace brother Alan after the All Blacks' stylish win in Sydney in 1987.   *John Selkirk*

Castres' aims for the 1993 season were realistically modest, to reach the play-offs which would rank them as one of the leading 16 clubs in France. They hadn't won the national championship since 1949 so their expectations of advancing much further were not great.

Whetton came into the team as a player. Not as the captain, that role belonging to 38-year-old Francis Rui. Nor as the coach, Alain Gaileu handling that duty.

"I obviously had an input into training and tactics," says Whetton, "but I was basically happy to fit in with their wants. Where I was able to make a significant contribution was in improving discipline and concentration."

Not ranked among the top eight clubs of France, Castres duly qualified for the quarter-finals and were drawn to play against Narbonne at the neutral venue of Toulouse, a game it won. However, because Castres had fielded five reserves (one too many) a protest by Narbonne was upheld and the game had to be replayed. Castres won again, more easily this time.

Now came the challenge, for its semi-final opponent was Toulon, the team most fancied to win the championship. But Castes was on a winning streak and against the odds, at Dijon, it completed a huge upset.

The club final in France more or less equates to the NPC final in New Zealand, except that is a more important social occasion, and it is always staged in Paris, at the magnificent Parc des Princes, where the stadium is always sold out. Castres' opponents would be another unranked team, Grenoble, coached by Jacques Fouroux – the blue and white of Castres against the red and black of Grenoble. "Just like Auckland against Canterbury," laughs Whetton.

Now Whetton knew the Parc des Princes because he had played there as an All Black in 1981 and 1990. But not one of the good men of Castres had ever set foot on the hallowed turf. When their bus pulled up at the stadium gates, none of them knew where to go. "Here was the Kiwi leading the Frenchmen to the changing room," says Whetton.

When the players walked out on to the field, in front of the 60,000 spectators, most of them started crying. "They were at rugby's Mecca," says Whetton, "and they were overwhelmed. In a lot of their minds, I know, they had achieved enough simply by reaching the final. When they started looking for their families in the crowd, I decided it was time to shepherd them back to the changing room and give them a calming talk. I had to remind them that participating in the final wasn't enough – they had to win."

The final was, in Whetton's words, one hell of a game. "It wasn't pretty rugby, but it was physical, tight and incredibly tense." Whetton scored his team's only try which allowed Castres to establish a 14-11 lead, an advantage they held to the finish, thanks to Grenoble missing two late, kickable penalty attempts.

At the final whistle, the Castres players, not to mention their supporters, were overcome with emotion. Coach Gaileu jumped on Whetton, another player jumped on Gaileu. All the others were in tears. "You had to be there to experience it," says Whetton. "I thought I'd had my share of highlights with the All Blacks and Auckland, but this was something again."

The players went forward to receive the Shield of Brennus, which, Whetton says, was rather like winning the Ranfurly Shield and the

NPC all rolled into one. They got to shake the hand of President Mitterrand and then they did a victory lap, to the delight of their fans.

Whetton had performed the haka soon after his arrival in France, but despite many requests he said he would not do it again until Castres got to the Parc des Princes. Now here was a reporter reminding him of his promise, so, live on television throughout France, the lone New Zealander involved in the championship final performed the Maori war dance, to everyone's delight.

The Castres team flew home by charter flight the next day to a tumultuous reception. "The whole town, in fact the whole region, was celebrating," says Whetton. "They streets in from the airport were lined with people while thousands had been waiting for up to four hours at the stadium by the time we arrived. There were speeches and toasts and the trophy was proudly handed around. Finally the president of the club announced that, by popular demand, Gary Whetton would perform the haka again. So I ripped off my shirt, and did it once more. It capped an incredible weekend, one up on the top shelf with all my favourite rugby memories."

The Gary Whetton story begins differently from most of the subjects in this book. He was a twin, for a start, he and brother Alan (who also qualifies for a chapter in *Rugby Greats Vol 3*) being born on December 15, 1959. And where most future All Blacks were scampering around a rugby field from age of five, Whetton started out playing soccer. "It was a size thing," he says. "They wouldn't allow me to play rugby – I was too big."

It was a long time before rugby appealed to Whetton. People told him he had potential, but he couldn't be bothered training. Brother Alan describes him as "fat and lazy" at the time. Because of his size, he was included in the reserves for the crackerjack Auckland Grammar School first XV of 1976, a team that included All Blacks-to-be John Drake and Nicky Allen.

He made the first XV the following year, as a seventh former, being overshadowed by brother Alan and a young first-five who came into the team during the season, Grant Fox. If Gary Whetton's dramatic emergence as a rugby player ahead of his brother in the following year could be attributed to one event, it was the three weeks he spent at the Outward Bound course at Blenheim. "For the first time, I had to extend myself," he says. "I returned fit, considerably lighter and with

The All Blacks check out a street side cafe during their tour of France in 1990. Sharing the occasion with Gary Whetton is physiotherapist David Abercrombie, coach Alex Wyllie and Grant Fox.   Fotopacific

a much more positive attitude to life."

In that 1978 season he made the Auckland third grade representative side from the Grammar club and the following year, after only three senior matches, he was selected for the New Zealand Colts. He was part of the Colts again in 1980, along with brother Alan, for the tour of Australia. They contributed mightily to the 'test' victory over the Australians in the curtainraiser to the All Black test at the Sydney Cricket Ground. The *Rugby Annual* records that the heroes of that narrow win were "Albert Anderson and the Whetton brothers Gary and Alan who starved Australia of lineout ball throughout the second spell".

Auckland coach Bryan Craies had identified special qualities in Whetton, and had introduced him to his squad in '80, giving him five outings, including the Ranfurly Shield defences against Horowhenua and King Country. Because the All Blacks were touring Australia at the time, none of those appearances was in partnership with Andy Haden.

However, the next year not only were Haden and Whetton the regular locking combination with Auckland, in September they were sensationally paired for the crunch test against the Springboks at Eden Park. This was the infamous Flour Bomb test. Whetton had come into the reckoning when Graeme Higginson broke his ankle. Initially, the selectors had gone for veteran Frank Oliver as a replacement but when the second test was lost, they sought an injection of youth.

What a situation for a 21-year-old to be introduced to the All Blacks. Because protestors were grimly determined to prevent the match going ahead, Auckland was virtually a city under siege. Whetton remembers the Red Squad surrounding the team hotel 24 hours a day.

On the Friday, coach Peter Burke arranged a workout at Mairangi Bay that would simulate the first 20 minutes of the test. "The weather was wet and cold," recalls Whetton, "the ground surrounded by police. We trained as if it was the test . . . twenty minutes, then thirty, then forty. In the 1990s, teams don't even train on a Friday, but here we were going hell for leather. There was mud and slush and guys were smashing into each other. It was awesome. When I got back to the hotel, I crashed. I felt as if I'd played my test already!"

The *New Zealand Herald* described Whetton as a "Babe in Arms" and questioned whether he was up to it. "The story implied that my selection represented panic stations by the selectors," says Whetton. "That added to the day's pressures."

Kick-off was at 3pm but because of the protestor threat, the All Blacks had to depart their hotel, on Auckland's north shore, at 8.30am. "Protestors had been outside chanting all night," recalls Whetton. "I don't think the players had much sleep. The Springboks were better off, I'm sure, being housed at Eden Park."

Installed in a room at Eden Park, the All Blacks had about four hours to kill. There were mattresses on the floor, but the drama of the occasion meant no one was sleepy. Whetton walked around. "I think if I could have got out of the match at that stage, I would have. I was feeling the pressure that much, and I was so unsure of myself and my own ability. I did not honestly believe I was an All Black."

Throughout the match a light plane buzzed the ground dropping flour bombs, one of which struck Gary Knight. Referee Clive Norling a couple of times asked the players if they wanted to call the game off. The captains said no. With time nearly up on the clock, Ray Mordt scored to make it 22-all, Naas Botha's kick to come. "The guys were feeling dejected," says Whetton. "All I could think of was, 'Here goes my career – I'm a one test wonder'. But Botha's conversion attempt missed and play continued, for ages as it turned out. I don't remember any of the circumstances of Allan Hewson's penalty goal, except suddenly we were ahead 25-22 and there was a desperate need to keep the Springboks out of our half. Then the final whistle, and elation."

Whetton wanted to swap jerseys with the player he marked, Louis Moolman, but the Springbok was unyielding. "You guys are cheats," he declared. Whetton couldn't see how the All Blacks had cheated. "I think he was upset that I'd had a pretty good day in the lineouts and that the referee had played a lot of injury time."

Whetton got his Springbok jersey, thanks to the South African manager who slipped it to him quietly later on. He went on to play 58 tests but says that incredible game in '81 remains his favourite. "I've had a lot of thrills and memorable wins since, but that one takes the cake. It wasn't just that it was my debut, it was the entire circumstances."

Far from being the 'one-test wonder' he had dreaded, Whetton went on to play three more tests in 1981, one at the August 23 Stadium in Bucharest against Romania, and two, at Toulouse and Paris, in France. As the All Blacks won all three encounters with Whetton and Haden in control of the lineouts, Whetton seemed to be assured of a lengthy tenure in the New Zealand pack.

At the Athenee Palace Hotel in Bucharest, Whetton and Haden encountered a major problem – they were approximately 6ft 6in, their beds no more than 6ft 4in. The ever resourceful Haden produced a spanner. The beds were dismantled, head boards dispensed with and mattresses placed on the floor. Problem solved. Except that when the maids entered their room there was, Whetton says, "lots of screaming and yelling!"

When the team for the Bledisloe Cup series against the touring Wallabies in 1982 was announced, Whetton was out and Higginson back in. "I was pretty shattered not to be selected," he recalls. Another second test defeat opened the way for Whetton's recall and he was reunited with Haden for the decider at Eden Park. Apart from missing the tour of England and Scotland the next year through injury, he would be an automatic test selection for the next nine years!

Whetton's career was blossoming. After sharing in the whitewash of the British Lions in 1983, he was off to South Africa, one of eight New Zealanders (including Ivan Vodanovich as coach) invited to participate in the Western Province centenary celebrations.

Everything went sweetly until five minutes from the end of the Western Province game at Newlands when, in a freakish happening, Whetton's knee was badly wrenched. He went down in excruciating pain. When it was examined the next morning, it was apparent he had seriously damaged the medial ligament. By chance, a gifted surgeon who had been working in the UK was on hand and available to operate immediately. "He said if I chose to travel back to New Zealand for the operation, the ligament would go mushy," says Whetton. "My best chance of a full recovery was for him to repair it then and there. I told him to go for it."

The damage turned out to be worse than expected, with the medial and cruciate ligaments both damaged, as well as cartilage. Whetton remained in hospital for five days with a huge cast on his leg and couldn't fly home for a fortnight. Because of the newspaper publicity, he became quite a celebrity and had an endless string of visitors, including politicians and Springboks.

When he did finally arrive back in Auckland at the beginning of August, it was with the knowledge that he was out of sport for up to nine months. Once the plaster was removed, he embarked on a concentrated course of rehabilitation involving swimming (every morning for seven months), deep massage and exercises.

He returned to rugby action when Auckland undertook an early-season trip to the UK and was back in the All Black jersey for the series against France and then on the tour of Australia with Bryce Rope's team when a significant absentee was Haden.

Haden's expertise was certainly missing when the All Blacks stumbled in the first international in Sydney, losing 16-9, with Steve 'Skylab' Cutler controlling the lineouts. Back in Auckland, Haden had studied the video of that game and devised tactics to counter Cutler at Ballymore. He handed four foolscap pages of notes and sketches to Mark Shaw, who was rejoining the team after a week's compassionate leave with his sick wife. Whetton and his locking partner Albert Anderson applied Haden's suggestions so effectively that they took out the lineouts 24-13 in the second test, allowing the All Blacks to stage a sensational comeback from 12 points down to win.

"I thought it was the end of the world after we'd lost that first test," says Whetton. "Andy convinced me it wasn't and produced the tactics to overcome Cutler. Our coach Bryce Rope didn't appreciate Haden's interference, but we won the second test, and that was all that mattered."

The 1985-86 seasons were difficult ones, with politics intruding into rugby, forcing the cancellation of the scheduled tour of South Africa the one year, with the players ignoring protocol and undertaking their own tour, as Cavaliers, the next. All the tourists, including Whetton, received a two-test suspension, interrupting a remarkable sequence of test appearances for the lock. Once reinstated, he would play the next 40 test matches without a break.

Whetton records divisions in the Auckland team in '86, directly relating to the Cavaliers tour. David Kirk, one of only two original selections to stay at home (John Kirwan was the other), assumed the captaincy in Haden's absence, which did nothing for Haden's humour upon his return, particularly as Kirk had been publicly critical of the venture. "David had received his visa but withdrew a few days before we took off for South Africa," says Whetton. "We felt in the circumstances he would have been better keeping his opinions to himself. It didn't do anything for team spirit when we were all back together." Notwithstanding the friction, Auckland withstood every challenge for the Ranfurly Shield which it had picked up from Canterbury in the Provincial Match of the Century the previous season. While Kirk survived as Auckland captain, he had the leadership of the All Blacks taken away from him for the tour of France. Following the series loss to Alan Jones' Wallabies, the captaincy was transferred to Jock Hobbs. If that was a surprise, so was Alan Whetton's non-selection.

The 1987 season would be a watershed in New Zealand rugby, with a new selection panel (John Hart and Alex Wyllie joining Brian Lochore) introducing an exciting new concept for All Black rugby. "There was a whole new approach, a new way of selecting," says Whetton. "I wonder whether people realise that, even now. The selectors decided upon a game of skill, pace and aggression and chose players to fit." One player who did fit, in the opinion of the selectors, was Alan Whetton, chosen at the expense of the now veteran Mark 'Cowboy' Shaw.

Gary Whetton

One of the secrets of New Zealand's World Cup triumph, in Whetton's opinion, lay in the planning between matches. Before the third pool match against Argentina at Wellington, the players were billeted at Pirinoa, a tiny farming settlement in the Wairarapa, and before flying off to Brisbane for the semi-final clash with Wales, they were quartered at Napier, again mingling with the locals and experiencing an inspiring afternoon at Te Aute College.

A fabulous campaign was completed in style at Eden Park with the French being hammered by 29 points to 9. The All Blacks were the champions of the world. And they would prove worthy of the title as they took the sport by storm over the next three seasons, going on to complete 50 matches (including 23 internationals) without defeat. Whetton would be involved in every one of them, consistently pulling down quality lineout ball and being a major contributor to the free-flowing, high tempo game that ran every opponent ragged.

Throughout this golden period the All Blacks were captained by Buck Shelford. But after they had laboured to defeat Scotland early in the 1990 season, he was controversially axed, the leadership being moved on to Whetton. While it was a huge honour, and the captaincy sat easily on his broad shoulders (for he was already captaining Auckland), it was his misfortune that cracks were beginning to appear in the previously invincible All Black machine. Cracks on the field, cracks with the coaching.

Alex Wyllie, who'd had the team since 1988, was now finding it a challenge to motivate the same players. The NZRFU, sensing this, in its wisdom chose to introduce John Hart as a co-coach for the 1991 World Cup campaign. It was a clanger of monumental proportions, about as logical as asking Sir Robert Muldoon and David Lange to form a coalition government.

Whetton was caught as the meat in the sandwich. "As rugby coaches and personalities, they were utterly incompatible," he says. "They had their own thoughts about who should be selected and their own ways of coaching. John was innovative where Grizz preferred the tried and true methods. If I socialised with one, I upset the other. I was in an impossible situation and meanwhile the team was going steadily downhill. I basically tried to tread a middle path and do what I felt was best for the players. Our manager John Sturgeon wasn't a Hart man – he was still supporting Wyllie, and that didn't help. The tragedy

Having been in the All Black team that lost heavily at Nantes four years earlier, Gary Whetton delights in the test victory in the same city in 1990. Fotopacific

was that we crumbled in a World Cup year, not in an interim year when it wouldn't have mattered."

Of the disastrous semi-final against Australia, Whetton says, after 10 years in the All Blacks, he could sense when everything was right and the team was going to win. "I didn't have that feeling in Dublin. The Australians were awesome. They'd beaten us in Wellington and Sydney in the previous 15 months, so psychologically they knew we were no longer invincible, and they took the game to us. Although we had a good second half, we couldn't crack their defence. They deserved the win."

It was particularly galling for Whetton and his men to learn that, by defeating France in Paris, England had progressed to the final. "We'd beaten them decisively in pool play. Now we were eliminated and they were through to the final."

The play-off for third against Scotland, midweek at Cardiff, would be Whetton's final outing as an All Black. In the trauma of losing at Dublin, almost everyone had overlooked the fact that his appearance there was his 100th for New Zealand (a figure achieved by only six other players). By taking the field against Canada in the quarter-final he had become his country's most capped player, eclipsing the record of 55 tests set by the legendary Colin Meads two decades earlier, a monumental achievement.

Whetton considered there was plenty of rugby left in him when he returned to New Zealand, but the new selection panel of Laurie Mains, Earle Kirton and Peter Thorburn decided they didn't want him. Eleven locks were invited to the All Black trials in Napier in April but, cruelly, Whetton wasn't among them.

Instead of playing for them, he got to appear against them, for the World XV, in the third international at Eden Park. Most unexpectedly, he was invited to participate by the World team coaches Bob Templeton and Brian Lochore. "I wasn't sure I wanted to play against the All Blacks," says Whetton, "but Bob and BJ convinced me it would be a good way to go out. I considered it a great honour and a challenge. I enjoyed the game although it was a strange feeling lining up against the men in black. No prisoners were taken that afternoon, I can assure you!"

Whetton captained Auckland in all 17 matches in 1992, his career in the blue and white jersey, and Auckland's season, coming to a jarring halt when Waikato unceremoniously upended them in the NPC semi-final at Eden Park, Waikato going on to thrash Otago in the final.

Whereupon, Whetton and his family packed their bags and headed for Castres and an experience he never dreamed was possible.

The Castres interlude completed, in 1994 he returned to Auckland where he now runs his own insurance broking business, catering exclusively to business and professional clients. His rugby involvement continues as an NZRFU staff coaching member while, on request, he has assisted clubs and provincial teams – "for the love of the game, not money".

His precious spare time is given over to his wife Jane and their three sons, William, Jack and Louis.

Jeff Wilson

To play for your country at rugby or cricket at 19 is an exceptional achievement. To play for your country at *both* rugby and cricket when you're only 19 is almost unbelievable. Yet that was the achievement of Southland's favourite son Jeff Wilson in 1993.

The story gets better. He didn't just make up the numbers, as you might expect of a teenager thrust into the international scene. In his third one-day cricket international he guided New Zealand to a sensational victory over Alan Border's Australians with a heroic innings of 44 not out. Eight months later, he scored a hat-trick of tries in his rugby test debut, against Scotland at Murrayfield.

No wonder they began calling him Goldie. It fitted his complexion, but to his teammates, he'd instantly become Golden Boy because of his amazing capacity to produce heroic performances, which is something he'd been doing all his sporting life.

This is the guy who as a fullback in the Cargill High School first XV scored 66 points, including nine tries, in a match against local rival James Hargest High School, who played cricket for Southland at 15 and who, according to prominent basketball coach Tab Baldwin, was good enough to represent New Zealand at that code as well. All of which led to a book, called *The Natural*, being published on his astonishing sporting career in 1994, before he'd even turned 21.

Inevitably, Wilson had to choose between rugby and cricket because of the overlap of seasons. Fortunately for New Zealand's rugby followers, he gave priority rating to playing for the All Blacks,

Jeff Wilson

Jeff Wilson . . . the first player to represent New Zealand at rugby and cricket in the same year. Mark Leech (Photosport)

which he has done with great distinction since that memorable first tour in '93.

Not that there haven't been a few hiccups for the Golden Boy. After his second test, against England at Twickenham, he was disconsolate at missing several important kicks at goal, in 1994 he 'bombed' the matchwinning try against the Wallabies in Sydney and at the World Cup in 1995, when suddenly the whole rugby world went crazy over Jonah Lomu, for the first time in his sporting career he lapsed into comparative anonymity as the All Blacks' "other wing."

You can't keep a good man down for long, however, and when Jonah Lomu was confined to the reserves' bench in South Africa in 1996, it was Wilson who produced two stunning tries at Pretoria to set up the All Blacks' first ever series victory over the Springboks on South African soil.

Wilson made a brief appearance at Shell Trophy level through the summer or 1996-97, long enough to rip through eventual champion Canterbury's batting (with a haul of 5/34) – leaving the national selectors lamenting his unavailability – before refocusing on the serious business of rugby and the Otago Highlanders' Super 12 campaign.

It was inevitable that Jeff Wilson would turn out a useful sportsman because his father Bill was a handy allrounder in the Southland cricket team and played rugby to senior club level while his mother Lynne represented Otago at tennis and has won three masters tennis titles. Both his uncle John and his brother Richard played cricket for Southland and Otago. They were all lumped together in the crack Appleby senior club team in 1988, Jeff the youngest at 14.

However, it wasn't at cricket, rugby or basketball that Jeff made his first overseas sporting trip. It was as an athlete. At the age of 10 he represented New Zealand in the shot put at the Pan Pacific primary school track and field meeting in Melbourne. He was unplaced, one of the few occasions in his life when he wouldn't be in or near the winner's circle.

He'd collected a stack of medals for sprinting and in field events at Southland and South Island championships but after Melbourne he never participated competitively in track and field again, for the simple reason that cricket took precedence.

Notwithstanding his exceptional achievements in rugby and

cricket, he nominates basketball as his favourite game and laments the fact that the opportunities to play it, as he has matured, are almost nil. When his Southland under-18 team won the South Island tournament in 1991, he was named the most valuable player at the tournament. His coach Tab Baldwin, later to move to Auckland, says that Wilson had the ability to play in the national league. "And if he fine tuned his skills, I don't see why he couldn't play for the Tall Blacks (the New Zealand basketball team). He is a freak. He has speed and strength but what separates him from his peers is his mental make-up. In the years I have coached in the United States and New Zealand, I have never met anyone with a mental attitude more suited to the world of sport."

On the way home from the 1993 All Black tour of the UK, he stopped off in the United States to stay with Baldwin and attended both professional and university basketball matches. When he was still living at home in Invercargill, larger-than-life photos of the great American stars Michael Jordan and Charles Barkley filled most of one wall of his bedroom.

Cricket became the main focus for most of his time at Cargill High School, particularly when he was elevated to representative status with Southland. He decided to give rugby a miss in 1988 to have himself in top shape for the new cricket season. However, George Hau, the coach of the Southland under-16 rugby team, was short of a fullback for the South Island tournament at Blenheim. He invited Wilson to make up the squad. Wilson accepted. And before you knew it, he was playing fullback for South under-16 against North at Athletic Park.

George Hau insisted on taking his star fullback to the next tournament, in Dunedin in 1989, from where he not only won South Island selection again but was also named in the New Zealand under-17 team to tour Australia early in 1990. That team, captained from lock by another Southlander, Jason Templer, won all five matches including the 'test' at Canberra. The star performer? Jeff Wilson, no less. According to the *Rugby Annual*, he was "the outstanding individual, demonstrating John Gallagher-type attacking qualities." Coach Bob Oliphant predicted that Wilson would go on to play for the All Blacks.

It was in 1992 that Wilson's rugby career began to explode into life and when he first began to believe that rugby perhaps had as much to offer as cricket. The game that propelled him into the national limelight was Cargill's clash with James Hargest. Wilson was hyped up for it because in the corresponding match the previous season he had been crudely dealt to in a ruck, emerging with ugly lacerations to his head. "I told our guys it was going to be all-out war," he says. "We were going to blitz them. And we did."

And how! Rather than meeting fire with fire, Wilson and Cargill were determined to overwhelm rough play with sheer talent. The game was won by 102 points to 6, with Wilson, operating from fullback, scoring nine tries and kicking 16 conversions for an amazing personal haul of 66 points! Not surprisingly, Wilson was hot property the next day as journalists, and radio and television interviewers descended on the school. Surprisingly, it didn't qualify him for a listing in the *Guinness Book of Records* because a South African called Jannie van der Westhuizen had scored 80 points in a club match in 1972.

Southland rugby bosses recognised they had an uncommonly gifted player in their midst. The Invercargill Metropolitan selectors asked the Cargill High principal if he would mind releasing one of his seventh formers for the match against Otago Country at Homestead Stadium. The principal agreed and Wilson, far from being overawed at finding himself in the company of hardened senior footballers, again became the star turn, scoring three tries and setting up another.

The Southland representative selector-coach Barry Leonard could not resist the 18-year-old and introduced him to his squad mid-season, trying him out at fullback against Canterbury in a non-championship match at Lancaster Park. Also debuting for the maroons that afternoon was a likely looking halfback called Justin Marshall.

Because Simon Forrest was performing so outstandingly at fullback – his 13 tries that season constituting a Southland record – the only spot available to Wilson was left wing. He quickly adapted and went on to represent the team with distinction, scoring one unforgettable try against Taranaki in Invercargill when he stepped former All Black fullback Kieran Crowley. The *Rugby Annual* noted that he displayed "remarkable skills playing out of position on the left wing".

Wilson went on to achieve further heroics for the New Zealand secondary schools team, a side he'd first represented in 1991. The

Jeff Wilson

Jeff Wilson and Justin Marshall relax on the beach at Durban during the 1996 All Black tour of South Africa   Andrew Cornaga (Photosport)

national team faced two internationals in '92, the first against Irish schools at New Plymouth. Wilson was at fullback, Carlos Spencer at first-five, Jonah Lomu at No. 8 and Chresten Davis at lock. The Irish surprised the young New Zealanders with their commitment, establishing a 13-nil advantage in the opening minutes and remaining in front till the dying seconds. A minute from time and trailing 24-25, New Zealand was awarded a penalty 40 metres out and near touch. It fell to Wilson to salvage the game at the death. The kick is vividly described by Jonah Lomu in his chapter. "The incredible thing is that the kick went in a huge arc," says Lomu. "The only time it looked like going over was when it got to the posts!" Wilson was lifted triumphantly in the air by Lomu while the shattered Irish boys, who'd been in front for 79 minutes and 59 seconds, slumped to the turf, many of them in tears.

There was even better to come from Goldie when the New Zealand boys toured Australia the next month. He warmed up for the 'test' in Sydney with a flawless goalkicking exhibition in the 65-7 romp against ACT in Canberra, converting all eight tries and adding three penalty goals for a personal return of 25 points.

Of his performance in the international, under lights at the Football Stadium, even the normally reticent Wilson talks enthusiastically. "It ranks as probably the most complete performance of my career," he says. "There were no flaws. Everything worked perfectly for me, whether I was fielding the ball, finding touch, making tackles, hitting the line or kicking goals."

Experienced critics were left gasping at his achievements, the greatest of which was a 75-metre try after he'd crash-tackled the Australian centre Brad Condon. "He didn't see me coming – I wiped him out," says Wilson. As the ball spilled behind the stunned Condon, Wilson scooped it up, sidestepped two players and sprinted threequarters of the field to touch down between the uprights.

A lot of people had come to watch Jonah Lomu, who'd been getting a lot of publicity, but it was Wilson who stole the show. And who got the boot . . . the Bronze Boot trophy awarded to the most constructive player in the test match. A penalty goal from halfway and a couple of great trysaving tackles were extra trimmings to his performance that night as the New Zealanders cruised to a 31-8 victory.

A season of astonishing achievement behind him, Wilson put away the rugby boots and donned his cricketing flannels. By the end of the summer he would be playing for his country! It wasn't surprising that the national cricket selectors turned to him after he'd claimed 5/48 in his Shell Trophy debut and batted doggedly for 100 minutes for New Zealand Minor Associations to deny Graham Gooch's Englishmen a win at Napier. He also scored 99 when sent in to open for Otago against Central Districts.

Before stepping into the international one-day area, however, he toured India with the New Zealand Youth side, along with emerging stars such as Stephen Fleming, Dion Nash, Matthew Hart, Justin Vaughan and Lorne Howell. He describes the experience as "six weeks of living hell", with most of the players victims of the dreaded Delhi-belly.

Back home, he appeared in the youth series against Australia, helping New Zealand to success with a quick 31 and six wickets in the third, deciding, test. That seemed a good note on which to wrap up his season of cricket. He packed his gear away and headed for Dunedin, to begin a new life as a trainee teacher, taking time out to join the Harbour Rugby Club and plot his winter schedule.

Life can be full of surprises and Wilson was almost disbelieving when New Zealand Cricket made contact to advise that he was required for the one-day series against the Australians. "I hadn't given selection for New Zealand a thought," he admits. "I thought if anyone was going to get the call-up from Otago, it would be Dion Nash."

After a less than memorable debut at Carisbrook, when he scored a 'duck' and took 1/58 from his 10 overs, he began to contribute. At Wellington he scored 14 and claimed two valuable wickets, but his moment would come at Hamilton. His team, chasing 248, was in trouble at 172/6 when he walked to the crease. Seventy-six runs needed from 10 overs – a tall order against bowlers of the calibre of Merv Hughes, Shane Warne and Steve Waugh. But Wilson thrives on such challenges. He clubbed 44 runs from 28 deliveries, including a towering six off Waugh, winning the game with a boundary. He punched the air with his youthful exuberance as he ran to the pavilion, New Zealand's newest cricketing hero.

Otago coach Gordon Hunter found he had an embarrassment of riches at fullback in the 1993 season. Test choice John Timu was there and former All Black Greg Cooper, too. So he didn't have to rush the 19-year-old Wilson who was playing impressively with Harbour. It wasn't until Wilson had made his mark with the New Zealand Colts that he became a regular in the Otago line-up. In the Colts' game against Thames Valley, Wilson accumulated 39 points from four tries, five conversions and three penalty goals.

Slotted in on the left wing, Wilson was soon a favourite with the Carisbrook crowd, particularly after a typical display of individual brilliance brought the dark blues a rare and cherished NPC victory over mighty Auckland. If the Otago captain John Timu had been near the action, Wilson might have ended up kicking for goal (with Auckland leading 21-18), but he was back downfield. So Wilson encouraged Jamie Joseph to take a tap and go for a five-pointer. Joseph responded. Suddenly Wilson had the ball 22 metres from the goalline with some awesome obstacles in between, obstacles in the form of Inga Tuigamala, Eroni Clarke and Shane Howarth. No trouble for a twinkle-toed teenager. He wrongfooted the first two and eluded Howarth to score in Waisake Sotutu's tackle. The applause had scarcely died down when he coolly slotted the conversion from the sideline. Final score: Otago 25, Auckland 21.

The following week he was Otago's hero again when he landed an injury time conversion from the sideline, and into a blustery southerly, to earn a 20-all draw with Wellington at Athletic Park. The kick wasn't without controversy, the ball having toppled over as he was about to commence his run in. Wellington coach David Kirk was critical of the referee for allowing him a second chance.

Otago scored a handsome victory over Waikato in Hamilton to advance to the final of the NPC against Auckland at Eden Park, but the efforts of Wilson and co weren't enough to stop Graham Henry's men recording what would be the first of four successive championship wins.

The NPC final might have signalled the end of Wilson's rugby season but the New Zealand selectors had a surprise in store for him – selection in the All Black team to tour England and Scotland. Well, after his performances for Otago and the Colts in 1993, it wasn't really a surprise. Most experts had been predicting it. What *was* a surprise was John Kirwan's absence. He'd been cast adrift after 10 seasons as an automatic selection. And also missing, having decided to give first priority to his business commitments, was Grant Fox.

It was Fox's absence that clinched selection for Wilson. Coach Laurie Mains said it was essential to have two specialist goalkickers and as neither of the first-fives, Marc Ellis and Stephen Bachop, or fullback John Timu kicked, the selectors had to look elsewhere.

There was great elation in the Wilson household at his selection while the media had a field day with the teenager who had become the first individual to represent New Zealand at rugby and cricket in the same year. Only six had achieved it previously – George Dickinson, Curly Page, Charlie Oliver, Eric Tindill, Bill Carson and Brian McKechnie. Wilson was disappointed that Kirwan wasn't touring – "I'm sure I could have learnt a lot from him," he says – and regretted the fact that his Otago teammate Paul Cooke had missed selection. "I feel as if I have taken his place," he said.

Wilson would be the busiest All Black on tour, being selected for nine of the 13 matches. Only Zinzan Brooke matched that number, but two of his appearances were as a replacement. The Wilson debut (one day before his 20th birthday) came at one of the world's great stadiums, Twickenham, against a London and South East Division team overflowing with international players. The home team, it transpired, had resorted to rugby espionage, placing microphones on the field where the All Blacks trained and circularising all the players with the information gleaned. Fortunately for coach Mains, an expatriate Kiwi flatting with one of the players spotted the newsletter and warned the All Blacks who changed all their calls.

Wilson marked his debut in appropriate fashion, scoring two tries, producing an exaggerated swallow dive to complete the first. However, he wasn't altogether satisfied with his performance, considering his tackling to be shoddy and his ball retention less than ideal.

Although selected as a goalkicker, he was given the kicking duties only once in the long run-in to the internationals, against Northern Division at Anfield, the ground more normally associated with the Liverpool soccer team, hardly the ideal preparation for someone who would have the kicking duties thrust upon them in the international against England.

Before that drama, however, Wilson would experience one of the most memorable afternoons of his rugby career. He'd been brought on tour as an investment for the future but when John Timu reverted to fullback there was a right wing berth available, one that had been occupied with some permanency for a decade by Kirwan. Against Scotland at Murrayfield, he flourished in the No 14 jersey, completing a hat-trick of tries and, for good measure, adding the wide-angled conversion (to bring up New Zealand's half-century) to the last of them. Only two other All Blacks – Frank Mitchinson in 1907 and Tom Lynch in 1913 – had scored three tries on test debut.

He owed his third try to Otago teammate Stu Forster, having rejected Forster's suggestion that they attempt a particular blindside move. "I was feeling so tired, I suggested to Stu he try something else," says Wilson, "but he was insistent. So we worked it, and I scored another try!"

Fortunes can change dramatically in one week, as the All Blacks in general, and coach Mains and new winger Wilson, in particular, were to discover. When Matthew Cooper dropped out with injury, the goalkicking duties – in fact, all the kicking responsibilities – against England at Twickenham landed firmly in Wilson's lap . It was a huge ask for a 20-year-old in his second test.

"I think the selectors were hoping I was still on a high from the Scotland match and wouldn't feel the pressure," says Wilson. "But I did feel it. I was focused, but it was just one of those days." He missed his first three shots at goal, leaving the All Blacks scoreless in the first half. They eventually lost 15-9. Wilson was disconsolate in the dressing room afterwards. "My teammates came over and said all the right things but you can't help thinking about how they felt. I'm sure they were thinking that if Grant Fox had been playing, they would never have lost. That's hard to live with. And it still is – it's hard to accept that you let the guys down, knowing what it meant to them."

Wilson was unreasonably severe on himself. The author wrote in the *Rugby Annual*: "It's unfair to blame Wilson for the team's shock demise. The root cause lay with the forwards. The loose forwards seemed to be a metre off the pace while the lineout became a source of consternation. A strength against Scotland, it became a liability against England."

A chance meeting with Grant Fox in a lift in Cardiff before the final match instantly sorted out Wilson's goalkicking woes. Their conversation lasted no more than 15 seconds, before the lift doors opened and Fox got out, but in that time he suggested to Wilson that he was approaching the ball too squarely and needed to take one more step out and away before commencing his run in.

"Foxy had spotted what I was doing wrong from the grandstand," says Wilson. "It immediately corrected the problem." The evidence came in the tour finale against the Barbarians. Wilson landed four super goals and kicked as if he hadn't missed once on the whole tour.

It's hard to believe the player who was the toast of Murrayfield and who was then entrusted with the goalkicking duties against England and the Barbarians could not command a place in the All Black line-up for the domestic tests in 1994. There were extenuating circumstances. Wilson had come into the new season carrying an ankle injury sustained while playing cricket for Otago. About the time he was challenging for selection (following the test losses to France) the selectors, eager to introduce a specialist goalkicker, switched Timu to the wing to accommodate Shane Howarth at fullback. With Kirwan having re-established himself in the No 14 jersey, suddenly there was no room at the inn for Wilson. Mains would comment in his biography that Wilson had "let his feet come off the ground a little", an indication that his absence from the test team was not entirely attributable to his form.

When Wilson *did* recapture his test position, at Kirwan's expense, for the one-off Bledisloe Cup game under lights in Sydney it would

Jeff Wilson

involve a nightmare experience comparable with his goalkicking disasters at Twickenham.

In the dying stages of a spectacular contest, in which the All Blacks, seemingly down and out at halftime, came roaring back in the second half, Wilson had the winning of the game in his hands. Having eluded the great David Campese as yet another classic All Black attack unfolded, he zeroed in on the goalline. But zeroing in on him at the same time was Australia's exciting new halfback George Gregan. Gregan won, his perfectly timed tackle knocking the ball from Wilson's grasp. Try lost. Match lost. For Wilson, more tears. Another experience to store in the Not To Be Repeated file.

With his focus totally on the Rugby World Cup, Wilson sacrificed his other great passion, cricket, through the summer of 1994-95, emerging from the summer camps, as fit as he'd ever been in his life. By 1995, the Kirwan challenge had dissipated. JK had retired (only to return in a Warriors jersey). Timu was no longer a rival either, having defected to league. Which left Wilson and a rejuvenated Lomu to handle the wing duties for the All Blacks, which they fulfilled brilliantly.

Although Wilson performed competently at the World Cup, he was completely overshadowed by Lomu, becoming known as "the other wing". He took it all philosophically. "The play seemed to swing Jonah's way more than mine during the tournament," he says. "I was just thrilled to be involved, especially after missing all those tests in 1994." He was totally enthused by the all-action game plan Mains devised for the World Cup. "Involving all fifteen players at high velocity made it fantastic to be involved." Having a sensitive stomach at the best of times, he was, unfortunately, one of the first to succumb to the food poisoning that beset the All Blacks 48 hours out from the final against the Springboks. He was affected on the Saturday and pulled out of the game at the threequarter stage in a distressed state.

In the wake of the World Cup, rugby would be shaken to its very foundations as a fierce dogfight developed between the establishment and WRC over the right to administer the new professional code. For a while, it seemed WRC would win. It may well have done so, had it been able to contract every member of the All Black World Cup squad. But WRC suffered a fatal blow when Wilson and Josh Kronfeld announced they were signing with the NZRFU. Wilson acknowledges it was probably the hardest decision he has had to make in his life. "I talked to people I felt would understand my situation – my employer Richard Reid (at Nike), my lawyer David Howman and my family. I obviously spent a lot of time talking to Josh. We had to make a quickfire decision. Everything was in front of us, but we had a deadline. It was up to us to commit ourselves. Without the support of the majority of the All Blacks, we took the decision to sign with the NZRFU. We both wanted to keep wearing the All Black jesey."

Benefiting from playing in the No 15 jersey for Otago in the NPC series, Wilson was preferred in his favourite position of fullback for the test against Italy on the All Blacks' end of year tour. "Fullback provides so many more opportunities for attack," he says, "and I'm a player who loves to attack". After a dazzling performance at Bologna (against Italy), Wilson was looking forward to becoming a regular in the position, but a painful shoulder injury forced him out of the first test against France, bringing an early finish to his rugby year.

Any thoughts he had of playing fullback for New Zealand in 1996 disappeared when a dashing young player from Manawatu by the name of Christian Cullen claimed the position. But it mattered not. Wilson appeared in all 10 internationals on the wing, scoring tries in four of them, including the brace that helped clinch the series at Pretoria.

Jeff Wilson dives in for one of the tries that gave the All Blacks their winning break against South Africa at Pretoria in 1996.   John Selkirk